The Making of the Raj

The Making of the Raj

India under the East India Company

Ian St. John

 PRAEGER

AN IMPRINT OF ABC-CLIO, LLC
Santa Barbara, California • Denver, Colorado • Oxford, England

Library of Congress Cataloging-in-Publication Data

St. John, Ian, 1965–
    The making of the Raj : India under the East India Company / Ian St. John.
        p. cm.
    Includes bibliographical references and index.
    ISBN 978-1-84645-014-3 (hardcopy : alk. paper) — ISBN 978-0-313-09736-2 (ebook)   1. India—History—British occupation, 1765–1947. 2. East India Company—History. 3. India—Civilization—British influences.   I. Title.
    DS465.S75 2012
    954.03′1—dc23   2011027596

ISBN: 978-1-84645-014-3
EISBN: 978-0-313-09736-2

16   15   14   13   12   1   2   3   4   5

This book is also available on the World Wide Web as an eBook.
Visit www.abc-clio.com for details.

Praeger
An Imprint of ABC-CLIO, LLC

ABC-CLIO, LLC
130 Cremona Drive, P.O. Box 1911
Santa Barbara, California 93116-1911

This book is printed on acid-free paper ∞

Manufactured in the United States of America

Contents

Preface

The story of the rise and fulfillment of British rule has been told often and this book does not seek to add another volume to this already well-stocked shelf. What it aims to supply is something complimentary yet altogether different. It seeks to trace the effects of the expanding British presence in India upon the lived experience of the Indians themselves. What, exactly, did the British assumption of hegemony in India mean for the people who actually inhabited the sub-continent? How were their lives affected? What differences, if any, did the fact of British rule make to the Indian way of life? Obviously, any worthwhile assessment of the consequences of British dominion in India must be contingent upon answers to questions such as these. Yet the issues at stake run far deeper than some imperial balance sheet. For what took place in India in the 18th and early 19th centuries was a decisive moment in the history of globalization. Two complex civilizations came into contact, each with a rich and sophisticated cultural history, and each embodying assumptions and ways of conducting affairs which, if sufficiently similar to allow elements of fruitful interaction, were also so different as to lead to numerous cases of incomprehension, misunderstanding, resentment, and exploitation. Those British merchants who first journeyed to India under the auspices of the East India Company did so with a view to utilizing India as a base for commercial operations, at first with the wider Far East, then increasingly within India itself. The idea that they should seek to reconfigure the society they encountered was simply beyond the range of their expectations or their imaginations. Yet as they found themselves interacting with

Indians themselves, so they ineluctably found themselves transformed
from an isolated element upon the margins of Indian civilization, their
connection with the Indian hinterland being mediated through the
mechanism of the cash-nexus, to active players in the Indian scene—
helping to make dynasties, assume responsibilities, exert power, and
formulate policies. The British, in other words, began to transform the
world they had sought, initially, only to profit from. And in so doing,
they stood for something far larger than they could ever really grasp:
they were the agents of a western assault upon the way of life of an
ancient Asian civilization. It was the beginning of an encounter that
has not ended—that has, if anything, intensified over the years and
become ever more complex, as people and ideas have flowed back and
forth between East and West. In retrospect the changes wrought by the
British in the days of the East India Company were tentative, uncertain, limited, fractured, partial. They were, nevertheless, profound for
all that: both in terms of what they meant for many individual Indians, for the political and economic organization of Indian life, for the
beliefs and modes of expression and communication of large sections
of Indian society, and for the foundations they laid for the more far-
reaching changes that were to follow after the Mutiny and the procla-
mation of the Raj. For all these reasons it is a story that should engage
the attention of any student of British, Indian, or global history, and
it is the aim of the pages that follow to provide it in a manner that is
concise, readable, and comprehensible to any interested reader.

The organization of this book follows a simple plan. In the first part
there is presented a basic narrative of the process by which the East
India Company went from being a small trading presence scattered
around the coast of India to becoming the dominant military, political,
and economic power in India—creating, in effect, a new British Empire
in South Asia. In the second part, the consequences of this assumption of Company rule for the people of India are laid bare through the
analysis of a number of key areas of Anglo-Indian interaction: the rural
economy; the patterns of trade and industrial production; the systems
of class and caste; the impact of the state; and the cultural and religious
life of the Indian people. The book concludes with a review of Indian
resistance to the practice of British rule, culminating in the Mutiny or
Rebellion of 1857 and the consequences of its suppression.

Clearly, any true assessment of the impact of Britain upon a society
so rich and diverse as that of India must become a history of India itself.
If such a thing were possible, it would require many more pages and a

far deeper knowledge of the nuances of Indian history—in particular within the context of different regions and communal forms—than this study could claim to possess. Our purpose is a more limited one: namely, to focus rigorously upon the interface between British policy and practice and the India which provided the context for this exercise in imperial manipulation. And this interaction, while far from the whole story of India or Britain in the years before 1859, was yet the most dynamic agent making for change, not only within the subcontinent, but in terms of Britain's relationship to the world and the wider character of the dialogue between East and West—initiating a process of mutual transformation whose ultimate results are still to be fully disclosed.

Part I

The Expansion of British Rule
1600–1859

1

First Impressions

By tradition, the first Englishman to set foot in India was one Father Thomas Stephens, an émigré Jesuit priest who journeyed from Lisbon to the Portuguese colony of Goa in 1579. Although reputedly an Oxford man, it is hard to imagine a less representative example of the race of men who were shortly to leave such an imprint upon the subcontinent, for whom the search for spices far eclipsed any corresponding interest in Christians. A more typical encounter occurred some 30 years later, when Captain William Hawkins—a veteran of Drake's journey to the South Seas and the tussle with the Spanish Armada—arrived as the British East India Company's emissary to the court of the Mughal Emperor, Jahangir. In its lobbying for trading privileges the Company, founded in 1600 by businessmen stung by recent price increases on spices imported into Europe by the Dutch East India Company, could not have chosen more appositely. Jahangir was a notorious drunkard and he and Hawkins indulged in long drinking bouts. The Englishman, who was a fluent Turkish speaker, entered with alacrity into the pleasures of courtly life, receiving a subsidy from the Great Mughal and agreeing to take an Armenian Christian as his wife. If Hawkins left Agra in 1611 with a hangover and more domestic responsibilities than he bargained for, he yet carried in his pocket something altogether more valuable: permission to establish a trading post at Surat on India's west coast.

British motives were transparent: to gain access to trading opportunities along the west coast of India, with its links to Persia and the Indonesian spice trade. But what about Jahangir? He had slender use for the British as trading partners. India was already a flourishing commercial center and there was little that Britain—a gloomy land of sheep farmers and wool merchants—could offer by way of exchange. What Jahangir did value was Britain's naval prowess and he hit upon the idea of playing off the British navy against the Portuguese, whose policy of forced conversions to Catholicism was an irritation he was keen to rid himself of. Accordingly, in 1612 and 1614 the East India Company broke Portuguese naval power in two engagements and emerged as the unofficial navy of the Mughal Empire. Both sides had reason to be pleased with the outcome and over the following decades the Company's presence along the Indian coast was allowed to extend, as they added trading posts or factories at Madras (1639), Bombay (1668), and Calcutta (1690). Of course, the British were not the only Europeans active in the region: besides the Portuguese, the French East India Company had a base at Pondicherry and the Dutch operated out of Ceylon. All were drawn to India as a staging post in the wider eastern trade in spices and textiles. For the Mughals the British were but one of a range of useful trading partners and for this first century the relationship between Indians and Britons was a purely commercial one. The impact of the British on the cultural life of India was marginal and neither side could have anticipated that this handful of traders would come to dominate the subcontinent.

What was the character of this India the British encountered in the 17th and early 18th centuries? It had, to begin with, a vigorous commercial culture. Market systems were well developed and facilitated active trading links both within India itself and beyond to Persia and Africa, China, and the Spice Islands (latter-day Indonesia). Though India produced relatively few spices, its Malabar coast was the center of a prosperous entrepot trade—and it was this that Europeans like the Portuguese, Dutch, and British wanted to tap in to. India's chief exports were silks, calico cottons, sugar, and opium. Cotton spinning and weaving was the national industry of India, and although most production occurred within a village context, there were centers that specialized in the export trade—notably Dacca in East Bengal, which in 1800 boasted 8,000 looms, a population of 200,000, and some 6,000 brick-built dwellings.[1] This trade was organized and financed by a sophisticated network of bankers and merchants, headed by such people as the Marwaris community from Rajasthan and the Jagat Sheth family of Bengal. Payment was made via bills of exchange known as *hundis*.[2] Beneath these leading financiers were myriad wholesalers and money-lenders who transacted with artisan producers and loaned them money for the purchase of raw materials.

This strong trading tradition underpinned a correspondingly developed urban culture. In the region around the Ganges in north India there were some 60 centers with populations above 10,000, with many more having populations of 2,000–3,000.[3] Of the larger cities some, like Dhaka and Benares, were commercial centers, others, notably Luknow, Lahore, and Delhi, were administrative and political capitals, and others combined these functions. Murshidabad was an example of the latter. As the capital of Bengal it was the site of government offices and attracted the residences of wealthy landlords and tax gatherers. Yet it was also an important banking center and impressed Robert Clive when he arrived there in 1757:

> This city is as extensive, populous, and rich as the city of London, with this difference that there were individuals in the first possessing infinitely greater property than in the last city.[4]

It was, indeed, the splendor in which the ruling elites of India lived that struck European visitors and made India a byword for opulent living. Sir Thomas Roe, Hawkins's successor at the court of Jahangir in Agra—though nominally representing not the East India Company but King James I—wrote to his Royal patron:

> Fame hath done much for the Glory of this place. Yet it cannot be denied that this King is one of the mightyest Princes in Asia, as well in the extent of territory as in revenue; equal to the Turk, far exceeding the Persian.[5]

Much of the industrial production of India was generated by the conspicuous consumption of the Mughals and their princely allies like the Rajputs of Rajasthan, and court cities tended to show concentrations of workers in the tailoring, jewelry-making, metal-working, construction, and paper trades.[6]

However, the striking achievements of Indian commerce should not eclipse the essential importance of agriculture. Land, its cultivation, control, and taxation, was the basis of the economy, the social hierarchy, organized religion, claims to status, and the sinews of state power. Approximately three-quarters of the population lived in villages. This does not mean that they were all primarily farmers. While the vast majority of rural Indians did engage in farming, many combined this with domestic industry. The distinction between agriculture and industry was always blurred—a state of affairs historians have come to label proto-industrial.

Central to the social organization of the countryside was the village community. This was an entity the British struggled to comprehend. A series of writers during the 19th century came to romanticize the Indian village, regarding it, not merely as the historical foundation of Indian society, but as a surviving relic of a way of life that had once been shared by the Indo-Aryan peoples of Europe.[7] Sir Charles Metcalfe's description of 1830 bears repeating:

> The Village Communities are little Republics, having nearly everything that they want within themselves, and almost independent of any foreign relations. They seem to last where nothing else lasts. Dynasty after dynasty tumbles down . . . but the Village Communities remain the same. In times of trouble they arm and fortify themselves; a hostile army passes through the country; the Village Community collect their cattle within their walls, and let the enemy pass unprovoked. . . . The union of the Village Communities . . . has, I conceive, contributed more than any other cause to the preservation of the people of India through all the revolutions and changes which they have suffered, and it is in a high degree conducive to their happiness and to the enjoyment of a great portion of freedom and independence.[8]

Now there *was* truth in this picture. The villages of India were indeed self-sufficient in many ways, characterized by a hereditary division of labor in which weavers, shoe-makers, and metal workers dwelt alongside farmers and shared in the collective output of the village in return for the manufactures they supplied. Even so, the villages were far from the self-sufficient and harmonious islands of Victorian mythology. Unsurprisingly, there were marked inequalities within the villages, with larger landholders able to exact labor services from those with limited land rights or no land or trade at all. These villages themselves were linked within regional trading networks, sending goods to market centers (signified by the name *ganj*) or beyond to major towns or ports for dispatch overseas. Merchants were active within the rural areas, arranging for the buying and selling of food and manufactured products and lending money to cultivators in straightened circumstances. One indicator of the integration of the village communities into the wider economy is indeed this use of cash: in Bengal, for example, most land taxes were paid in cash and the rural banking system was well developed.[9] The prime source of the Mughals' fabled wealth was the tax they levied upon the land. The collection of these taxes was often farmed out to wealthy individuals known as zamindars (which means, literally, "holder of land"), and the burden was high—reaching up to one-half of the gross produce of the village. The Indian village, in short, was neither isolated, homogenous, nor unchanging.

Even so, beneath the busy exterior of trade, cash, and industry, India's economy manifested one structural weakness: technological backwardness. Methods of production, on the land and in manufacturing, were simple and static. There were hardly any labor-saving devices and no attempt had been made to utilize non-human sources of power. In many parts of India ploughs lacked iron shares and did little more than scratch the surface; cow dung was burned as fuel rather than used as manure; carts were rare and oxen capable of pulling them even rarer. The artisans of India were unrivalled in manual skill, but they worked in ways that had hardly changed in centuries. "Both early modern Europe and medieval China," writes Raychaudhuri, "were far ahead of mid-eighteenth century India in such crucial fields of technology as the use of wind and water power, metallurgy, printing, nautical instruments, and basic tools and precision instruments."[10] In the 18th century, this conduct of a flourishing trading culture upon a traditional technical base was far from unusual, and there is no reason to countenance the views of those nationalists for whom India was on the verge of an industrial revolution when the British arrived. It is nonetheless undeniable that the underdevelopment of India's productive potential exposed it to the power of the one nation that, among all others in the world, was to take the exceptional step of revolutionizing its systems of production.

Politically, India had been subject to the imperial sway of the Mughals since the early 1500s. This empire, elaborated by a succession of great rulers such as Babur, Akbar, and Shah-Jahan, was one of the most impressive—administratively and culturally—in the world. Yet it was also about to enter a long phase of decline. By the late 17th century its rulers were struggling to maintain the authority of the center against the challenge of rival states, notably the Marathas, a struggle which drained the Mughal state of power and resources. As the imperial grip weakened, there arose a tendency for provincial governors and previously allied princes and local elites, like the Rajputs and the Jats, to wrest for themselves freedom of action. Accordingly, the 18th century was a period of state formation within India as the once-commanding empire broke apart.[11] Within this context there was a struggle for power, as new dynasties were founded, old ones were disinterred, and military adventurers took advantage of the vacuum left by the contracting reach of Mughal power.

The flux and instability of 18th-century India made a vivid impression upon the British, forming the backdrop—and justification—for traditional narratives of British conquest. India, it was said, was in a state of anarchy and decline, rapine and pillage. As Percival Spear wrote in a popular history of modern India:

> The British found a country in ruins. . . . Not only did they encounter dismantled fortresses and deserted palaces, but canals run dry, tanks or reservoirs broken, roads neglected, towns in decay, and whole regions depopulated. . . . India was exhausted and for the moment without inspiration. . . . Everywhere the links between the rulers and the people had been snapped. . . . The rule of force was universal and politically there was no hope.[12]

From this perspective, the East India Company was pretty much forced to uphold law and order amidst the void left by the Mughals, for only then could it continue to trade and India continue to prosper. With no Indian power able to maintain stability, the reluctant British found themselves, by default, called upon to found the *Pax Britannica*.

Such lurid depictions of 18th-century India are now considered inadequate and self-serving. To begin with, India was not in a state of disordered decline. If it had been, it would be hard to explain why so many Europeans were keen to expand their trading connections with it. Of course, war and uncertainty damaged trade in some places and some times. Banditry was rife between Delhi and Agra; western Bengal and Orissa were ravaged by the Marathas; irrigation decayed in the lands between the Ganges and Jamna Rivers; agriculture was seriously disrupted in Assam by the armies of rival chieftains, and so on.[13] But for most of India, this remained a period of growth and new opportunities. Population was rising, the new mouths being fed by an expanded agricultural output, itself reflecting an overall extension of the cultivated area. As a result, there were no serious famines in the first six decades of the century. Land revenues were still collected in cash, which suggests that foodstuffs were yet being marketed. Trade, too, was flourishing in these years with, notes Chris Bayly, European merchants purchasing ever-greater quantities of cloth and saltpeter.[14]

The second point to have emerged from recent research has a deeper significance, not merely for our understanding of Mughal decline, but for the whole narrative of British intervention. For it is now argued that it was the economic prosperity of late Mughal India, not its stagnation and decline, that undermined the authority of the empire.

As Marx would have predicted, it was cash and commerce that dissolved the old structures of power. Contrary to traditional accounts, which have the Mughal regime rotting, like a fish, from the head as various misguided and self-indulgent rulers squandered their golden heritage, it was, rather, dismembered by the rise of confident and well-resourced groups with the capacity to challenge its authority successfully. Groups like landlord-warrior elites who extracted increased revenue from the land and used it to build up their private armies; successful peasant cultivators-cum-warriors like the Jats and the Sikhs; the merchants and bankers who financed governments and negotiated with European tradesmen; the so-called scribal castes—the literate men employed to transact state, commercial, and financial business; and the Brahmin priests who played an increasingly important role in bestowing theocratic legitimacy upon socially upstart rulers such as the Marathas. It was the prosperity and prestige of these groups that allowed them to contest Mughal hegemony and effectively found new states—a process that can be witnessed in such strategic territories as the Punjab, Bengal, Hyderabad, Mysore, and Oudh.

So India was indeed in a state of flux—but a flux symptomatic, less of social decay than of dynamism, as new groups and individuals emerged willing to throw off Mughal domination and found innovative types of state. And it was into this restless, shifting, evolving India that the East India Company found itself drawn, adding, in the process, one more element making for a reconfiguration of the subcontinent.

2

Indians and the Making of the Raj

If commerce unraveled the old India, it also created the conditions for the new. When the bid for all-India supremacy by the Marathas, the most formidable of the post-Mughal political entities, ended in defeat outside Delhi at the hands of an Afghan army in 1761, it looked as if the subcontinent would break up into a patchwork of autonomous states of varying sizes—more akin to the map of Europe than the preceding Mughal Empire. That this did not happen was the consequence of the British. And here we have the single biggest impact of Britain upon India: the fact that the Mughal Empire had a successor in the shape of the British Empire, an empire that, in turn, was to bequeath the states of India, Pakistan, and Bangladesh today. This comparatively simple political configuration of the subcontinent is the most visible legacy of British rule.

Yet at this point two things must be grasped. First, the British Raj that ultimately emerged was neither planned nor envisaged at the commencement of the process. Any suggestion that the East India Company would come to occupy the imperial throne vacated by the Great Mughal would have appeared outlandish to Britons and Indians alike. Second, the expansion of British power within India was not something thrust upon passive or resisting Indians by a masterful colonizing race. Important sections of Indian society have as fair claim to be considered the architects of the Raj as the British themselves. Put another way, the Raj did not just happen to Indians; as befitted the dynamic nature of 18th-century India, they played a leading role in making their own history—even if that history unfolded in ways unanticipated by the chief actors. If Indians never *willed* British conquest, they unwittingly helped to make it happen.

The paradox of this outcome should not obscure the logic behind it. For the British were deeply implicated in the forces that were making the new India. Most obviously, the Company, by its trading activities, fuelled the growth of the market economy. It purchased cloth, silk, indigo, saltpeter, and spices like pepper and cardamom for export, paying for these goods with silver that was much needed by India's merchants and government exchequers. In the conduct of its inland trade, the Company was heavily dependent upon the services of merchants, bankers, and scribal castes who negotiated with producers, transported goods, supplied working capital, and exchanged money. By this means powerful reciprocal interests were created: numerous Indian groups—farmers, money lenders, artisans, merchants, rural and governing elites—had a stake in the East India Company and the Company had a stake in them. The Company based its operations in a series of fortified factory ports, notably Calcutta, Madras, and Bombay. Many Indians were drawn to these towns, not just for the economic opportunities they offered, but for the protection they provided from the instability beyond their walls. In 1668, Bombay's population was 10,000; within six years it stood at 60,000.[1] By the end of the 18th century, the population of Madras was some 25,000. Eclipsing them all was Calcutta. In 1797, it was estimated to be the home of 10,000 Indian shopkeepers, with a total population of 200,000 by 1822, a further 100,000 entering the city each day to work.[2] A new urban culture emerged in these so-called Black Towns, distinct from, but inextricably bound up with, the activities of the European community and with a vested interest in its continuance. And then there was the very thing that had first won Jahangir's respect for the British: their naval power. Both Bombay and Calcutta sustained extensive merchant fleets that carried Indian goods along the coasts and also across to the Middle and Far East. Alongside these trading vessels were ships of war, and in 1674, Shivaji, the formidable leader of the Marathas, signed a treaty with the Company in the hope that he would gain its naval support in his prolonged struggle with the Mughals.[3]

But what was it that induced the British to take the fateful step beyond being merely one among many commercial players within the Indian dynamic to enter what Chris Bayly has described as the military bazaar that was 18th-century India?[4] Most important was the pervasive connection between politics and economics that existed in the India of that time. In the absence of an established institutional framework, the exploitation of economic opportunities was dependent upon the concomitant political and security conditions being created and sustained. Merchants were among a number of social groups competing for ascendancy, yet the British had obvious cause to favor them. It was, as we shall see, a conspiracy of bankers and merchants that drew the Company into the internal political affairs of Bengal. On the Malabar coast of Southwest India the British assumed formal control so as to defend the position of the Moplahs, a very useful merchant class who helped them in conducting inland trade, against the Hindu Nayar chieftains, who were the dominant group within the region. In Gujarat, it was the Marathas who were the threat to local merchants, who urged the Company to capture the castle overshadowing Surat and extend their territories into the hinterland—both of which they did. Political influence was itself highly remunerative, as when the Company pressed the nawabs of Bengal into allowing them to trade inland without the need to pay customs duties. Indeed the prime mover behind the growth of the British Empire in India was the belief among those who administered the Company that political power was a route to riches. That this equation was in fact fallacious supplied, ironically, the impetus to continual expansion as the Company chased the elusive dividends of power.

What gave the Company the ability to play the game of Indian politics was its formidable military presence. A condition for all those competing for position in the new India was the capacity to command military resources. Sikhs, Rajputs, zamindars, Marathas: all could put armed troops in the field and the Company was no exception. The composition of its army was no exception either. For the East India Company army was a mercenary force, recruited among groups with a martial tradition who were prepared to sell their services to the highest bidder. For them the Company was a good employer, for it could afford to offer high and, more important in an India where arrears of pay were notorious, regular wages. Increasingly recruiting among the Rajput and Brahmin castes of the territory of Oudh, by 1805 the army had grown to 155,000 men, of which European-born troops and officers made up little more than a tenth. It was, in other words, an Indian army that conquered India for the British. What gave this army an edge was, first, the British control of the seas, which meant it could transport and supply troops speedily along the coast, and second, the training and leadership the British officers provided. If the Indian sepoys were not always *well* led, they were *bravely* led by charismatic and risk-taking officers who installed a degree of discipline unfamiliar among purely indigenous forces. The result was an army that quickly gained a reputation for invincibility in the face of apparently impossible odds and, as such, its services were much prized by Indians prepared to call upon the British to assist them in their local power struggles. Of course, as civilian leaders throughout history have discovered, it is far easier to persuade an army to enter the political fray than it is to induce it to leave.

The third element in the equation of Company intervention was the presence of a European rival in the shape of the French East India Company. The latter, under the visionary leadership of Dupleix, was the first to see that it could put its military superiority to profitable account by acquiring territory in India—for with land came tax revenue.[5] The French focused their efforts in the Karnatic region of South India, deploying their army to overthrow the ruler (or nawab) of the state of Karnataka, replacing him with one Chandra Singh, while in Hyderabad another French protégé, Salabat Jang, was made nizam. These transactions brought land and wealth to the French; unfortunately, they also brought them into collision with the British East India Company, which had no wish to see a French Empire emerge in the hinterland of its own port of Madras. Step forward Robert Clive. Company clerk turned military adventurer, Clive was the epitome of the sort of man for whom the maelstrom of Indian politics offered the chance to gain a personal fortune, make a reputation, and—it turned out—found an Empire. In a characteristically audacious move, he captured Karnataka's capital of Arcot in 1751 with a force of just 200 European troops and 600 sepoys—only to find himself besieged by a French-led army of 10,000. Clive's defense of Arcot lasted 50 days before he was relieved by a Company force and a body of cavalry sent by the Marathas—writing, thereby, one of the most glorious chapters in the mythological history of the Raj. Thus freed, Clive and the Company's forces proceeded to capture and execute Chandra Singh and place their own candidate upon the throne of Karnataka. Dupleix's schemes were in ruins and with them French ambitions in India.[6] But for Clive the events in the Karnatic were pregnant with meaning. First, he had apparently shown that with brave and audacious leadership the Company's Indian troops could carry all before them; and second, that the Company was not confined to dealing in cotton piece goods and spices: it could break dynasties and make kings, opening before itself a destiny far removed from that envisaged for it by its merchant-founders. These lessons he was shortly to apply in the state of Bengal.

With its lands watered by the Ganges and Brahmaputra Rivers, its strategic location for coastal and East-Asian trade, its thriving cotton weaving industry, and its 40 million inhabitants, Bengal was the richest and most fertile region in India. Appropriately enough, it was here that the themes in Anglo-Indian relations we have traced were played out most explicitly. Bengal had represented a central buttress of the Mughal Empire, being administered on the emperors' behalf by viceroys designated by the title of nawab, who remitted a rich revenue stream to the coffers of the Mughal treasury. Yet it was precisely this economic prosperity, combined with its location at the eastern extremity of the Empire, that allowed the nawabs to rest for themselves evergreater autonomy from the early 1700s. By the 1740s, Bengal was a classic successor state, ceasing altogether to pay tribute to Delhi and under the stewardship of one Ali Vardi Khan, who had forcibly seized the nawabship in 1740, filling the high offices of state with family members.

However, Khan's position was never unquestioned and even the quickest glance at the characteristics of his reign dispels any lingering stereotypes of oriental despotism. For one thing, the Khan's were Muslims ruling a state where Hindus had a slight numerical edge and, more significant, dominated the most influential positions in terms of access to political and economic power—accounting, for instance, for the large majority of bankers, merchants, tax collectors, and administrators. Muslims, by contrast, were most typically found among the ranks of the poor peasant cultivators. Even within a Muslim context the Khan dynasty was isolated, originating among the Shias from the North West, whereas the local population were Bengali converts to the Sunni branch of the faith. One consequence of this was that the nawabs found it difficult to staff an adequate army—itself a real draw back as the ever-sanguine Marathas were intruding into their territories, being eventually induced to desist in 1751 by the payment of an annual tribute of 1.2 million rupees and the effective cessation of the province of Orissa.[7]

The root of the nawab's weakness was finance. Founding a new state and running a mercenary army required money, and for this the state became dependent upon the financial resources of some key interest groups. First among these was the Hindu banking Jagat Sheth banking family. Jagat Sheth means literally Merchants of the World, and within the world of Bengal finance, this was no idle boast. Their influence was profound: peasants afflicted by harvest shortfall, zamindar tax collectors struggling to meet their obligations, merchants in need of credit, European traders requiring to exchange currency: all turned to the Sheth's. The government was no exception and Marshall writes that the Sheth's were virtual partners in government, managing state finances and even controlling the Bengal mint.[8] Another influential element within the state were the zamindars—the hereditary class of largely Hindu tax collectors. Though they did not own the land they taxed, they did exert authority over the cultivators, dispensing local justice and police services and maintaining bodies of armed retainers. The zamindars were evidently a force to be reckoned with; yet what made this especially so was the process of consolidation which had been occurring among their number for some years. By 1740, 60 percent of the nawabs' revenue came from just 15 zamindars, operating over territories of 10,000 square miles or more and commanding—as in the case of the Burwan Zamindari—an armed militia of 30,000. Like the Sheth's, these wealthy zamindars were effectively partners in government.

If the nawabs were dependent upon the activities of the large bankers and revenue collectors, they were reliant, also, upon the prosperity brought to their territory by the operations of the East India Company. Calcutta was the Company's most thriving base. Silk, cotton textiles, sugar, and saltpeter were all purchased by the Company from across Bengal and shipped toward London and East Asia. Exports to London alone amounted to £400,000 per annum in the 1740s. These goods were paid for chiefly with silver, the Company infusing £200,000 of this precious metal yearly into the Bengal economy.[9] In recognition of the vital part played by the Company in the commercial dynamism of Bengal, it had been granted, in 1717, the privilege of trading its goods free from customs duties.

Bengal, then, was in a state of delicately poised equilibrium: ruled by an alien usurping nawab who was dependent upon, and correspondingly checked by, the services of Hindu bankers, hereditary tax collectors, and British merchants. It was this equilibrium that imploded in 1756 when the death of Ali Vardi brought his 20-year-old grandson Siraj-ud-Daula to the throne. With the impetuosity of youth, Siraj was resolved to be no conciliatory nawab, content merely to preserve his position through playing one group against another. He was determined, rather, to assert his authority against the various groups that had come to hem it in. If he had pursued a divide and conquer strategy, moving against the various interests in turn, he might have been successful.

He chose, instead, to initiate coercive policies against all simultaneously, alienating all the key players within Bengal. "He made no distinction between vice and virtue," commented one Muslim Chronicle, and soon became "more detested than Pharaoh."[10] Stalwarts of his grandfather's government—notably Rai Durlabh, the Hindu head of administration, and Mir Jafar, Commander-in-Chief of the Army—were dismissed to make way for his own favorites. Merchants, zamindars, and bankers found themselves confronted with demands for cash. In the case of the Jagat Sheth's, 30 million rupees were demanded—protests being met by a physical assault upon the leader of the house and threats of forcible circumcision and conversion to Islam. European traders were pressed to make loans also, the Dutch East India Company agreeing to pay 450,000 rupees and the French 350,000.

The British East India Company faced similar cash demands but, unlike the other European companies, refused to pay and instead commenced work to enhance the defenses around its base of Fort St. George in Calcutta. For Siraj this was an unacceptable provocation, and when his demand that the work cease passed unheeded, he sent a force into Calcutta in June 1756. The fort was poorly defended by only 514 men, many of whom were Swiss mercenaries. When the governor fled to a boat in the harbor, the troops consoled themselves with the contents of the wine stores and the fort was quickly overrun. What happened next has been the subject of much dispute and even stronger expressions of feeling. The remaining European troops, along with the sepoys and various European and Anglo-Indian civilians still left within the fort, were placed in an airless prison cell some 18 feet by 14 feet—the infamous Black Hole of Calcutta. Deprived of air and water and trampling each other underfoot, a number of the prisoners died in the sweltering heat of the Bengal night. Exactly how many perished is unknown: original claims of 123 fatalities out of 146 are now discounted, and a number closer to 44 finds greater favor. We will never know for sure since no count was made of the numbers of prisoners actually taken. But the details of the case were of little concern to the British; what mattered was the image of scores of British men and women struggling to breathe while Siraj, the model of oriental cruelty, "slept off his debauch." "Nothing in history or fiction," to continue the extravagant words of the historian Lord Macaulay in 1840, "approaches the horrors which were recounted by the few survivors of that night."[11]

However dark were the events of the Black Hole, they constituted a crisis for the East India Company—as well as for the significant sections of Bengal society who had become dependent upon the Company's financial and trading networks. A relief force of 900 European troops and 1,500 sepoys was immediately dispatched from Madras under the command of Clive. Little difficulty was encountered in ejecting Siraj from Calcutta and forcing him to come to terms, according to which the Company was to be restored its trading privileges, while its army was to defend Bengal against incursions by the likes of the Marathas.

Thus far, only the status quo ante had been restored. What happened next was the step that would lead to the founding of a British Empire in India. Quite simply, powerful vested interests within Bengal came to the conclusion that their security and prosperity would be best served by the ejection of Siraj from the nawabship. Among those taking this view were the Jagat Sheths, the great Sikh merchant Omichand, and the aggrieved Jafar. From their perspective, the presence within Bengal of a powerful Company army was a heaven-sent opportunity and they entered into negotiations with Clive to bring about this political revolution. If the conspiracy did not originate with Clive, he was quick to sense the opportunities it presented—for personal enrichment as much as for the profits of the Company. His experience of the Karnatic showed that kingmaking was more than feasible, while the rich province of Bengal represented a prize altogether more alluring. For if the Company could secure a share of the revenue of Bengal, then it might cover its operating costs, leaving the monies it raised through trade as pure profit. It was just this scenario that was to motivate the first phase of the Company's territorial expansion within India.

By early June 1757, the plot had been laid, the central element being the wealth of the Jagat Sheths. Clive's army was to overthrow Siraj and put Jafar on the throne. For this service the Company would receive enhanced trading privileges, gifts, and compensation amounting to around £1,250,000.[12] Now all that was required was to engineer a battle. Clive wrote a letter to Siraj cataloging the Company's grievances with his administration and then led a force of 1,000 Europeans and 2,000 sepoys to confront the nawab's army of 50,000 at Plassey on June 23, 1757. The engagement was ragged and unfocused—not least because most of Siraj's army was in fact loyal to Jafar and the conspirators. With his army disintegrating Siraj fled the field, only to be captured and put to death by Jafar's son, Miran. With good reason did Pannikar describe Plassey as "a transaction, not a battle."[13]

It had been the ostensible object of Plassey to place in office a nawab prepared to respect the old balance of power within Bengal, which had

permitted private traders, bankers, tax farmers and European merchants to pursue their interests within the context of a post-Mughal
state. Yet no such balance proved attainable. Even had it wished it, the
East India Company could not return to a blameless life of commercial accumulation. For one thing, it had become a zamindar in its own
right, having been granted revenue collection rights over 900 square
miles in order to pay for the upkeep of its army. This army was itself
the dominant political fact in Bengal: it had unmade one nawab and
made another, who thereafter existed on its sufferance. At the same
time, the Company was consolidating its economic dominance of the
state. It had secured monopoly rights to the trade in such vital products as salt, indigo, and betel nut, while its employees set about exploiting the political influence of the Company to force favorable trade
deals with up-country merchants and artisans. All of this trade was
tax free, and the nawab's revenues were undercut at the same time
as he was subject to a series of financial demands from the Company,
which believed he had a personal fortune of £40 million hidden away.
Inevitably, state finances were soon heading into crisis and Jafar was
unable to make the payments the Company demanded to cover the
burgeoning costs of defending Bengal against the Marathas. But when
the Company demanded the secession of three further provinces in
order to make its revenue receipts secure, Jafar refused.[14] As far as the
Company was concerned, Jafar was proving unreliable and ungrate-
ful, and it was decided in 1760 to replace him as nawab by his son-
in-law, Mir Kasim—who repaid the service by granting the requested
territorial concessions and handing out a further £200,000 in gifts to
Company officials.

Unexpectedly, Kasim's initial tractability belied a more steely political purpose. Determined to reassert the independent authority of the
nawab, he withdrew his court to the western province of Bihar, refused
to accept a British resident, began rebuilding an army on European
lines, and demanded that the Jagat Sheths withdraw from political
activity. Having become accustomed to the idea that it could dictate
policy to the nawabs, the Company was uneasy at these developments. When Kasim next proceeded to try to end the practice whereby
Company officials trading in a *private* capacity exploited concessions
granted to the East India Company as a corporate body, the Company
again resolved on regime change. Kasim was deposed and Jafar—who
was willing to promise the British complete freedom of trade—was
restored in his place. Unwilling to take this result lying down, Kasim

assembled an anti-Company coalition, which included the Mughal Emperor Shah Alam and Shuja-ud-Daula, the ruler of the neighboring state of Oudh—the largest province of the Mughal empire. Battle was joined at Buxor in October 1764. This was a far more significant encounter than Plassey, with regard both to the intensity of the fighting and the consequences of the outcome. Once again, a disciplined and resolute Company army prevailed over a much larger force. In so doing, the power of the Company was asserted, not merely in Bengal, but across North India, as the Mughal Emperor was humbled in the face of Company firepower and the nawab of Oudh was allowed to retain his position only upon the sufferance of the British. In Bengal, the nawab was reduced to a mere figure head: the Company effectively controlled the administration, receiving from the Mughal Emperor the technical title of diwan, which meant that it was legally entitled to run Bengal's taxation system in return for a yearly tribute of £272,000. An annual sum of £33 million now flowed the Company's way, money it could use to cover its costs, purchase goods for export to Britain, and expand its armed forces—which numbered 25,000 men in 1768 and 40,000 in 1784. After Buxor, the people of Bengal could be in no doubt that they were subjects of a new and alien government—though what, precisely, this exotic power represented was as yet unclear, not merely to Indians, but to the Company's directors in London, the British government, and not a few of those who had brought about this state of affairs.

To summarize, there was no British conquest of Bengal as such. The extension of British power occurred *via* the East India Company and proceeded in piece-meal fashion over several years. Even then it was not initiated with this end in view, followed no preconceived plan, and was certainly not endorsed by politically-conscious opinion within Britain. What, says Lawrence James, drove events forward were the actions of a few "private enterprise imperialists" motivated by the prospect of monetary gain.[15] These men, also, possessed no plan and were drawn into the vortex of Bengali politics by sectional interest groups who wished to utilize the military services of the Company in their own power struggles with the erratic and domineering Siraj-ud-Duala. But if the likes of Clive had no blueprint for conquest they were, after Plassey, guided by something far more revolutionary in its implications: a principle. This principle stated that it was permissible to use force to reconfigure the internal politics of Bengal if this appeared the path of greatest net benefit to the Company. The interests, rights, and attitudes of Indians themselves were an irrelevance, except insofar as they affected the consequences of a line of policy. It was an exercise in "realeconomik" which had, crucially, no inherent stopping point. On the contrary, the course taken in Bengal might well extend further into India if the balance of advantage seemed to require it. Such a pursuit of personal gain unfettered by any consideration of the interests of the host community was without precedent. Not for nothing did the East India Company quickly become a kind of Frankenstein's monster, feeding upon the fruits of its own avarice.

3

Bengal and Beyond

Owing to the complicity of strategically situated Indians, the clumsy miscalculations of a succession of nawabs, and the discipline of the Company army, the assumption of power in Bengal had proven comparatively easy. The question of what, precisely, to do with it raised altogether more intractable issues. It was not the *purpose* of Company rule that was in doubt: it was to raise sufficient revenue from Bengal to cover its outlays—the day-to-day costs of administration, the expense of sustaining a sizeable Company army, and, above all, to fund the purchase of Indian goods for export to Europe, ending, thereby, the unpopular practice of paying for Indian goods with scarce British silver. All the money generated by selling goods in Britain and elsewhere would thus be cleared as pure profit. In economic terms, the annexation of Bengal was a coup, though the ideal of a self-sufficient Company was never realized. While Indian tax revenues were certainly adequate to cover the purchase of goods for export—ending, from 1757, the inflow of British bullion—the costs of administration and defense had an inconvenient habit of rising in line with the extent of territory controlled, so that the British lion in India always gave the impression of chasing its own tail.

If the ends of Company rule were clear enough, what had still to be resolved was *how* this sizeable, populous, and complex state was to be administered. The Company lacked the two prerequisites of effective government: personnel and knowledge. In 1756, there were a mere 751 British nationals in Bengal amidst a population of 40 million. Even by 1773, the Company could call upon the services of only 250 employees and agents, a figure that had crept up to 400 by 1800.[1] Further disabling the effectiveness of the Company was ignorance: the

British knew little of the language, customs, land tenure, or tax system of Bengal. In this context, they had little option but to delegate to Indians as many administrative functions as possible, being content to set the parameters of policy and oversee their commercial interests. This was the approach to government characterizing the governorship of Warren Hastings (1772–85). He saw the British as primarily supervisors, respecting the cultural traditions of Bengal and leaving as much as possible of the old Mughal system of governance in place—making extensive use of the services of Indian clerks, tax collectors, merchants, and bankers.

This policy of arm's-length regulation had everything to recommend it but its consequences. Predictably, the Indians to whom discretionary authority was devolved took advantage of the situation to forward their own interests, siphoning off funds for themselves, taking bribes, dealing harshly with those subject to their revenue demands, and colluding in corruption. Just how prevalent these practices were remains unclear owing to the very paucity of information that accorded Indians privileged positions in the first place; but the belief that Indian agents were corrupt and ineffectual soon became commonplace and contributed to a policy of Anglicizing the higher levels of Company administration—with results that subsisted throughout the history of British rule and played a not unimportant role in radicalizing those educated Indians who were barred from lucrative governmental careers.

However, it was the conduct of the Company and its own employees that posed by far the greater threat to the sustainability of British dominion. This body of merchants, unexpectedly finding themselves in control of an apparently rich territory, could not resist the temptation to appropriate larger and larger sums for private and corporate gain. Possessing monopolies in the trade of key commodities, they found it easy to intimidate producers into selling goods at ruinously low prices which they then passed on to consumers for inflated sums. Worse still, Company employees, being only moderately remunerated in a land where life expectancy was short and the universal ambition was to amass a fortune and return to Britain, took to private trade to supplement their earnings. Armed with certificates exempting them from internal customs duties, they were able to drive native merchants out of business and call upon the military services of the army to pressure artisans into parting with their goods at knockdown prices. All the while, the chief engine of state finance, the land tax, was being continually ratcheted up to bankroll the Company's operations and dividends.

In 1764–65 the land revenue realized £0.8 million; in 1765–66 £1.4 million; in 1771–72 £2.3 million; and by 1775–76 £2.8 million.[2] "Such is the little regard which they show to the people of these kingdoms," lamented the writer of the Siyar Mutakharin, "and such their antipathy and indifference to their welfare, that the people under their dominion groan everywhere, and are reduced to poverty and distress."[3]

The inevitable issue of this conduct was to plunge Bengal into an economic and financial crisis. In 1769, the Company's resident in Murshidabad informed the directors in London:

> It must give pain to an Englishman to have reason to think that since the accession of the Company to the Dewani the condition of the people of this country has been worse than it was before, and yet I'm afraid the fact is undoubted. . . . This fine country, which flourished under the most despotic and arbitrary Government, is verging towards its ruin while the English have so really a great a share in the Administration.[4]

The fact was that the endemic poverty of the Bengal masses, and the corresponding backwardness of its agriculture, meant that the province could never generate the kind of revenue needed to fund both the needs of the state and the private speculations of Company servants. What surplus revenue the land did yield was fast swallowed up by the ever-vociferous demands of the military, which accounted for 43 percent of Company spending in the years 1760 to 1800.[5] By seeking to extract excessive sums from Bengal, the inexperienced East India Company helped to precipitate, in 1770, the first serious famine in living memory when the monsoon rains failed—leaving up to 10 million people, or a quarter of the population, dead.

Tragedy for the people of Bengal threatened ruin for the Company. News of its assumption of the diwanship had provoked speculative buying of Company stock as investors sought a slice of this license to print money. But amidst the devastation of 1770, revenues slumped, failing to cover even military expenses let alone annual dividends. Having well and truly feasted upon the goose that laid the golden eggs, the Company was forced to turn to the British government for an emergency loan of £1 million.

These events were of greater moment for the future of British rule in India than the lauded victories at Plassey and Buxor. For the view now crystallized in London that the Company could no longer be allowed to do as it pleased in India. It had, quite simply, to be saved from itself if Bengal, and Britain's wider interests in India, were to be preserved.

The result was twofold. To begin with, in 1773 Parliament passed the Regulating Act, which asserted, for the first time, the principle that the Company was answerable to Parliament for its conduct in India. A council of five was established to administer the affairs of Bengal, the Company appointing two members and the British government three, one of which was to be the governor-general—the first occupant of the post being Hastings. A supreme court was also set up in Calcutta with the remit of holding Company employees to account for their conduct—including toward the native population.

Of course, as Judith Brown points out, it was all very well asserting the principle of government control over the Company: that control had also to be made effective.[6] This required a much tighter and more direct supervision of Indian administration than had prevailed hitherto, and in 1786, Lord Cornwallis was sent to India to make this happen. Cornwallis was determined to replace the freebooting imperialism that had bedeviled Bengal with a constitutional government overseeing the application of laws to which all were subject. He was convinced that the miasma of corruption into which the state had sunk was attributable to the policy of working closely with Indians, who were, he believed, inherently given to embezzlement and fraud. To excise this supposed source of infection, he proceeded with a policy of Anglicizing the influential positions within the administration, confining Indians to a purely subordinate support role. Company officials were themselves to be given limited scope for discretion—and hence corruption—in their dealings with the subject population, most notably with the decision to fix permanently the amount of the land tax to be paid, ending the possibility of negotiating payments on an *ad hoc* basis. Good Whig that he was, Cornwallis similarly insisted upon a separation of executive and judicial functions: revenue collection officers lost their previous powers to enforce local justice, with Indians and Company officials alike being subject to the rule of law enforced by a network of courts and magistrates. In 1789, the abuses perpetrated by Company officials when trading in a private capacity were ended when all private trade was made illegal.

What did these developments mean for Indians? The worst abuses of Company rule were checked and some stability restored to the framework of the economic and fiscal system after the vortex that had been unleashed with the overthrow of Siraj-ud-Duala. Yet these benefits came at the price of a fundamental shift in the status of Indians themselves. At the commencement of the Company's governing odyssey Bengali interest groups were partners in the making of policy, initiating the moves against a capricious nawab, hiring the services of Clive's army, and administering the revenue system on behalf of his successors. With Cornwallis's drive toward Anglicization and the introduction of British constitutional models, these once-powerful indigenous groups found themselves marginalized from the center of power, forced to operate, henceforward, within parameters set by the Company and, ultimately, the British government. More generally, there began what Spear characterizes as a "widening of the racial gulf" between Indians and British administrators. As the government of Bengal became "more English and more Olympian," there was an end to the previous socializing of men such as Hastings, Chapman, and Palmer with Indian rajahs, Brahmins, and Muslim learned men. Hastings's friend, General Palmer, lamented the result:

> I observe with great concern the system of depressing then adopted by the present government and imitated in the manners of almost every European. They are excluded from all posts of great respectability or emolument, and are treated with mortifying hauteur and reserve.[7]

Even so, it would be a mistake to exaggerate the abruptness of the transition represented by Cornwallis's reforms. Whatever the ideology of the Company Raj, the logistics of British government continued to dictate events on the ground. And here it remained the case that British officials were few in number, often possessed little knowledge of the local language or customary practices, and were frequently moved from one district to another. As Brown remarks, "the British officer was literally stranded in a sea of ignorance and incompetence."[8] All of these circumstances rendered British power as dependent as ever upon the active cooperation of key Indians—the Indians who kept the village accounts, staffed the courts, translated for the sahib, served as clerks, and manned the police force and army. Less than 400 European officials, however talented—and the Company's servants were a generally mediocre and poorly educated bunch—and even if supported in 1803 by something like 18,000 white troops, could not hope to build an empire in Bengal, let alone India as a whole. The Raj was as much the creation of Indians as it ever was the British.

The expansion of British power beyond Bengal is a subject often treated in exhaustive, even loving, detail—only gaining in bewildering complexity as a consequence. To describe it here would take us far from the intention of this volume. It will suffice for our purposes if we can grasp the logic which underlay the uneven, but unidirectional, spread of British dominion.

It must first be understood that there was no one factor making for the acquisition of territory. The process took place over too long a time (almost a century separated Plassey from the final absorption of the Punjab in 1849); involved too many very different governor-generals (each operating beyond the effective reach of Company headquarters in London); was a response to too great a diversity of local circumstances; and reflected the opportunism of too many military and civilian adventurers, for any single motive to possibly account for what transpired. If one factor were to be singled about beyond all others, it was the perennial need of the Company to pay its way. As the scale of its military and governmental operations increased, the Company needed to collect ever-larger sums of revenue and conduct ever-larger volumes of trade. This, in turn, required economic stability and predictability—the ability of merchants to carry on their trade without threat of plunder, attack, or uncertainty. The question, quite simply, was would these objectives be better met if the Company left the individual rulers in singular possession of their states? Or would it be better for the Company to deploy its preeminent military power to conquer unstable and threatening provinces once and for all? There was no singular answer to this question. Where a state was seen as posing a real threat to the Company or its trading allies it was prepared to undertake military action against it. Where the potential for disruption was more theoretical than real, or where the state possessed a more general strategic importance in the wider scheme of British dominion, then methods short of outright occupation were utilized. The general outcome, though, was the same: bit by bit the Company extended its authority across India until there were no organized powers able to contest its hegemony.

There were three notable examples of the Company using its military muscle to remove perceived threats to its position. The first occurred in the southern state of Mysore. Like Bengal, Mysore provided a characteristic example of an 18th century post-Mughal state. Originally ruled by a Hindu dynasty, in the 1750s a Muslim military adventurer, Haider Ali, assumed ever-greater power as commander of its military forces, and when the maharaja died in 1766, he stepped forward to take control. Ali was ambitious to expand the power of Mysore, and this brought him in to conflict with the neighboring states of Hyderabad and the Hindu Marathas, as well the Company with its base at Madras. A series of wars followed in which the British allied with the nizam of Hyderabad and the Maharatas against Ali's territorial pretensions. Ali prevailed in a number of engagements—even threatening Madras at one point—until, in 1781, he was defeated by a Company army led by Eyre Coote.

Though Ali died the following year, his ambitious state policy was continued by his son, Tipu Sultan. Again, Mysore's dynamism and expansionist tendencies brought it into collision with its regional rivals, and in 1792, a Company-led alliance that included Hyderabad, Travancore, and the Marathas dealt a decisive defeat to Tipu, who was forced to make a humiliating peace under which he relinquished half his territories and had to pay heavy indemnities to the Company and its allies. But still Tipu's Mysore was not broken. Resolved to avoid enfeebling bankruptcy, believing, "It is far better to live like a lion for a day than to live like a sheep for a hundred years," Tipu Sultan moved quickly to rebuild his power—increasing taxes, centralizing his state, developing an army along western lines, purchasing modern weaponry, and carrying out incursions into the prosperous western coastal region. With Britain locked in conflict with France in the wake of the 1789 Revolution, Tipu made a deliberate attempt to cultivate French support, praising republican ideals, calling himself Citizen Tipu, and sending agents to Paris to acquire up-to-date weapons.

The Company, now headed by Lord Wellesley, was determined to remove any threat of French intervention, and in 1798 launched a last campaign against Mysore in alliance with the nizam of Hyderabad. The army, commanded in the field by Wellesley's brother Arthur, the future Duke of Wellington, drove Tipu into his capital of Seringapatam, where he was killed sword in hand in 1799. Mysore was dismembered, much of its lands being shared between Hyderabad, the Marathas, and the British, while the remaining central province was placed under a descendant of the old Hindu rulers whom Ali had deposed. Notwithstanding his ultimate failure, Tipu remains an iconic figure in Indian history: the rare example of a ruler prepared to stand up to the British and who showed that it was possible to respond creatively to defeat rather than simply allow his state to become an emasculated element within the Company's system of domination. If, it is implied, other Indian leaders had proven equally courageous, the tide of British conquest might have been reversed. In practice, however, the fate of Tipu signaled the fact that personal bravery could not gainsay the Company's great advantage in resources and manpower, and far from rallying other rulers behind his resistance, his expansionist policies alienated regional powers like the Marathas and Hyderabad and caused them to cooperate with the British in his destruction. It was only subsequently that the Tiger of Mysore came to take his place in the lists of Indian patriots.

Although the Marathas had assisted the Company in its conflict with Mysore, they had themselves already been involved in military operations against the British and the relationship between the two potential rivals to pan-Indian hegemony remained tense. The Marathas had proven a very provoking thorn in the side of the last great Mughal Emperor, Aurangzeb, and it was his obsessive pursuit of final victory over the Maratha leader Shivaji that had pointed the way to Mughal decline. Unexpected defeat at the hands of an invading Afghan army shattered Maratha aspirations to found a pan-Indian Empire. Even so, they remained a formidable military presence across large swathes of the subcontinent, controlling territories stretching from Delhi and Agra in the north, to Orissa in the east, and the borders of Hyderabad in the south. At the root of the expansionist instincts of the Marathas was the inhospitable character of their center at Poona in the upland of the Western Ghats, which meant that if large armies were to be maintained they would have to live by extorting supplies from the more fertile lands they had conquered. Clearly, an expansionist and militaristic state of this kind posed a challenge to the British interest in stable and prosperous trading conditions. Indeed, the Company found itself coming under pressure to take action on behalf of Indian trading partners—such as the cotton merchants of Gujarat who feared Maratha incursions and at whose behest a series of territories around Surat were annexed by the Company.

What appeared to bring the Marathas within the range of British military power was the fact that theirs was not a centralized empire at all, but a loose federation of five separate dynasties, each responsible for its own affairs and only loosely connected to the center by kinship ties. At the center itself sat the peshwa, traditionally the head of the confederacy and, since the 18th century, a hereditary title born by one of the five Maratha dynasties, the Brahmin Raos. In 1802, the then peshwa, Baji Rao, indebted and under pressure from the other Maratha chiefs who wished to make him their cipher, fled Poona and turned to the Company for help. Wellesley, the governor-general, forgetting the federal nature of the Maratha polity, believed he could use the peshwa to assert authority over the Marathas in general and agreed to restore him to the throne on condition that he accept a Company force and resident and cede lands to pay for the operation. Rao accepted and was restored as peshwa by Wellesley. Predictably, the other Maratha warrior-rulers, notably the Scindhias of Gwalior, the Bhonslas of Nagpur, and the Holkars of Indore, refused to be bound by Rao's treaty with the Company and war broke out. In 1803, Scindhia and Bhonsla were defeated by a Company army under General Lake and forced to relinquish territory—Scindhia handing over his lands north of the Jumna River, which included the old Mughal capitals of Delhi and Agra (and the old Mughal himself, in the shape of the blind Shah Alam), as well as Gujarat, while Bhonsla of Nagpur gave up the eastern state of Orissa, a byword in oppressive and impoverishing administration. However, an attack on Holkar failed, and at this point, with the Marathas weakened but not wholly subdued, Wellesley was recalled to London.

Only in 1817 were accounts finally settled with the Marathas. What brought matters to a head was a military assault initiated by Lord Hastings (governor-general, 1813–23) against the Pindaris, a group of irregular horsemen originally attached to the Marathas, but who by the 1810s had swollen into a force of some 20,000 robbers and bandits of all religions and castes—what W.W. Hunter characterized as "the *debris* of the Mughal Empire"[9]—who preyed on the property of local merchants in the Deccan and undertook raids which carried them as far as Madras and Bombay. Not taking any chances, Hastings assembled a large army and surrounded the Pindaris with a "ring of iron and steel," gradually tightening his grip, rounding up the Pindari bands and either destroying their leaders or forcing them to come to terms. Unnerved by such a large Company force on his borders and suspecting it might next be deployed against him, the peshwa Baji Rao decided to launch a bid to free himself from Company control. His attack on the British residency in Poona sparked a more general Maratha revolt that was joined by the Bhonsles of Nagpur and Holkar of Indore. Resolved to end the Maratha threat, Hastings sent against them an army of over 100,000—the largest the Company had yet fielded. One by one, the resisting Maratha chiefs were defeated and surrendered. The office of peshwa was abolished, lands were confiscated, Holkar was forced to make a treaty of alliance with the Company, and the Bhonslas were deposed in favor of a more compliant ruler. By this means, the once-feared Marathas were humbled and, with their armies disbanded, many of their soldiers turned to Company service to secure their livelihoods.

The third of the autonomous states with the fighting potential to rival the Company was the one the British feared most and against whom they delayed taking action the longest: the Sikhs of the Punjab. As with Bengal and Mysore, the Sikh dynasty that ruled the Punjab was of comparatively recent origin. Originally a reformist Hindu movement which shared aspects of Islamic teaching—notably a monotheistic conception of God—the Sikhs had gradually evolved into a militant, warrior brotherhood. They resisted Mughal rule in its later stages and the demise of that Empire saw a number of Sikh bands operating within the Punjab. These disparate groups had been welded together by 1820 into a single Sikh state by Ranjit Singh, dominating a region in which Muslims were in a majority. Under Singh's leadership, a formidable army had been created known as the Khalsa. Well trained under the guidance of French and Italian mercenaries, and equipped to European standards, it boasted 45,000 infantrymen armed with modern muskets, 800 pieces of artillery, and 26,000 cavalrymen. In 1837, Emily Eden, the sister of the then governor-general, Lord Aukland, traveled into the Punjab and recorded the impression made by a review of Singh's army:

> All the gentlemen went at daybreak yesterday to Ranjit [Singh's] review, and came back rather discomfited. He had nearly as many troops out as [we] had; they were quite as well disciplined, rather better dressed, repeated the same military movements and several others much more complicated, and, in short, nobody knows what to say about it, so they say nothing, except that they are sure the Sikhs would run away in a real fight. It is a sad blow to our vanities![10]

In these circumstances, the Company had little choice but to acknowledge the Punjab as a useful buffer state between its own territories and the more turbulent Northwest Frontier and Afghanistan.

However, the death of Singh in 1839 inaugurated a period of instability and faction fighting within the Punjab as the army became increasingly restless and politicized, seeking to dominate the state. In 1845, a section of the army attacked the state of Jammu and then crossed the Sutlej River—the nominal dividing line between the Sikh and Company territories. The Company, conscious of the strategic sensitivity of the Punjab, took this as a *causas belli* and declared war in December 1845. The British were very nervous: as James observes, the Sikhs were the only modern army they had confronted in India and defeat could spell ruin for the Company. Accordingly, an army of

54,000 troops was assembled—a fifth of the entire Company forces.[11] The battle was bloody for both sides. What undid the Sikhs was their poor leadership. Their generals expected to lose and were keen to make terms with the Company. They fought a purely defensive campaign and waited to be attacked. A series of intense assaults followed which eventually broke Sikh resistance, allowing the Company to occupy the capital of Lahore.

However, the Company remained reluctant to annex the Punjab, preferring to impose a punitive peace. Reparations of £1.5 million were imposed, fertile land on the Sutlej forfeited, the territory of Kashmir was detached and given to the pro-British Hindu, Gulab Singh, and a British resident (the charismatic Henry Lawrence) established in Lahore, supported by a garrison of Company troops. These new arrangements lasted merely two years. To the underlying instability of the Punjab were now added the grievances of numerous groups who felt they had suffered from the British dispensation: members of Ranjit Singh's family, including his widow, the Maharani Jandin; officials and zamindars who had been sacked or slighted by Lawrence; and thousands of discharged members of the Khalsa. An uprising began which saw several British officers killed and the Second Sikh War commenced. The new governor-general, Lord Dalhousie, convinced of the benefits of British rule and keen to extinguish the remnants of Sikh autonomy, reportedly declared: "Unwarned by precedent, uninfluenced by example, the Sikh nation has called for war; and on my word, sirs, war they shall have and with a vengeance."[12] Once again the Sikhs made the mistake of opting for defensive tactics and again the British hit them hard with large armies. Both sides took heavy losses, but it was the Sikhs who were forced into retreat and surrender. This time the Punjab was annexed in 1849, carrying British territory to the Indus and removing the last real threat to British hegemony.

The Company was acutely aware of the need to consolidate its hold over the rich and volatile frontier zone of the Punjab and the result was one of the most successful exercises in social and political engineering in the history of British rule. Under the so-called Punjab System overseen by the brothers Henry and John Lawrence, administrators traveled around the countryside on horseback, dispensing rough and ready justice and overseeing the construction of roads, bridges, and schools. Irrigation projects which favored the agricultural communities of the Jullunder and Rechna Doabs, who had supplied the backbone of the Khalsa armies, were prioritized and tax assessments kept deliberately low (at around 25 percent of the value of output). The Sikhs, as a minority within the Punjab, preferred British to Muslim rule—and especially one which so explicitly favored their interests. Indeed, half of the old Sikh army took employment in the Company forces. These events were rich with future significance. As Chris Bayly remarks, Lawrence's Punjab System was "the India of the Crown in gestation." It was an India where the acquiescence of rural society was to be bought by a progressive fall in the weight of the land revenue and agricultural growth, and by attempts to associate powerful villagers with an alien government.[13]

But these examples of armed conquest were atypical. The Company's preferred option was to stop short of outright annexation. War was an expensive and risky undertaking—and by 1806, the Company's debts stood at £29 million. It was also regarded as bad for business—which, for the Company directors in London, was the fatal objection. In 1767, the board of directors warned the president of Calcutta that to extend the Company's territories beyond Bengal, Bombay, and Madras would "lead from one acquisition to another until we shall find no security but in the subjection of the whole, which by dividing your force would lose us the whole and end in our extirpation from Hindustan." Parliament echoed this refrain when it declared in 1783, "to pursue schemes of conquest and expansion of dominion in India are measures repugnant to the wish, the honor, and the policy of this nation."[14]

The Company's preferred method for securing the stable borders and trading environment it wished for was by means of the system of subsidiary treaties. Under this arrangement an Indian ruler was allowed to retain his *de jure* independence on condition of signing treaties of alliance with the Company, accepting the presence of a Company resident who would monitor the internal affairs of the state, and agreeing to the deployment of a body of Company troops for defensive purposes, the costs of which they would have to bear themselves. Predictably enough, such draconian terms tended to put the states affected under considerable strain—with the result that they began to manifest the very symptoms of instability, incompetent government, and internal strife it was the ostensible object of the Company to avoid. As Thomas Munro ruefully observed, "the subsidiary system must everywhere run its full course, and destroy every government which it seeks to protect."[15] The Company, truly, had a happy knack of creating the very conditions that would bring about the expansion of an Empire it claimed never to wish for.

The most important—and also classic—example of this process was witnessed in the powerful Mughal successor state of Oudh. Chris Bayly's dissection of the unfolding events in this state is a model of analysis.[16] In Oudh the demise of the Mughal Empire left a small elite of Muslim warriors, literati, and gentry in control of a largely Hindu countryside. Under the terms of its subsidiary treaty, this state had to pay the British an annual sum of 7.5 million rupees in return for the stationing of Company troops to protect it from internal and external enemies. However, the pressure of this huge financial demand disrupted the fragile and multi-layered political system. Demands from revenue collectors forced local notables into revolt throughout the 1780s and 1790s, while the army was in a state of constant disaffection over arrears of pay. When the nawab died in 1797, the British resident, suspicious of the loyalty of his son Vazir Ali, had Ali declared illegitimate, replacing him with the more pliant Saadat Ali Khan, who had long been under British tutelage. In 1798, Ali tried to raise a rebellion in alliance with Rajput warriors. Wellesley feared incursions by Afghanistan and pressed Ali Khan to resign. He refused but was forced to cede all his western territories and those along the Ganges and Jumna Rivers to the British. Although the rump of Oudh survived until its final annexation in 1856, it was severed from its most valuable trade routes and reduced to the status of an economic backwater.

So did the British never seize territories out of motives of simple imperialist aggrandizement? The closest any governor-general came to manifesting a belief that annexation was a good in itself, both for the Company and the Indians, was Richard Wellesley. Appointed in 1798, he believed that India would only be stable when a paramount power was able to enforce the public peace upon the various states of the subcontinent, and that the Company had no choice but to perform this role. A policy of *laissez faire* was not an option and risked leaving India open to the machinations of Britain's deadly rivals, the French. Wellesley had no compunction about interfering in the internal affairs of Indian states: he considered India's existing rulers to be oppressive usurpers, with the British, accordingly, appearing in the guise of liberators. Emboldened by this ideology, and well assisted by his two brothers Henry and Arthur, Wellesley set about crushing the remaining rivals to British power and bringing the whole subcontinent under British domination. Within six years he had destroyed Tipu's Mysore, broken the power of the Marathas, and doubled the extent of the Company's territories—as well as making an extensive series of subsidiary treaties. Predictably, however, the board of directors found such rest-less expansionism destabilizing and costly, and Wellesley was recalled in 1804 before his ambition to dominate the entire subcontinent had been realized.

The governor-general who most nearly matched Wellesley's san-guine imperialism was Lord Dalhousie (1848–56), a Victorian in the liberal-progressive mode who was convinced that the Company had every right to exploit "every just opportunity which presents itself" to consolidate its rule—by absorbing territories located amidst its ex-isting possessions or which occupied strategically sensitive positions upon its borders. Dalhousie's belief that territorial expansion would strengthen the Raj economically and politically was not new, but his deployment of the Doctrine of Lapse added a new cynicism to the pro-cess that unnerved the remaining rulers of India and helped prepare the ground for the implosion of the Mutiny in 1857. Under the Doc-trine, any ruler who was childless would no longer be able to adopt a son and heir, as had previously been the custom under Hindu law, his territories instead reverting to the Company as the paramount power. By this neat expedient, which Dalhousie justified by arguing that the benefits to the governed of coming under British rule far out-weighed the costs of breaking with a tradition of dubious legitimacy, some seven states were added to Company control, including Satara (1848), Udaipur (1852), Jhansi (1853), and Nagpur (1854). Besides also overseeing the annexation of the Punjab with the Second Sikh War, Dalhousie annexed the surviving territories of the king of Oudh on grounds of corrupt, inefficient, and oppressive government: "The Brit-ish government," he declared, "would be guilty in the sight of God and man if it were any longer to aid in sustaining by its countenance an administration fraught with suffering to millions."[17]

Thus, by the time of Dalhousie's departure from India in 1856, the disposition of the Company's territories had assumed the broad out-lines they would retain until the end of British dominion in 1947. In the northwest lay the lands of the Punjab, running up toward the foothills of Afghanistan, while in the northeast was Bengal and Bihar. Linking these two great northern provinces were the annexed lands of Oudh and Rohilkhand. Running southwest from Bengal was a great swathe of territory in central and eastern India, much of it—such as Orissa, Nagpur, and Berars—being acquired from the Marathas. Similarly, the old Bombay presidency in the west had expanded to include the Maratha homelands of the Western Ghats. Finally, in the south, was the territory commanded by the Madras presidency. As such, two-fifths of India yet remained technically outside the Company's jurisdiction, instead being governed by an array of princes totaling over 700 in number and occupying states varying in size from a few square miles to imposing kingdoms like Hyderabad. Even so, most of these independent states had signed subsidiary treaties acknowledging the Company as the paramount power.

So how had it been possible for a commercial company that arrived in India to trade, and which always decried that it had any formulated strategy of territorial expansion, to subdue the whole of the subcontinent and establish a pan-Indian Empire? Though this question has engendered considerable controversy, the essential explanation is straightforward enough. Quite simply, in any given military standoff the forces deployed by the Company and its allies were too great to be withstood by any resisting Indian ruler. This, after all, was the story of the wars against Bengal, Mysore, the Marathas, and even the Sikhs. Two elements combined to produce this state of affairs.

To begin with, there was the strength of the British. This was compounded out of an admixture of three elements whose relative weight varied over time. First, there were the Company's material resources, with its access to the London money market, its developing capacity to extract revenue from the Indian territories it controlled, its lucrative trading networks, and unrivalled command of the sea. Second, there was the quality of its army and officers: well organized and drilled; receiving higher and more regular pay than its Indian counterparts; possessing weapons that were superior to most of those it faced; mobilizing the power of the infantry (a force historically treated with contempt by the Indians, who put their faith in the cavalry and massed ranks of elephants, which now proved easy prey to well-organized musket fire[18]); with a high level of morale and self-belief; and led by officers who were generally better and more determined than those of the enemies they confronted. Lastly, there was the ability of the Company to form crucial alliances with, on the one hand, significant regional powers like Hyderabad, the Sikhs, and even the Marathas, and, on the other, influential interest groups within states, such as the rising merchant and banking classes, all of whom believed they had a vested interest in being seen to collaborate with the British. At the time of Plassey the Company's resource advantage over the nawab was non-existent: the Bengal Army far exceeded Clive's force in numbers and the finance for the campaign came largely from disaffected elements within the Bengal state. What was crucial in Bengal was Clive's charismatic leadership and the hollowness of Siraj-ud-Daula's position as key groups within his own army and administration conspired to overthrow him with British assistance. Of course, once having acquired its Bengal foothold, the Company's resource base expanded exponentially as it gained access to land revenue and could afford to recruit much larger numbers of Indian troops. By the time of the war against the Marathas, the Company enjoyed advantages in all three areas: it could deploy an army of 120,000, better equipped and trained than those it faced, and led by talented officers like Lake and Wellesley, as well as having the support of Indian allies, notably Hyderabad. With this set of assets the Company was effectively unstoppable. Each victory brought an enhanced reputation for invincibility in addition to more resources and the absorption of former warrior-opponents into its army—the Marathas after their final defeat in 1817 and, still more strikingly, the Sikhs after 1849, who quickly became the backbone of the Indian Army.

The second factor was the corresponding weakness of the Indians who sought to resist British conquest. The Company never had an absolute advantage over India as a whole, and if the Indians had somehow united *en masse* to fight Company intervention, the British would have been driven into the sea by the sheer weight in numbers. Yet such an eventuality was never a possibility. India in the 18th century was a land of numerous states forging their identities and institutions in the wake of the demise of the Mughals. As states formed and flexed their muscles, and as new dynasties emerged and adventurers took their chances, there was no basis for collective action of any kind. Quite the reverse: in a dispute with a ruler, the East India Company could expect assistance from neighboring states harboring grievances or ambitions toward it, or look to assistance from *within* the state from groups at odds with the governing elite—be it merchants, or disaffected sections of the army, or descendants of usurped rulers. Indeed, for many of India's rising commercial, scribal, and gentry groups, the Company had a positive appeal, with its active support for trade and the importance it attached to upholding property rights—which contrasted favorably with the often capricious and despotic practices of state rulers.[19] Thus, in the case of Bengal, alienated elements within the state fell over themselves to conspire with the Company in ejecting the hated Siraj: the Jagat Sheth financiers, zamindars, and senior figures within the government and army. Without their encouragement and money, it is unlikely that Clive would have tried to depose Siraj and found the Empire. The Marathas, too, were weakened by their faction-ridden polity, with five centers of power each as ready to fight with each other as unite against the Company, as well as by the hostility of groups like the Gujaratis and Hyderabad, who were only too pleased to see the Maratha threat removed. In Mysore, Haider Ali and Tipu Sultan were keen to challenge the British; yet they had been equally keen to threaten their neighbors and had themselves usurped power within Mysore, while their attempts to found a strong centralized state capable of confronting the Company offended Hindu merchants and village leaders.[20] Thus their essential isolation meant they were doomed in the face of the Company's military, economic, and diplomatic resources. Finally, the Sikhs, too, were a minority group within the state they dominated. They were riven with factions battling for supremacy, and their military leaders were more willing to do deals with the British than fight them. Thus not only did Indian states fail to unite against the Company—they often as not worked with it in its conflicts with specific state rulers, and even those states that *did* resist were fatally undermined by internal divisions and rivalries.

None of this should surprise us. Recall again Bayly's remark to the effect that the company was sucked into the military bizarre that was 18th-century India. As an army, the Company was but one player in an India of over 700 political entities, while as a trading body it was a lucrative source of revenue for merchants, financiers, and governments. For any given state, there was every reason to use the Company in its rivalry with some more threatening neighbor; while for any given aggrieved interest group within a state there was every reason to call upon the Company for assistance in removing a corrupt or persecuting elite. In neither case did those working with the Company imagine that they were helping to construct a new alien Empire in India. They were, rather, acting rationally to forward their own interests amidst the uncertain and competitive environment of post-Mughal India.

Of course, by each of them making specific deals and compromises with the Company, they unwittingly made it, not one player among many, but the paramount power within the subcontinent. There was, in other words, a collective logic at work which carried the Company to power—but it was a logic that was immanent in the situation and which only became manifest as events unfolded. It was not understood or willed by the individual Indian states or interest groups on the one hand, or by the Company on the other. Clive, for example, the man who has a better claim than any to have set the process running, never intended to conquer India as a whole and explicitly counseled against the idea of carrying Company rule beyond Bengal and Bihar. This was true of the great majority of governor-generals, who saw their role as stabilizing the position they inherited. True, Wellesley did envisage a *Pax Britannica* for India—but he was only in power for six years before he was replaced with Cornwallis, who was dispatched for a second time with the specific brief of making peace at any price. It was the logic of Indian realities that made the British Empire in India—not the preconceived strategies of the Company or its Indian allies.

Part II

The Experience of British Rule
1600–1859

Having traced the process by which the British East India Company came to found an Empire in India, the question must now be posed: in what ways, and to what degree, was the lived experience of Indians affected by the rise of British power? Opinion upon this issue divides along two distinct fault lines: namely, the *extent* and *nature* of the British impact.

Taking the latter schism first, for some, such as Karl Marx, British rule acted as a solvent upon customary Indian society, initiating it into the current of progressive Western-inspired change. As a commercial enterprise representing the interests of a Britain itself undergoing its own transformation into a capitalist, industrial, society, the East India Company could not but intrude modern market systems into a previously self-sufficient peasant economy. At the same time the Company was the vehicle for a wide set of enlightenment ideals, introducing not only the insights of modern science and medicine, but such concepts as liberalism, utilitarianism, nationalism, and democracy. From this perspective, British rule represented, however unconsciously, a catalyst for change, leaving India by 1858 a radically altered country on the threshold of modernity. To quote Marx's analysis of 1853:

> The British were the first conquerors superior, and therefore inaccessible, to Hindoo civilisation. They destroyed it by breaking up the native communities, by uprooting native industry, and by levelling all that was great and elevated in the native society. The historic pages of their rule in India report hardly anything beyond that destruction. The work of regeneration hardly transpires through a heap of ruins. Nevertheless it has begun.[1]

Curiously enough, another widely held narrative sees the effects of British rule in diametrically opposed terms. Indian nationalist writers, in particular, have regarded the hand of British power as essentially stultifying. The India of the 18th century was, they believe, a dynamic and creative place, characterized by rapid social change, a marketized economy, a flourishing artisanal sector on the verge of its own indigenously generated industrial revolution, and the emergence of modern states. All this dynamism was suppressed by exploitative colonial rule, which destroyed Indian industry, obliterated the independence of emerging states, stifled debate, and entrenched the position of feudal elites who conspired with the British in obstructing progressive classes and movements. India's natural evolution toward modern institutions was thereby stymied, bequeathing a legacy of arrested development, which continues to bedevil the subcontinent even today. The reflections of Jawaharlal Nehru, Congress leader and first prime minister of independent India, in his 1946 book *The Discovery of India* are symptomatic of this approach:

> Nearly all our major problems to-day have grown up during British rule and as a direct result of British policy: the princes; the minority problem; various vested interests, foreign and Indian; the lack of industry and the neglect of agriculture; the extreme backwardness in the social services; and, above all, the tragic poverty of the people.[2]

However different, these rival interpretations unite in regarding the Company's impact as profound, for good or ill. An alternative viewpoint holds that the effects of British rule were, in fact, much more limited. Superficially, an empire had been created that dominated the subcontinent. But, as Brown points out, in reality British rule was a weak and precarious thing. To begin with, two-fifths of India remained subject to independent princes who continued, within limits, to rule according to the traditional mores of deference, courtly display, nepotism, and feudal dependency. Yet even within British India, the European presence was slight and ephemeral, with no capacity to engender fundamental shifts within traditional society. The essential function of Company officials was to extract the land tax and uphold law and order. Beyond this, they had neither the inclination nor the remit to reconfigure Indian society. Even had they wished to do so, British administrators were too few in number and too dependent upon the assistance of Indians themselves for this to be a realistic possibility—if anything, writes Brown, they were "imprisoned by the forces of Indian society."[3] British rule, that is to say, was geographically wide but socially and culturally shallow, and was powerless to affect the underlying dynamics of Indian society, which antedated British rule and postdated its demise.

Confusingly, there is significant insight in all these perspectives upon the first century of British rule and it is tempting simply to assert that the truth lies somewhere between all of them. The reader would be forgiven, however, for regarding such a verdict as altogether too trite and wonder what kind of truth it can be that claims to synthesize such radically opposed opinions. And as if matters were not sufficiently involved, another issue needs to be raised: namely, our concept of traditional India itself. For recent research has increasingly suggested that the widely held picture of an Indian society of village cultivators hidebound by caste rules and saturated by Hinduism was, in fact, not traditional at all, but something which came into existence only in the 18th and early 19th centuries and owed not a little to the impact of Company rule.

What is at stake, therefore, is not just the nature of British rule, but the meaning of India itself, and this is something that is more than hard to grasp: it is an idea that has lived more vigorously in the minds of historians, polemicists, and anthropologists than it ever has in the minds of Indians themselves.

4

Landed Society and British Rule

It was inevitable that the countryside would provide the location for the most pervasive and profound interaction between Indians and their new colonial masters. Agriculture was the mainstay of Indian national life and land the most coveted resource—supplying the essential sustenance of the majority of the population as well as underpinning hierarchies of status and power. Land was likewise the foundation of the Raj, for the more prosaic reason that the land revenue represented the staple income of the government. The land tax had traditionally provided the sinews of state finance, but this dependence increased under Company rule as the cult of free trade meant that the Company was deprived by Parliament of its monopolies in eastern trade, internal customs duties were dismantled, and British goods were imported at duties that hardly ever exceeded 5 percent.[4] By 1891, customs duties yielded only 2 percent of government income.[5] Burton Stein does not exaggerate when he writes, "all aspects of the Company's operations—the Civil Service, the judiciary and the Company's commerce—were now centred on land revenue administration."[6] The issue to be considered here is the extent to which British revenue collection and related activities impacted upon the character of Indian rural life. Conventionally it has been held that the British revolutionized agrarian relations in India, though the magnitude of this impact has been questioned increasingly by historians who place greater emphasis upon the continuities with pre-Company rural conditions.[7]

It is essential, if what follows is to be understood, that the nature of landed property in India at the time of British conquest be grasped. In India, nearly all those born into a rural community had some hereditary entitlement to the land, though the extent of these entitlements varied widely. This did not mean that people actually owned pieces of land of varying size. What it meant was that people, grouped in families, villages, jatis, or tribes, had the customary right to either access pieces of land or control who did. What people inherited, in other words, was not a certificate giving exclusive ownership of a piece of land, but rather a certain extent of customary rights to make use of the land in return for paying tax revenue and rents to the state or tax-collecting intermediaries. As a corollary of this, there was no commercial land market. Hereditary access rights could not be bought or sold, and if an individual died or was unable to sustain cultivation, his land would be merged into the holdings of the village—it was very rare for land to pass beyond such networks to strangers.[8] Equally, if a peasant failed to pay his rents to the landlord he might be threatened, beaten up, or have his possessions seized—but he would not expelled from the land. R. C. Dutt summed up the traditional land system of India with admirable concision: the state was entitled to revenue from the land; rural landlord elites were entitled to customary rents in return for paying revenue to the state; and the ryots (peasants) had hereditary rights to their holdings subject to the payment of customary rents to the landlords.[9] Everything was regulated by local custom. Even units of land measurement were physically and socially conditioned, the basic unit, the bigha, being defined as the amount of land necessary to support a family according to the needs of its caste.[10]

It should not be inferred that Indian rural life was some kind of communal idyll. For access rights to land were distributed very unequally. Rural elites controlled tracts of land of varying size, which they rented out to small cultivators and from whom they often collected land taxes on behalf of the Mughal Empire or its successor states. These elite families exercised considerable power at the local level, often maintaining bodies of armed followers and dispensing law and order within their domains. The zamindars of Bengal are the most famous of these landlord elites, but there were comparable groups across India. In South India, for example, Dharma Kumar describes how powerful families dominated the life of each village, collecting land revenue, organizing public works, and lending money.[11]

At the other end of the scale were small peasants who were effectively tenants of the larger landholders. In most cases, the land to which they had access was insufficient to meet their family's subsistence needs and they had to eke out their incomes through laboring work on other farms or by engaging in manufacturing activity. In north

Bengal, for example, this was true of some 50 percent of peasant families.[12] What held the small cultivator back was not so much a shortage of land—there was, in fact, a plentiful supply of land in India into the 19th century. The constraint was resources: cultivating land required labor, tools, and livestock to clear and farm it and these the poorer farmers lacked. A pair of oxen could plough between three and six acres, so a farmer who could afford only two such animals could not feed his family from his holding.[13] Within this context, most land was devoted to supplying the basic consumption needs of the cultivator or for local exchange within the village. There was little land to spare for the growing of cash crops.

Britain's engagement with the rural life of India was overwhelmingly governed by the need to collect the land tax. Yet this was no mere matter of fiscal policy: issues arising out of the assessment and collection of the revenue went to the heart of the character and consequences of British rule in general.

As the Company's officials contemplated the levying of the land tax, two main questions intruded themselves. First of all, who was to be liable for the payment of the tax: individual peasants, kinship groups, villages, or rural elites? In considering this matter, the British got themselves involved in a very different, and much more convoluted, inquiry: namely, who could be legitimately said to *own* the land? Now there was no logical connection between these two questions. Just because someone is assumed to be liable for a tax on certain resources does not mean that they thereby own them. Many tenants, for example, pay taxes liable on the property they occupy, yet do not own that property as a result. This was still more obviously the case in India where, as we have remarked, nobody, strictly speaking, owned the land at all.

It was this simple distinction that the Company conflated. Carrying with them the ideological framework of 18th-century Britain, where private property in resources like land was held to be the basis of social order and material progress, they simply could not countenance the idea that the land of India was not owned by someone. And it was this owner, they believed, who was ultimately responsible for the payment of the land tax. This ideological construct of the Company was pregnant with wide-ranging implications, since it gave rise to what was, perhaps, the single most important consequence of British rule. For when the British, predictably enough, were disappointed in their search for an Indian landowning class they resorted to the next best thing: they created one. That is to say, they took the revolutionary step of introducing into India the idea of private property in land.

Besides the question of *who* should pay the tax, there was also the issue of the appropriate *level* at which to set it. Here, too, the debate was shot through with theoretical presuppositions as it became a battleground for competing perspectives within the influential schools of British political economy. The role of landlords and the economic function of rent were explosive issues in a Britain that was itself fast industrializing in the context of a society still dominated by a landed elite which seemed, to many in the middle class, to be profiting parasitically from the prosperity trade and industry were generating. These controversies spilled over into the Indian scene through the medium of James Mill. Besides being a political radical and evangelist for the new science of political economy and its allied doctrine of utilitarianism, Mill had also written a monumental history of modern India—despite never having visited the country—on the strength of which he had been employed as an administrator in the London office of the East India Company. From this base, he was able to exert a pervasive influence upon the direction of Company policy in India—and this included the area of revenue assessment. Mill was a proponent of the theory of rent developed by his friend David Ricardo, according to which the rental income yielded by land was an unearned surplus arising from the fact that fertile land was a resource scarce in supply. As such it did not, unlike the wages of labor or the profits of entrepreneurs, serve any economic function and could and should be creamed off by the state for the good of the community. This basic doctrine came to provide the justification for the taxation policy of the Raj, the goal being to secure for the Indian government all revenues in excess of those necessary to cover the costs of cultivation. Unfortunately, this neat theory proved impossible to apply scientifically in the Indian context, and the attempts to do so had parlous consequences for the development of agriculture.

Bengal was the first province in which these questions were posed and became the *locus classicus* of the land question in British India. Collecting the revenue from Bengal was a critical matter for the Company: it needed the money to meet the cost of its purchases of Indian goods for export, as well as to cover its burgeoning military and civil expenditure and cross-subsidize its Madras and Bombay presidencies. In Bengal, the land tax, under both the Mughals and the successor regimes, was not collected by state officials. Instead, the responsibility for gathering the land revenue was contracted out to a complex mix of intermediaries, ranging from small village maliks in Bihar to the powerful class of mainly Hindu hereditary tax farmers known as the zamindars (literally "holders of land"). These zamindars collected the revenue from tracts of land and in return for so doing were permitted to retain a share of the proceeds. This right to collect the land revenue and take a cut for themselves was their property and they could buy and sell it. They did not, however, own the land itself, to which they had no exclusive rights.

By the 18th century, these zamindars had become wealthy and powerful men, employing networks of officials and sub-contractors to collect taxes over areas that could run into thousands of square miles. Operations on such a scale required the maintenance of law and order and the zamindars effectively acted as a layer of local government, enforcing laws, judging and punishing offenders, and commanding bodies of armed followers. The zamindar of Burdwan, for example, could call upon a militia of 30,000, besides a personal household of troops. The nawabs, in other words, depended upon the zamindars for the bulk of their income and for the maintenance of law and order; in return the zamindars expected a free hand in running their territories and made a large margin of profit on their collections.[14]

The Company government of Bengal did not trust the zamindars, believing that they kept back too much tax revenue for themselves, did not tax evenly, and were prone to corruption and favoritism—all of which was probably true. The standards of tax assessment were indeed very rudimentary: the basic assessment of tax liability in use had been carried out in 1722, being itself the first since 1582, and the level of revenue a cultivator could expect to pay depended upon such matters as his status (the rich paid less than the poor), the length of his occupancy, kinship ties, and custom. Being, however, novices in the complex world of Bengal tax gathering the Company lacked the requisite information and resources to assess and collect the revenue themselves. In 1772, they chose, instead, to auction to the highest bidders the right to be a zamindar for a period of five years. This expedient was soon exposed as a failure. Eager to retain their territories the zamindars made unrealistically high bids and even after exploiting their cultivating tenants to the greatest extent were unable to meet their revenue commitments. Calls for a new approach naturally arose, led in India by Philip Francis, a member of the governor-general's council who was well read in the economic theory of the day. According to Francis, the root cause of the low revenue-yielding capacity of Bengal was the fact that the zamindars had no vested interest in raising the productivity of the land. Not only did they have no proprietorial rights over the land, but any increased production they might bring about would simply be used to justify enhanced tax assessments. Francis's recommendations were radical, namely to recognize the zamindars as the owners of the land and fix their revenue obligations in perpetuity, so that they would have an incentive to improve their land and pocket the greater profits it yielded.[15]

Francis's views found favor in England, and in 1786 the Board of Directors resolved that a Permanent Settlement of land in Bengal be made and the Whig, Lord Cornwallis, was sent out to implement it. This he did in 1793, announcing a dual scheme of land and revenue reform to apply to the Company territories of Bengal, Bihar, northern Madras, and parts of the United Provinces. First, he recognized the zamindars as the owners of the land they raised revenue for. They were to go from being tax farmers to gentry landowners on the British model, the lesser cultivators who actually toiled in the fields now being given the status of tenant farmers. "At one stroke," says Hardy, "the zamindar of Bengal, whether colonizer, freebooter, Mughal revenue agent or tax farmer was converted into modern Indian landlord."[16] The zamindar had the right to levy whatever rents he wished upon the cultivators, being then required to pay a certain amount of that revenue as land tax to the state. The zamindars could pass land on within their families, sell it if they wished, and, crucially, if a tenant cultivator failed to make his rent-cum-tax payments, he could be replaced by someone else. As such, the zamindar approximated to a British landowner—yet with one conspicuous difference: he was not the outright owner of the land he controlled. Ownership was held to reside with the state that had created him, and if the zamindar failed to make the tax payments to the Bengal government for which he was liable, he could be expelled from his land holding and replaced by someone else. In effect, what the British had done was rent to the zamindars the right to collect what revenue they wished from their tenants.[17]

Secondly, with regard to the amount of the tax to be paid, Cornwallis took the irrevocable step of permanently fixing its absolute amount. Each zamindar would henceforward be liable to pay an annual sum that would remain the same in perpetuity. This was the famous Permanent Settlement. Although this initial settlement was high (26 million rupees or £3 million), it was expected to decline relatively thereafter as agricultural output increased, allowing the zamindar to pocket ever larger sums as his reward for promoting rural development. At the same time, Cornwallis relieved the zamindars of their traditional policing and juridical functions, and required them to disband their armed retainers.

The motives behind this attempt to cut the Gordian knot of revenue gathering in Bengal have been intensively debated. According to one much-favored explanation, the objective of the Permanent Settlement was to create in the zamindars a privileged and loyal landlord class that would act as a bulwark to British power. As the Marxist R. Palme Dutt wrote in 1940, it "was recognised that, with the small numbers of English holding down a vast population, it was absolutely necessary to establish a social basis for their power through the creation of a new class whose interests, through receiving a subsidiary share in the spoils, would be bound up with the maintenance of English rule."[18] More recent writers to lend their weight to elements of this viewpoint include Chris Bayly, for whom the Permanent Settlement was designed to reinforce social control and settle areas of north Bengal, and Peter Robb, who sees it as a socio-economic device to encourage political allies and social stability, in addition to promoting economic advance.[19] Even so, this explanation has been increasingly called into question. The immediate effect of the Settlement was to push many zamindars toward bankruptcy, which was hardly conducive to pro-Raj sentiment, while the simultaneous measures to strip the zamindars of their policing and judicial roles suggests they were not regarded as co-partners in the governance of Bengal. Most important, it is pointed out—for instance by B. Chaudhuri—that the British position in Bengal was already secure and the need to create a collaborationist intermediate class can hardly account for such a radical step.[20]

Another interpretation sees Cornwallis as engaged in the attempt to reproduce the British governing system into India. By entrenching the zamindars as a rural elite comparable to that which still dominated local as well as national government in Britain, and fixing the revenue available to the state, he was thereby hoping to create the conditions for a minimal state—one which devolved responsibility for local government to the zamindars and which could not easily access additional funds to cover higher spending. For Brown such measures accorded readily with Cornwallis's Whig predilections, while Robb emphasizes the intention to avoid the kind of arbitrary exactions by the state that were seen as symptomatic of indigenous Indian regimes, generating a pervasive uncertainty which discouraged investment in improved agriculture.[21]

A third school of writers discounts the idea of a considered ideology of good governance, conceiving of the Permanent Settlement as, rather, an administrative expedient designed to solve the immediate problem of securing a reliable income stream given the deficiencies of the state in terms of an adequate bureaucracy and local knowledge.[22] "The objective," wrote Nehru, "was to collect as much money in the shape of revenue and as speedily as possible."[23] As such it testified to the early modern character of the Bengal government and represented an admission that the Company was not yet in a position to collect the tax revenue itself. To quote Robb again: "That the zamindars were given private property resulted from an accident of timing as well as a theory of economic development."[24] Support for this perspective is provided by the fact that, once the necessary state resources for the conduct of revenue assessments had been accumulated, the Permanent Settlement model was abandoned.

However, the most currently favored interpretation of the Permanent Settlement presents it as a deliberate attempt by the Company to stimulate economic growth. It was widely believed that Bengal was a province in decline—to which the famine of 1769–70 bore visible testimony—and that the root cause of this was not the grasping and incompetent conduct of the Company, but the fact that no one had vested ownership rights in the land. "The security of private property," wrote the governor to the board of directors in 1772, "is the greatest encouragement to industry, on which the wealth of every state depends."[25] By making the zamindars stakeholders in the land, and not mere tax gatherers, and by securing to them the fruits of any extra agricultural output in terms of enhanced rents, it was hoped to create a climate of agricultural improvement driven forward by a class of improving landlords such as had overseen the agricultural revolution in Britain. As Cornwallis himself declared, Bengal's "agriculture must flourish before its commerce can become extensive." Here the fixity of tax demands was important: variable tax liability would discourage a zamindar from investing in agricultural improvements, as he would expect to find himself subject to increased tax liability as a result. In this manner, the zamindars were to metamorphose from parasitical tax gatherers into the hitherto unlikely role of improving landlords and saviors of Bengal and East India Company finances.

If the motives behind the Bengal settlement have occasioned much debate, this has been still more true of its consequences. For some, notably the usually trenchant critic of British economic policy in India,

R. C. Dutt, the Permanent Settlement was "the wisest and most successful measure which the British nation has ever adopted in India"
since it allowed the Indian people to profit from their own exertions
and removed the damaging effects of uncertainty. The whole rural
community had benefited, he wrote in 1906, and since its introduction,
Bengal had been spared the kind of devastating famines that continued
to afflict those areas with variable tax assessments.[26] Unfortunately,
R. C. Dutt's sanguine assessment has been altogether untypical—with
most commentators, then and since, expressing severe reservations as
to the results of the Settlement.

How heavy was the initial assessment levied on the new zamindar land owners? The received view that it represented an exorbi-
tant increase on former liabilities has been questioned by Marshall,
who estimates that the total tax burden placed upon Bengal alone, at
22 million rupees, was some 18.5 percent larger than the last assessment
made prior to 1757—a significant increase, but "less crippling than is
sometimes supposed."[27] However, Chaudhuri points out that any assessment beyond that pre-dating Company rule must be considered
excessive in that it failed to take into account the effects of the 1769–70
famine, which had reduced Bengal's population and the extent of its
cultivated area by up to one-third.[28] What *is* clear is that the tax burden
as a share of the value of output did steadily decrease as anticipated:
the initial figure of 45 percent of the value of agricultural production
in 1793 had fallen to a mere 1.7 percent by the late 1930s.[29] Indeed, it
was this very contraction in the share of the tax take that evoked criticism from within the ranks of the British administration as the costs of
government continued to increase and the Bengal settlement not only
failed to capture a share of the rising prosperity of Bengal, but actually
declined in real terms owing to inflation. As a tax system the Permanent Settlement came to be considered insufficiently flexible and this
was one reason why it was not rolled out across India.

What were the effects upon the zamindars? The initial tax assessments placed them under much pressure and many were unable to
meet their obligations—in the first five years of its operation some
10 percent of the set tax proved unrecoverable. The great zamindari
estates that had formed by the 18th century began to break up, being
simply too unwieldy to be conducted with sufficient rigor to meet
the high charges to which they were subject. Land was accordingly
sold on a large scale: in Bengal between 1794 and 1807 lands on which
41 percent of the government's revenue was raised were put up for

sale.[30] The transfer of land was especially rapid in Orissa. Although only being brought within the Permanent Settlement in 1804, by 1818, 52 percent of Orissa's 3,000 initially recognized proprietors had been ejected from their estates for failure to remit their taxes.[31]

It used to be thought that much of this land was bought by a new class of prosperous merchants from the likes of Calcutta who functioned as absentee landlords and, untrammeled by custom or sentiment, were prepared to extract as much money as possible from the peasants.[32] This did happen to a degree—the most famous example being the extensive purchases by the Tagore family—and the new market in landed property made it much easier for commercial wealth to flow into land. But research now suggests that the impact of land sales on the social structure of rural areas was much more limited. To begin with, as the larger zamindari estates broke up, it was prosperous tenant farmers who stepped in to acquire it. In north Bihar in 1790, there were 1,351 registered landowners; by 1850, this number had nearly trebled to 3,018, and by the 1890s it had exploded to 31,893.[33] In like manner they subcontracted the right to collect the revenue on parts of their estates to smaller tax farmers known as patnis. By 1819, the zamindar of Burdwan had created 1,495 such patnis. In Jessore, the number of people liable for tax returns rose from 100 in 1793 to 3,444 in 1809.[34] Where zamindari estates were sold off they tended to be bought by neighboring landowners, with the consequence that the social composition of the zamindar class changed remarkably little. In effect what the land sales associated with the Permanent Settlement brought about was a trickling down of land ownership rights to the more substantial class of peasant cultivators and a redistribution of land holdings *within* the existing rural elites, as the zamindars who were able to cope with the new demands—mainly the small to medium-sized concerns—took advantage of the plight of their larger neighbors to add to their holdings.

These zamindars who were able to weather the initial storms began to prosper from the early decades of the 19th century as Bengal's rising population pushed up rents relative to the fixed tax burden. "For many," writes Marshall, "running a zamindari was becoming a very profitable business," and this was reflected in a steady rise in the value of land from the 1810s onwards. With rapidly amassing wealth, the zamindari class was indeed loyal to the Company that had entrenched them as landowners and many maintained impressive establishments. "Even if," continues Marshall, "they did not rule the countryside as their predecessors had done under the nawabs, they still exerted very powerful local leadership. Even newly founded dynasties became patrons of learning and religion."[35]

But what of the key motive of promoting rural development? It is now recognized that this did not happen. Although the zamindars had an incentive to make improvements, the institutional and cultural context within which they operated did not favor innovation. It was a straightforward matter for them to pocket the rising revenues yielded by population growth and rising prices, and few took significant steps to invest in the land. To increase output they found it easier to extend the cultivated area rather than intensify production on existing holdings. They remained, fundamentally, what they had always been—middle men, with actual production decisions being taken by peasant cultivators. These peasant cultivators were, indeed, the chief losers from the Permanent Settlement. To raise the revenue necessary to cover their tax liabilities the zamindars naturally turned to squeezing greater rents from their tenants. In doing so they were assisted by two factors: first, as legal owners of the land, the zamindars were able to turn to the courts to enforce payments of monies owing; and second, the historic shift which coincided with the introduction of the Permanent Settlement from a land-surplus to a land-scarce economy greatly enhanced their capacity to raise rent demands. The British had foreseen that the zamindars would seek to shift the tax burden onto the cultivators and the Permanent Settlement included measures to protect their interests—including a ban on ad hoc revenue demands (known as cesses) and provisions for rent payments to be set down in writing and fixed for periods of 10 years. But illiterate and desperately poor peasants dependent upon the local landowner for access to increasingly scarce land were in no position to enforce such terms, and the Company did little to intervene on their behalf. As a result official survey reports from regions like Rangpur in northern Bengal in 1815 described how "the arbitrary oppression under which the cultivator of the soil groans, has at length attained a height so alarming, as to have become by far the most extensively injurious of all the evils under which the district labours."[36] In sum, the whole social system of agriculture remained embedded within customary practices and dependencies and the looked-for agricultural revolution of Bengal did not materialize.

As the Company Raj extended beyond Bengal, with it went the same issues of revenue collection. At first attempts were made to follow the

Permanent Settlement model, as in the vicinity of Madras, where the Hindu poligars were regarded, like the zamindars, as a hereditary gentry class. By the 1830s, one-third of the Madras Presidency was under the fixed-payment zamindari system.[37] But this was not typical of subsequent revenue assessments, which sought to create, not landlord elites, but a class of prosperous peasant cultivators.

In South and Western India, the *ryotwari* system was generally adopted. This entailed recognizing individual peasant cultivators (ryots) as the owners of the land, who thereby became liable for the payment of the land tax. As the system's chief architect, Sir Thomas Munro, explained:

> The registered occupant of each field deals directly with Government, and so long as he pays the assessment he is entitled to hold the land forever and cannot be ejected by Government, though he himself may, in any year, increase or diminish his holding or entirely abandon it. . . . Inheritance, transfer, mortgage, sale, and lease are without restriction; private improvements involve no addition, either present or future, to the assessment.[38]

The level of the land tax was not fixed, but instead was to vary with agricultural and market conditions, the amount the land could reasonably be expected to bear being set by a district collector on his regular tours of the areas for which he was responsible. During these tours he would classify fields according to their soil and produce and set a tax rate for a limited period of time. In the Punjab and Northwest Frontier Province a further variant on this tax regime was represented by the *mahalwari* system, under which the land tax was levied upon a village unit, the amount payable by each member to be apportioned by the village itself. By the end of the 19th century, around half of British India was assessed for land tax under the ryotwari system, with the zamindari and mahalwari settlements accounting for the remainder.[39]

Why was the Bengal model of permanent revenue settlements on a landlord class not copied more widely? In much of India there was simply no zamindari class to hand and little possibility of making one. The poligar elite of Mysore, for instance, had already lost their status at the hands of Haider Ali and Tipu Sultan.[40] There was also the growing dissatisfaction with the workings of the Bengal settlement—and in particular a determination to avoid an inflexible revenue base which would not adjust to changing price and prosperity levels, while Stokes has emphasized the growing influence of utilitarian thinking in

Company policy making, with its hostility to landlords as essentially parasitic beneficiaries of economic progress.

More significant was the Company's growing capacity to undertake detailed revenue assessments. When Cornwallis settled Bengal, the Company lacked the staff and expertise to oversee a system that adjusted taxation according to local circumstances. As the Company's own knowledge base expanded, it was able to contemplate the intensive measuring and monitoring implied by the up-country tours of district revenue collectors. It now became possible, in theory, to adjust revenue demands in line with farming conditions. "Increasing exploration, information, and bureaucracy," writes Robb, "had given the Company the confidence to attempt closer administration, while claiming enhanced respect for Indian traditions."[41] Chris Bayly similarly observes that by the 1820s nearly all districts had revenue survey maps going way beyond anything possessed by the Mughals. The company's capacity to assess and enforce revenue payments was unique in Indian history.[42]

Lastly, there was the role of individuals like Munro and the members of the Madras Revenue Board. These men wanted to stabilize traditional Indian society rather than artificially force it into a mould owing more to British practice. However, they disagreed sharply as to the means by which this should be accomplished. The Madras Revenue Board wanted to shore up the traditional Indian village communities through the deployment of the mahalwari system, believing—correctly as it turned out—that the ryotwari system of individual proprietorship would only hasten their dissolution. In a strongly worded memorandum of 1818, they criticized the advocates of a ryotwari settlement:

> In pursuit of this supposed improvement, we find them unintentionally dissolving the ancient ties, the ancient usages which united the republic of each Hindu village, and by a kind of agrarian law newly assessing and parcelling out the lands which from time immemorial had belonged to the Village Community collectively.[43]

The unnamed target of these words was Munro, the champion of the ryotwari system in the Madras Presidency. In the clash between these two scenarios it was Munro who enjoyed the backing of the board of directors and in 1820 he returned to India as governor of Madras and proceeded to implement his ryotwari settlement—though he was unsuccessful in his campaign to have the settlement made permanent in the manner of Bengal, which he regarded as necessary if the peasants were to be incentivized to make improvements.[44] Here the role of Mill was important. He, too, favored the ryotwari system, for the classical liberal reason that it would promote individualism, but he also wanted variable tax assessments as only then would it be possible to capture the economic rent for the state.[45]

In the light of the above evolution of British agrarian policy before 1858, what can we say were the leading consequences of British rule for Indian rural society?

First, and most significant, was the introduction of the concept of private property in land into the Indian countryside. This reform struck at the heart of the customary shared usage of resources and dealt another blow to the already ailing Indian village community. With ownership rights in land came the possibility of trading it, and an active land market arose. To cite the case of the Aligarh district, 2 percent of land holdings changed hands per annum in the period 1838 to 1858.[46] Around Benares, 40 percent of proprietary rights were sold between 1800 and the mid-19th century.[47] In such situations, there are always winners and losers: while some peasants defaulted on their rents or taxes and were forced to sell all or part of their landholding, others were able to add to their farms and so increase their revenue-earning potential. These more prosperous farmers might employ the poorer peasants as laborers, or enter into sharecropping arrangements with them. The number of peasants who actually held a proprietary right in land (and were thus responsible for the payment of land taxes) was in fact quite small. In Mathura district, one in three of the male population had land rights; in the area of Muzaffarnager near the Ganges Canal the ratio was as low as one in six. The "proprietary body," says Stokes, "was very much a rural elite."[48]

Second, the high and regular demands of the Company for cash gave an impetus to the development of commercialized agriculture as peasants were forced to sell a greater share of their output.[49] This effect should not be exaggerated: even under the Mughals, most land revenue was collected as cash and therefore peasants were already marketing a portion of their produce. More important than the tax regime in promoting the marketization of agriculture were improving road, river, and latterly rail communications and the growth of urban centers like Bombay and Calcutta. Prior to the arrival of the railway, observed William Digby, villages producing a surplus crop would store it to offset bad times; now the surplus was shipped off by rail to be sold.[50] European merchants engendered a demand for specific products in demand beyond India. The most famous was indigo, a dying agent used in Europe's burgeoning textile industry. Realizing the commercial potential of the crop, the Company assiduously encouraged its cultivation and output increased rapidly from the late 18th century. However, the European planters who conducted the trade in regions like northern Bihar drove notoriously hard bargains with local peasants, who were reduced to a position of dependency through chronic indebtedness. Equally controversial was the Company's promotion of opium, the entire output of which it purchased for export to China in order to finance its imports of tea and silk. Production grew strongly, from 4,000 chests per annum in 1789 to 50,000 in the 1860s.[51] In another attempt to reduce its trading deficit with China, the Company encouraged the establishment of tea plantations in India. These were a genuinely new feature in the Indian scene—funded and run by European capital and employing wage labor in remote, purpose-built communities. By the mid-19th century remarkable results were being achieved—exports leaping from 144,161 lb. in 1847 to 3,343,663 lb.—though the localized and specialist nature of the tea plantations meant that their crossover effects upon more general farming practice were minimal.[52] The Company was less successful in its efforts to stimulate cotton farming in India with a view to supplying the British textile industry: American cotton varieties performed badly, while the fibers yielded by Indian cotton were too short for use in Lancashire mills. Thus, though the total volume of crops produced for market increased, commercial agriculture remained an essentially marginal extra within the context of Indian farming as a whole, which continued to be subsistence oriented. Perhaps its main effect was to widen still further rural inequalities as larger, more prosperous, farmers were able to exploit new opportunities. In this respect, comments Marshall, cash crops probably "contributed more significantly than British revenue policy had done to increasing the differentiation among the rural population."[53]

A third feature linked to Company policies was the growth of peasant indebtedness. This was not a new feature of the Indian scene— Stokes concludes, "the moneylender's grip predated British rule" in Central India[54]—but its effects became ever more pervasive under the impact of British policy. Holt Mackenzie estimated in 1832 that more than three-quarters of all Bengal farmers were in debt.[55] For many, accumulating annually sufficient cash to be able to pay the land tax was a major challenge. What placed them under particular pressure was the fact that the Company was very tardy in adjusting its revenue demands if harvests were poor or prices low. In such situations, cultivators were often unable to meet their tax demands and, if they were not to lose their land entirely, were forced to borrow at high interest rates from Hindu moneylenders or from their more prosperous neighbors. Once incurred, few peasants were ever able to pay off their debts, which were inherited from one generation to the next, rising cumulatively, placing these unhappy families in a position of total dependence upon their creditors—forming, in effect, a new kind of bonded labor.[56] Once their crop was harvested, the proceeds would be paid to the creditor, who would then advance them sufficient funds to meet their revenue demands and supply their basic needs, and so would the cycle be perpetuated, year upon year. The moneylenders did not want to take over the land—they preferred to control the cultivator and his crop since by this means they were able to take a large share of whatever net revenue the farm generated after the land tax had been extracted. Further strengthening the moneylenders' hands was British legislation which meant that, for the first time in India, a lender unable to realize a debt was permitted to seize the land as collateral and sell it. With laws limiting maximum interest rates also being repealed in 1855, the operations of moneylenders became increasingly resented. In the Faridpur district of Bengal, J. C. Jack recorded interest rates of "never less than 36 percent" in the years 1906 to 1910.[57] Not for nothing were moneylenders usually the first target of any peasant protest movements. Lawrence James relates how, during the 1854–55 uprising of the Santhals of Midnapur, insurgents hacked off the limbs and head of a moneylender, chanting "four annas," "eight annas," "twelve annas," and "quittance" with the final stroke.[58]

Two further developments associated with Company policy should be noted. One was irrigation. In Mughal times, India had boasted impressive canal and irrigation systems, yet these had fallen into disrepair and the Company made a start at upgrading them. During the 1810s and 1820s work went ahead to renovate the Jumna Canal system in north-central India, the benefits yielded encouraging the Company to embark—in 1841—upon the construction of a new Ganges Canal, which by 1856 ran to some 1,400 kilometers and brought regular water supplies to 600,000 hectares across the Doab.[59] Progress in the south was much more limited and owed everything to the personal enthusiasm of the engineer Arthur Cotton, who through such schemes as the damming of the Coleroon and Krishna Rivers brought a million acres of paddy field into cultivation.[60] Eye-catching though these projects were, however, they were highly localized in their impact, and it is generally recognized that the Company significantly underinvested in irrigation works. Despite being financially profitable, even if judged in terms of only the transport dues and increased revenue assessments they yielded, "the Company's attitude," writes Edwardes, "remained parsimonious and . . . the Directors authorized expenditure only with reluctance and . . . under the strongest pressure from administrators in India."[61]

The Company exerted, finally, a conspicuous impact upon the natural environment of India.[62] Here the most tangible effect was deforestation. The clearing of forestland for strategic purposes had long been a policy of Indian rulers, for whom trees were seen as providing a haven for groups threatening the state—ranging from rebels and bandits to the armies of enemy powers. The Company perpetuated this tradition. As Bayly notes, when Arthur Wellesley drove roads through the forests of Malabar he cleared the land of trees for one mile on either side. Similarly, forests sheltering the Pindaris bands were destroyed.[63] More important was the impact of Company-promoted activities. Cotton cultivation depleted the soil and pushed farmers into virgin forest lands; tea plantations replaced trees in the Assam and Bengal Hills; and demand for teak for ship and building construction led to extensive felling in the western forests. In addition, peasants, seeking to escape high revenue assessments, settled in erstwhile forest districts. By the 1840s, large tracts of India, such as the Deccan and Mysore, were effectively treeless, bringing environmental damage in the form of soil erosion, reduced rainfall, and higher temperatures.

Besides these specific effects of Company rule, there were two broader shifts occurring within the country districts which, while not solely a consequence of Company policy, emerged out of conditions the Company helped to create. Both were linked to growing pressure on the land. In the 18th century it was labor, not land, which was the scarce resource in India. There were large tracts of unfarmed land and, if a group of peasants found the terms imposed by the local landholder or tax gatherer too irksome, they could shift their entire village into the uncultivated waste. Even in an economically prosperous region like Bengal agricultural activity was constrained by a lack of labor: in Chittagong in 1761 only 25 percent of the available land was cultivated.[64] When famine struck Bengal in 1770, one-third of the farmed land went out of cultivation.

However, the balance between land and labor shifted decisively in favor of the former from the early 19th century. To begin with, the population of India, stagnant for most of the 18th century, entered upon a growth trend around 1800, which carried it from some 200 million to 255 million at the time of the first census in 1871. Second, the decline of the traditional artisan sector under pressure from factory-made British imports took from peasants the chance to earn a livelihood from non-agricultural pursuits. As village and cottage industry employed less people there was a growth in the numbers seeking to make a living through farming. Nineteenth century India exhibited the curious phenomenon of a country with a rising share of the labor force engaged in agriculture. With this process operating in conjunction with a growing total population, the result was an inexorable decline in the average size of land holdings. In a noteworthy 1917 study, Harold Mann, Director of Agriculture for Bombay, catalogued the changing landholding pattern for a village in the Poona district of Maharashtra. Whereas in 1771, the average size of a holding was 40 acres, in 1818 it was 17.5 acres, in 1820–40 14 acres, and by 1914 was reduced to just 7 acres. As Mann summarized:

> In the pre-British days and in the early days of British rule the holdings were usually of a fair size, most frequently more than 9 or 10 acres, while individual holdings of less than 2 acres were hardly known. Now the number of holdings is more than doubled, and 81 percent of these holdings are under 10 acres in size, while no less than 60 percent are less than five acres.[65]

These ever-more diminutive land holdings yielded a precarious livelihood. Mann believed that any holding of less than 10 acres could not maintain its owners, while even somewhat larger farms were vulnerable to harvest failure, illness, or excessive tax demands.[66] Thus was reinforced the tendencies toward peasant indebtedness, forced land sales, landless laborers, and the various features associated with inequality and absolute poverty in the Indian countryside.

Population pressure was one factor behind the second long-term shift associated with the period of Company rule: namely, the extension of settled cultivation into previously marginal areas. Yet other forces encouraged this process. One was the creation of private property in land. It was a dogma of the British that the waste, communal, or uncultivated land of India had to belong to somebody and was settled upon individuals when the revenue assessments were carried out. With possession of land came a liability for tax and those thus favored were now under pressure to make it pay by bringing it under the plough.[67] A third element behind this extension of the cultivated area was the imposition of law and order, which meant that landed proprietors felt more confident in extending their farming operations into previously wastelands.

Why was law and order a factor here? It was because what the British habitually referred to as wasteland was not waste at all, being, in fact, utilized by a whole range of social groups. There was, to begin with, the poor of the villages who turned to the surrounding wooded and uncultivated land to supplement their meager livelihoods. This loss of a collective amenity contributed to the increasingly precarious position of the lower echelons of the village hierarchy, while with all land now somebody's property the poor were deprived of their previous ability to migrate away from onerous tax and rental demands: peasant farmers were thus rendered more immobile and liable to the exploitative practices of rural elites.

Next, there were the nomads and pastoralists who did not practice settled arable farming, but rather moved with their flocks and herds over wide-ranging areas. Such groups as the Gujars, Mewatis, Bhattis, and Rangar Rajputs played an important part in the economy of India, moving their herds of goats, sheep, cattle, and horses between grazing lands, yet they increasingly found their traditional migration routes blocked by new villages of arable cultivators and conflict often resulted. In this clash between settled and nomadic agriculture, the British consistently sided with the former, associating migratory pastoralists with criminality, martial traditions, damage to crops and property, and a low propensity to pay tax. By this means, the old culture of the nomads declined and with it came a deterioration and shrinkage in India's horse and livestock resources.[68]

Besides the nomads, a second group to suffer at the hands of the village cultivators were the so-called tribals. These were social groups inhabiting remote and unchartered territories and who existed outside of the mainstream of Hindu culture. They were often ethnically distinct and preserved ways of life that pre-dated the Aryan invasions, having never been formally incorporated into any of the Empires that had risen and fallen on Indian soil. As the quest for cultivable land intensified, these tribals found their previously secluded realms intruded upon by the paraphernalia of village life—landed property, tradesmen, moneylenders, the land tax, Hindu ritual, and the gradations of caste. Before long, the hill tribesmen found themselves in debt and forced to seek agricultural work in an effort to raise cash. Resentment at this subversion of ancient ways of life prompted tribals to turn to guerrilla warfare and open insurrections, the most notable including the Paika insurrection in Orissa (1817–18), the Kol rebellion in Chota Nagpur, Bihar, (1831–32), the Bhil rebellion in Khandesh (1818–31), the Khasi rebellion (1829–33), and the Santhal rebellion of West Bengal (1855–56). The Company intervened to suppress such protest movements, not merely because of their determination to uphold law and order and support the claims of settled cultivators, but because they looked upon forests as a commercial resource and objected to tribals collecting forest produce, grazing animals, and felling trees.[69] Thus the Bhils of the Khandesh region of the Deccan plateau, classed as early as 1804 as an incorrigible and hereditary criminal class, were subject to pacification wars in the 1820s, their tribal lands being portioned out among those prepared to make terms with the state, and a series of irregular Bhil corps were formed as part of the Indian Army—proving themselves, says James, "excellent soldiers, loyal to the Raj during the 1857 Mutiny, and always willing to suppress disorders among their own people."[70] Even then, traditional attitudes were slow to change—on both sides. As late as 1883, Sir Lepel Griffin described "the true Bhil" as "the child of the forest and will avoid hot work or plough if he can steal enough to get drunk upon."[71]

Now these incursions of settled village cultivation into the lands previously dominated by nomads and tribals had one very significant effect. For it was now, under the auspices of Company rule, that the India that has come to be regarded as traditional and even unchanging actually became ubiquitous. Prior to the 18th and early 19th centuries, many Indians were not peasant cultivators, did not live in villages, and did not subscribe to the leading tenets of the Hindu or Muslim faiths. The Company left a significantly more arable, village-centered, static, rural, and Hindu India than it found. To quote Bayly:

> India as it is commonly conceived, a land of settled arable farming, of caste Hindus and of specialist agricultural produce, was very much a creation of this period. The stranger, older India of forest and nomad where the agricultural frontier was as often in retreat as on the advance, began to disappear. The more homogenous society of peasants and petty moneylenders which emerged in the later 19th century was a more appropriate basis for a semi-European colonial state.[72]

Paradoxically, therefore, the Company by its modernizing reforms and protection of landed property, helped to bring into existence the traditional India that entered into the consciousness of such diverse groups as colonial administrators, Indian nationalists, foreign observers, writers, poets, social reformers, historians, and anthropologists. It was, perhaps, the ultimate example of the Victorian invention of tradition.

How, then, can we summarize the impact of Company rule upon the actual tillers of the soil? No rural system is ever characterized by uniformity of experience and 19th century India was far from being an exception. Besides the obvious point that in a complex country such as India every generalization can be contradicted by contrary instances, there is the more piquant fact that the impact of Company policy varied across the country due both to differences in those policies and their implementation—such as the zamindari versus ryotwari settlements—and the contrasting opportunities and potentialities cultivators in different regions enjoyed. Bearing in mind all these caveats, the following would appear to be reasonably safe characterizations of the rural scene of India under Company rule.

First, the peasant cultivator was subject to high cash demands for tax revenue. Not that this was a new thing—all Indian regimes had squeezed the cultivators for revenue and the Mughal successor states had ratcheted up the level of tax demands as they attempted to found new dynasties and governing systems. In Bengal, for instance, revenue demands at the time of British conquest amounted to around one-half of total output, similar rates being reported in the South.[73] Under the Marathas, tax rates in the Deccan were said to be so oppressive that entire villages were driven out of production.[74] The problem was that the British took these tax levels as their benchmark and under the Company tax rates reached as high as 55 percent of gross output.[75] This was onerous enough, but the effect of these tax burdens was made all the more significant by the rigor with which the company insisted upon payment. The Company was, on balance, a more efficient tax collector than the successor states—"a cow cannot gender in a village," commented the outspoken critic of British rule, Digby, in 1901, "but note is made of the calf that is born . . . not an acre of land is sown or the crop from it reaped without the officers under [the Viceroy's] direction knowing fully what is done."[76] It wielded a bigger stick, too, as the introduction of the concept of private property in land meant that a defaulting peasant could face eviction, either by the Colonial government or by a zamindar landholder. By the early decades of the 19th century, the Company in Bengal was collecting its revenue demands in full.[77] In the Bombay territories, acquired in 1818, the land revenue collected had doubled within four years.[78] The districts around Delhi were notorious for the severity of their revenue assessments in the first decades of the 19th century, and when a village failed to render up the specified amount, Company troops were billeted there until the sum was collected. Stringent assessments of this kind rendered some villages unsustainable: the district of Sonepat, which in 1821 boasted some nine villages, had become deserted by 1842, forcing a halving of the assessment.[79]

Of course, the British needed the land revenue badly, but they justified their high tax demands in terms of Mill's doctrine of rent, according to which all revenue in excess of that necessary to cover costs of production was pure surplus with no economic function. Only in the 1830s was the rigor of the tax system diluted by officials on the ground who sought to render it more sensitive to the ability of the peasantry to pay. This was the Bombay Survey System developed by Wingate and Goldsmid.[80] In West India, the extent of cultivated land began to increase as a result—though even by midcentury significant amounts of uncultivated land remained.[81]

Now the basic effect of the high taxation levels was to leave the peasant cultivator with a minimal surplus for investment in improving his land. Living hand-to-mouth, the main challenge each year was to generate enough cash sales to cover the tax demand. "Neither native nor European agriculturalist," wrote Bishop Herber in 1826, "can thrive in the present rate of taxation. Half the gross produce of the soil is demanded by Government, and this . . . is sadly too much to leave an adequate provision for the peasant."[82] Reinforcing this effect was the declining size of land holdings, due to pressure upon the land, and the increasing resort to marginal land. The peasantry of India consequently lacked either the means or know-how to improve their technique of production and had, in any case, little incentive to do so as any increased productivity was likely to bring higher tax assessments. The zamindars were meant to be exceptions to this rule—but as we have seen, the Permanent Settlement proved a failure in this regard.

The upshot of these circumstances was essentially static levels of technique and soil productivity. It does not require a close reading of the theories of Malthus to recognize that the position of the peasantry was a highly precarious one, confined within ever-diminishing landholdings, forced to have recourse to increasingly marginal land, and in all probability indebted to local money lenders—who extracted a high price for tiding their clients over hard times and who could, ultimately, seize the farm in lieu of bad debts. By the time the state, the landlord, the moneylender and the merchant had all made their claims upon the produce of his labor, the peasant might well find himself with little more than a third of his original output to feed his family and invest in its future. In meeting the demands upon him, the peasant was more dependent than ever upon the output yielded by the farm itself since the relentless march of cheap manufactured goods from Britain meant that the possibility of supplementing rural incomes through, say, cotton spinning and weaving had receded. Equally, he was loosing customary access rights to additional resources yielded by the forests and uncultivated lands around the village. One implication of this was the increasing use of animal dung in place of wood as a fuel—which had the crucial drawback of depriving the land of much needed manure.[83] In consequence the typical cultivator had little alternative to hiring himself out as a laborer to larger landholders.

Overall, it is generally believed that the material condition of the typical farmer remained static over the first 60 or so years of company rule, reflecting the stagnant levels of output per head.[84] It was the scope for continuing to extend the cultivated area that enabled the growth in food output to just about keep pace with the rising number of mouths to be fed, leaving the mass of the population no better or worse off. But if the cultivator's real income remained stable, his *vulnerability* increased. Living hand-to-mouth on a cramped holding, with little opportunity for alternative sources of income, facing tax demands which left him little margin for investment, and in debt to money-lenders and local landowners, the cultivator—whom all recognized as the foundation of the Indian social and economic system—was in a wretched condition and one which could easily shift over into disaster if the rains failed or disease ravaged crops or if market conditions yielded falling prices and sales. Only after 1921 did average life expectancy in India rise above 25.[85]

This malaise of the typical farmer was most tangibly evidenced by the appalling incidence of famines, the ever-present threat of which hung like a pal over the lives of the poorest peasants and threw into question the boasts of the superior nature of British over-indigenous government. Episodes of extreme scarcity were no stranger to India, but they became, if anything, more common under British rule and extracted a high cost in loss of life and livestock. In the last 30 years of the 18th century, official records enumerated four major instances of famine or serious shortage. The years 1800 to 1850 saw 12 such incidents—including the great North Indian famine of 1837–38, which carried away an estimated one million lives—while the period 1850 to 1900 yielded some 19 cases, culminating in the terrible West Indian famine of 1899–1900, whose mortality level was placed at 1,250,000 by the Famine Commissioners.[86] For much of this period the British had no famine relief policy, preferring to rely on the beneficent workings of supply and demand which, it was believed, would see to it that food was shipped from areas of surplus to those of scarcity—overlooking, of course, not only the absence of necessary communications, but the fact that the poor had no money to purchase any such supplies that did arrive.[87] It was only in the 1840s that the colonial state began to evolve a more interventionist response, drawing up for each province a famine code that specified measures for famine prevention and relief—which, if it did not lift the incidence of famine, at least attenuated its impact.[88]

Yet this story of stagnation and nascent Maltusian crisis was not the only one to emerge from the Company Raj. For there were also cultivators who prospered during these years. These were the peasants who, enjoying larger or better situated or more fertile holdings, had a greater command of resources such as livestock, seeds, water, and implements and were therefore better able to take advantage of the emerging opportunities for market production—opportunities linked to rising urban demand, company orders for export goods, and the improving transport and irrigation infrastructure. Such peasants were able to utilize their greater wealth to add to their land holdings by buying land from their struggling or dispossessed neighbors, whom thy might employ as laborers or with whom they might enter into sharecropping arrangements. It was these peasants, likewise, who were able to purchase factory-made goods or build more substantial houses made of brick. In Bengal this rising class of substantial peasant cultivators, known as *mandals*, took a leading role in village politics, acting as village headman and sometimes acquiring revenue-collecting rights themselves, and were strong enough to resist excessive revenue demands by the zamindars—even leading violent opposition.[89] India had, in other words, its own emerging kulak class and there was an ever-widening range of experience within Indian agriculture, with striking inequalities within villages and between regions. From mid-century, this balance between winners and losers began to shift somewhat in favor of the former as prosperity linked to rising food prices and declining tax burdens began to suffuse itself through Indian agriculture more generally.

What, lastly, were the implications of Company rule for the social hierarchy of village life? These are especially hard to pin down. Undeniably, sections of the old rural elites did lose out amidst the new Company regime—families who failed to respond to commercial opportunities or were unable to squeeze their tenants rigorously enough and who could not, therefore, meet the initially high revenue demands. Yet the implications of this were more limited than has often been assumed since much of the land thus relinquished was actually bought up by more successful sections of the old elites. There was no fundamental shift in the social or caste composition of the leading landholders. Equally, the land market brought into existence by the British did not function in textbook fashion. Caste hierarchies and group and kinship ties continued to regulate access to land. Interest rates, too, were linked to social standing: those from lower caste and status groups had to pay higher premiums than those in more favored positions. Although zamindars lost many of their former governing powers, they retained their status within the rural communities. However, there was, says Bayly, a shift in the basis of their authority. Old semi-feudal systems of military power, kinship ties, and dependent labor gave way to more commercial attitudes. Zamindars were more guided by commercial considerations and often favored lower castes as tenants as they were more amenable to commercial pressure.[90]

At a more humble level, village leaders, like the Patels of West India, who had previously collected tax revenues for whole villages and acted as another layer of government at village level, were marginalized by the introduction of personal ryotwari assessments. And there was, probably, some increase in the numbers who had no land at all—a position bringing much stigma within rural communities. Just how many more peasants found themselves landless has been a matter of dispute. While a critic of British rule like R. Palme Dutt could refer confidently to the rising proportion of landless agricultural laborers, more recent writers have questioned this picture. Markovits, for instance, points out that around 20 percent of Indians were already menial laborers in the pre-British period, while Bayly observes that while some were loosing their land due to the pressure of tax and interest demands, others, such as untouchables and low-caste groups, were acquiring land for the first time as previous bars on their access to the land were lifted. Like Markovits, he concludes that the share of rural workers who had no access to the land remained stable at approximately 20 percent.[91] Such stability seems counter-intuitive in view of the mounting population pressure upon the land and the decline in access to communal land resources, and it is likely that the existence of the landless poor revolved much more around the casual cash-nexus than it had in less commercial, semi-feudal, days.

Overall, the structure and character of Indian rural life changed remarkably little. None of the reformers' visions for India, reflects Brown, came to pass.[92] Beneath the appearance of a hegemonic and reforming Company, the day-to-day experience of the average peasant cultivator continued to be shaped by far deeper and longstanding patterns of life. India was a land of small cultivators providing primarily for subsistence needs when the Company arrived, and so it remained when the Company was wound up as a governing institution in 1859. The old hierarchies persisted and were probably only compounded by the widening gap between the minority able to profit from enhanced market possibilities, and the majority who could not. The share of total output that was sold for cash remained broadly stable at 15 percent, and absolute consumption levels also appear to have changed little. In this sense neither the prophets of imperial progress, nor the nationalist lamentations of decay and demoralization, find vindication from the first century of British rule.

5

Commerce and Industry under Company Rule

The Company was not in India to fight wars, annex territory, or restructure the agrarian system; it was in India to make money from trade. It was accordingly all the more ironic that the means taken by the Company to ensure its commercial ends—culminating in its becoming the paramount power in the subcontinent—came to consume the bulk of its energies, displacing, thereby, the very economic motives that were the raison d'être for the entire operation. Underlying this dialectical evolution was the fact that Britain's trading relationship with India developed in a manner that subverted the mercantile assumptions upon which the Company was constituted. Coinciding with the Company's rise to political power was a descent into economic obsolescence, which meant that it could be pensioned off in 1859 as a faintly absurd anachronism. For Indians, likewise, their experience of the Company as a commercial concern—though never straightforward or one-dimensional—was always imbued with profound implications for the character of their economic and social life.

Under the terms of its founding charter, the Company was to enjoy a monopoly in British trade with the East. The Company had the sole right to ship goods between Britain and India and to conduct British trade with other Eastern nations such as China. The goods imported by the Company into Britain consisted, as we have seen, of an eclectic mix of primary and processed items, ranging from spices and saltpeter to silk and cotton textiles. These items were acquired by the Company from an extensive network of Indian producers, this up-country trade being transacted on the Company's behalf by a body of local Indian merchants, who then shipped the produce to Calcutta or, to a lesser extent, Madras or Bombay, for shipment beyond India. These Indian *banians*, with their knowledge of trading conditions, sources of supply, and local languages, were, like the zamindars who collected its taxes and the sepoys who fought its battles, one of the central pillars of Company rule, without whom it could not have contemplated administering so vast an Empire with so few men. In return, these Indian mercantile families, like the Carrs and Tagores, grew very wealthy through their participation in Company trading networks.

Besides exports from India, the Company made a large part of its profits from its conduct of the trade in tea from China—which yielded some £17 million between 1793 and 1810. The cost of this Chinese tea was met by the export of opium from India to China—despite the repeated attempts of the Chinese government to bar its import, resistance being overcome through a series of opium wars. The cultivation and trade in opium within India was regulated closely by the Company, which held a monopoly in the crop.

The basic problem the Company faced was that, although there existed a ready European market for Indian goods, Indians displayed a much more limited demand for British imports (and indeed for any other nations' products, India having a notoriously low propensity to import). As a result, British trade with India was in deficit, the difference being covered by a net flow of gold and silver bullion from Britain to India. Thus, at midcentury the Company sold British goods in India to the value of around £240,000 per annum, but this was well short of the value of Indian goods sold in Britain, the difference being covered by net flows of gold and silver bullion to India of between £700,000 and £1 million each year.[1] India was happy to receive such inflows of precious metals, for which she had a strong indigenous demand and little by the way of domestic production (she had no silver mines at all). Bullion imports ensured a buoyant money supply and an upward tendency in prices.

However, in an economic climate still shaped by mercantilist assumptions, this loss of precious metals to India was deeply unpopular within Britain, and the Company was widely regarded as a threat to both British industry and gold reserves. Accordingly, it became the Company's goal to generate sufficient money within India to cover its purchases of Indian goods—thereby obviating the need for a reciprocal flow of bullion and leaving the Company with a clear profit on its export sales. It looked to the tax revenue from its conquered territories to supply these funds. To an extent this happened: in Bengal, the Company's purchase of Indian goods out of its tax revenues (confusingly called its investment) rose to £400,000 in 1765 and £1 million in the late 1770s[2] and the inflow of precious metals was replaced by a net drain of gold and silver to Britain, exposing Bengal to the problem of de-monetarization and falling prices. Even so, the acquisition of territory was far from the license to print money that had been expected for the simple reason that as the governed area increased so did the costs of administering and defending it. Between 1792 and 1809, the Company actually made a loss of £8 million.[3]

What was the impact upon India of the Company's trading activity? India already had a well-developed trading economy—which was, of course, why the Company was so eager to do business there. Still, the Company's operations almost certainly enhanced India's trading op-portunities. The Company was a large purchaser of key goods, which then gained access not only to British, but European and eastern mar-kets. Bengal's main export to Europe was cotton piece goods, and this trade was encouraged by the Company, exports rising from 550,790 to 777,237 pieces over the course of the 1780s and 1790s. Exports of sugar, silk goods, indigo, and opium were also promoted. "Early Brit-ish rule," says Marshall, "powerfully stimulated the demands for the products of eastern India," the total value of Bengal's export trade in-creasing from 3 million rupees in 1777 to 15 million rupees in 1797, 45 million rupees in 1813–14, and 60 million rupees in 1828.[4] It wasn't only the official operations of the Company that were important here: nearly all its employees supplemented their relatively low salaries by engaging in private trade in products such as opium, betel nut, salt, and tobacco. By 1763, notes Brown, private trade in Bengal alone was worth over £500,000.[5] When, in 1772, fears concerning the corrupting effects of this private trade led to its prohibition, it continued by means of the so-called Agency House system, whereby Company employees deposited their money with Indian merchant houses that proceeded to invest it on their behalf. By this means, the emergence of a new Indian commercial class was encouraged, with many going on to form their own joint-stock trading companies.

Further encouraging Indian producers to take advantage of these commercial opportunities was the greater degree of law and order prevailing within Company territories and the priority given to the protection of property. In the decades following the decline of Mu-ghal authority cross-India trade had been disrupted by the activities of armed bands like the Marathas, who compromised the principal trade route running from Surat in the West via Agra to the Hooghly River.[6]

The Company lifted the Maratha threat, broke up the Pindari bands, and restored the Mughal network of fortified rest houses on the major roads, all of which encouraged merchants to undertake more extensive and frequent journeys. As security increased, moneylenders were more willing to extend their operations into rural areas, declining rates of interest testifying to the diminishing degrees of risk associated with this advancing money. "The reality of *Pax Britannica* for much of rural society," observes Chris Bayly, "cannot be doubted."[7]

Even then, some caveats must be entered. The stimulating effect of Company trade was localized, being largely confined within areas such as the Ganges Basin, with their access to the populous city and port of Calcutta. While Ganges River trade increased by 1,200 percent between 1785 and 1834, other areas were relatively untouched by commodity production. The cost and difficulty of transport remained a powerful disincentive to trade. Roads, insofar as they existed at all, were little more than dirt tracks unsuited to wheeled traffic, oxen carrying pack loads being still the predominant means of carriage, with the result that long distance trade was largely confined to expensive luxury items and certain mass consumption staples like salt and grain.[8] And still, while the absolute volume of Indian trade was high, it remained limited as a share of the economy. Even so late as the 1950s it was estimated that as many as 43 percent of rural transactions were in non-monetary form and in the 19th century this figure was very likely to have been above 50 percent.[9]

However, the trading relationship between Britain and India was shortly to be revolutionized by the unanticipated emergence of modern factory industry in Britain during the late 18th century. Whilst industrialization removed, on the one hand, a large part of the British market for Indian manufactures, it also exposed India to competition from goods that possessed a quality, and often a price, advantage over indigenous products. This competition struck, not only at India's domestic markets, but at its wider trade as well—exports of cloth from Madras to Southeast Asia, for example, contracting by some 40 percent between 1824 and 1850 in the face of the growing British presence.[10]

Reinforcing these shifts in comparative economic advantage was tariff policy. Whereas the East India Company had initially represented a vehicle for the import of cheaper goods from the east, its role was now transformed as British industry, with all the boundless energy of adolescence, saw India as a substantial export opportunity and expected the Company to open up its markets to its products. Commercial and manufacturing pressure within Britain achieved a victory in 1813 when, under the terms of the Company's Charter Renewal, it was deprived of its monopoly of Indian trade. At no point were Indian interests considered. Quite the reverse: tariff policies systematically disadvantaged the Indian producer. Thus, while British imports into India were subject to minimal tariffs of between 2.5 and 3.5 percent, Indian manufactured exports to Britain were discouraged by significant and often deliberately prohibitive duties—as Table 5.1 summarizes.

Indian goods were also subject to disadvantageous terms *within* India, for whereas British goods were exempt from internal customs duties, domestically produced goods were subject to a series of taxes and transit duties that added significantly to the cost of production. Whenever, during the manufacturing process, a product underwent a change of form—say, from raw cotton to yarn to cloth—a tax was imposed, the total tax payable in the case of cotton goods amounting to some 17.5 percent.[11] A further series of duties was imposed as goods were transported to market. Each of the principal towns and markets was surrounded by customs posts levying duties of between 2.5 and 10 percent by value, and long-distance trade brought the merchant up against a succession of customs points, each of which meant more delays and more opportunities for corruption. Thus in 1832, a trading boat travelling between Hardwar and Calcutta had to pass some 106 separate customs posts.[12] These duties had a damaging effect on Indian enterprise and were denounced by a series of British observers, including Holt Mackenzie, Charles Trevelyan, and Lord Ellenborough. "No less than 235 separate articles," declared the latter in 1835,

Table 5.1.   Import Duties on Indian Goods as a Percentage of Value

	1812	1824	1832
Muslins	27	37	10
Calicoes	71	68	10
Other cotton goods	27	50	20
Goats wool shawls	71	68	30
Lacquered ware	71	63	30
Silk manufactures	Prohibited	Prohibited	20

Source: R. C. Dutt, *Economic History of British India,* 1:294.

"are subjected to Inland Duties. The tariff includes almost everything of personal or domestic use, and its operation, combined with the system of search, is of the most vexatious and offensive character, without materially benefiting the revenue."[13] Such criticism, occurring within a context of an increasingly prevalent belief in the virtues of free trade, helped to pave the way for the gradual lifting of internal duties. In 1836, Lord Bentinck removed all the customs posts in Bengal, while in 1843–44 Lord Ellenborough, now governor-general of India, oversaw the abolition of inland duties in Sind, Madras, and Bombay. However, although the majority of internal duties had been lifted by 1847, they had by then, says B. Chaudhuri, "effectively constricted commerce," offering "differential advantage to foreign imports" and discouraging "regional specialisation."[14]

The British Industrial Revolution, working in conjunction with the policy of opening up India as a market for manufactured exports, led to a radical restructuring of Anglo-Indian trade. Exposed to the chill blast of foreign competition, cotton weaving—traditionally India's leading export industry—went in to rapid decline. In 1811–12, cotton piece goods made up one third of India's total exports by value. By 1834–35 this figure was 7 percent, and by 1850–51 a mere 3.7 percent. And while Indian producers lost access to export markets they faced, as Table 5.2 shows, stiffening competition at home.

Between 1843 and 1939, India was the largest single outlet for the British cotton industry. The damage to Indian industry represented by these imports, and the role of British tariff policy in reinforcing British industry's competitive advantage, was lamented by several contemporary observers. Writing in 1837, Montgomery Martin alleged that Britain had done "everything possible" to "impoverish . . . the miserable beings subject to the cruel selfishness of English commerce. . . . Under

Table 5.2. Cotton Textiles imported into India from Britain 1815–55

Year	Cotton textiles imported (millions of yards)
1815	1
1824	25
1835	50
1845	230
1855	450

the pretence of Free Trade," he continued, "England has compelled the Hindus to receive the products of the steam looms of Lancashire, Yorkshire, Glasgow, &c., at mere nominal duties."[15] The orientalist H. H. Wilson went further:

> The history of the trade of cotton cloths with India . . . is . . . a melancholy instance of the wrong done to India by the country on which she had become dependent. It was stated in evidence that the cotton and silk goods of India up to this period could be sold for a profit in the British market at a price from fifty to sixty percent lower than those fabricated in England. It consequently became necessary to protect the latter by duties of seventy and eighty percent on their value, or by positive prohibition. Had this not been the case . . . the mills of Paisley and of Manchester would have been stopped at their outset. . . . They were created by the sacrifice of the Indian manufacture.[16]

With a similar, if less dramatic, process at work with respect to goods like wool textiles, iron, pottery, glass, and paper, India became, for the first time in its history, a net importer of manufactured products. To pay for these imports India was pushed toward the greater export of primary products such as indigo, tea, linseed, opium, wool, and raw cotton. Thus, while the total volume of Indian exports increased strongly—quadrupling in volume and value between 1814 and 1858—and while she continued to enjoy a trading surplus with Britain, the *composition* of her trade shifted from secondary to primary goods. So whereas, between 1811 and 1850, cotton textiles declined as a share of exports from 33 to 3.7 percent, raw cotton grew from 4.9 to 19.1 percent, sugar from 1.5 to 10 percent, and opium from 23.8 to 30.1 percent.[17] As Robb summarizes:

> Broadly speaking, between the 1780s and 1860s, India moved from being an exporter of processed goods and an importer of bullion, to being an exporter of raw materials and an importer of manufactures.[18]

The irony here was that the British, despite having cornered the Indian market, never capitalized upon it to the extent they had anticipated. The mass of the Indian population were simply too poor to be in a position to purchase British-made factory goods, a deficiency exacerbated by the heavy revenue demands of the state and the decline of India's previously leading industries. Even after the ending of the Company's trading monopoly in 1813, Asia as a whole accounted for less than 10 percent of total British exports. What is more, the new trading regime established in the wake of the Industrial Revolution effectively spelled the end of the Company as a going commercial concern. While European demand for its main manufactured export—cotton piece goods—collapsed, it was forced to admit into India manufactured goods which, besides paying little in the way of tax, cut away at the mainspring of Indian economic dynamism—and hence the state's revenue-raising powers. The company protested at the destruction of Indian industry, but could do little to prevent it. Increasingly seen as an obsolete hindrance to trade, one by one the Company's commercial privileges were taken away, until in 1834 it was even deprived of its one sure source of earnings—its monopoly on trade with China. Henceforward, the East India Company became, in effect, a solely political institution.

The transformation of India in the direction of a primary producing economy, symptomized by the expanding share of the population engaged in agriculture, was to become one of the key nationalist indictments of British rule—that it deindustrialized India and rendered it a dependent colonial economy. The "unjust commercial policy of England," wrote R. C. Dutt, "discouraged and ruined the manufactures of India," it being "the settled policy of the ruling nation . . . to convert India into a land of raw produce only" so as to provide both a market for British exports and a guaranteed source of essential raw materials.[19] This said, British tariff and industrial policy cannot be regarded as merely a device for the impoverishment of the Indian people. The Industrial Revolution, beginning in Britain but soon spreading to Europe and beyond, was a fact that was bound to impact upon a traditional economy like India. True, high protective tariffs could have defended Indian producers from its destabilizing effects, but at the cost of denying Indian consumers access to cheaper cotton and other industrial goods. Any true assessment of the effects of cheap factory-made imports on the livelihoods of the majority of the Indian population must complete the near-impossible task of balancing the gains to consumers against the losses of the industrial sector and the secondary effects of these changes in areas such as the increasing pressure of population upon the land.

However, deindustrialization was not the only economic legacy of Company rule to be subject to nationalist criticism. A second key indictment centered around the infamous drain of wealth from India to Britain. According to this argument, the problem with Company rule was not so much that it taxed heavily or made large profits, but that it was an alien presence in India and sent any surplus monies it made back to Britain to line the pockets of its directors, pensioners, and suppliers. Previous rulers, though frequently originating from beyond India, settled permanently, which meant that the revenues they generated were spent within India, helping to stimulate local trade. This was not true of the Company, whose shareholders and pensioners lived largely in Britain, nor for its employees, whose goal was to make as much money as quickly as possible for remission home—mindful always of the precarious life expectancy of the early British settlers in India, which averaged 40 in 18th-century Bengal. As Edmund Burke declared in 1783, "Every rupee of profit made by an Englishman is lost forever to India."[20]

The monies transferred annually by the Company itself were known as the Home Charges. These included dividend payments to the owners of Company stock, interest on loans raised in England, the cost of administering Company affairs in London, the pensions of retired Company officials, and payments for members of the British army serving in India. In its mid-18th-century hey day, the Company was making profits of £500,000 per annum and paying dividends of 7–8 percent.[21] After the Company ceased to trade in 1834, its shareholders were guaranteed 10.5 percent of the Indian government's total revenue. The service charges on the Indian debt were another significant item as the total debt rose quickly, from £7 million in 1792 to £70 million in 1857. The £40 million of costs entailed in suppressing the Mutiny of 1857–58 were also imposed on India, and by 1877, the debt was standing at £139 million, much of it raised in London. Between 1813 and 1850, the annual Home Charges varied between £1.5 and £3.5 million.[22]

This, it must be emphasized, was the official transfer of funds from India to Britain. To this must be added the money sent back by Company officials trading and investing in their private capacity; an appreciable share of employee salaries; and the profits made by merchants, plantation owners, shipping interests, and the like. This private wealth drain exceeded the official sums, and according to Chris Bayly, a total of around £6 million was being transferred annually from India to Britain by 1820.[23] This outflow of money to Britain represented a debit in India's balance of payments and was funded out of her continuing surplus on physical trade with Britain.

There was thus a continual hemorrhaging of money from India to Britain for which no return was received—in effect a 'tribute' of

Empire. For critics of British rule this wealth drain was a major—even principal—cause of India's poverty as it deprived indigenous businesses of capital at the same time as it helped to fund Britain's Industrial Revolution. The economist W. T. Thornton, writing in 1880, believed the economic drain had "tapped India's very heart-blood" and "has dried up the mainspring of her industrial energy." Dadabhai Naoroji, Professor of Mathematics in Bombay and later MP for Finsbury in the UK, led a sustained campaign against the drain of wealth, arguing that it undid such beneficial effects of British rule as law and order. In his *Poverty and Un-British Rule in India* (1901) he claimed that the wealth drain, by impoverishing Indian producers, left her wide open to foreign competition and exploitation by external capital.

> The lot of India is a very sad one. Her condition is that of a master and a slave: but it is worse; it is that of a plundered nation in the hands of constant plunderers with the plunder carried away clean out of the land. In the case of the plundering raids occasionally made on India before the English came, the invaders went away and there were long intervals and security during which the land could recuperate. . . . But nothing of the kind is true now. The British invasion is continuous and the plunder goes right on with no intermission and actually increases, and the impoverished Indian nation has no opportunity whatever to recuperate.[24]

This argument regarding the deleterious effects of the wealth drain did not go unchallenged. In 1911, Theodore Martin pointed out that, owing to the British connection, India was able to raise money in London at favorable rates of interest, the savings thus made more than offsetting the drain in wealth.[25] According to Coupland, in the period to 1939 the interest paid on India's external (British) debt averaged 3.5 percent, compared to the 5.5 percent paid by Japan.[26] Similarly, Vera Anstey claimed that India's interest payments on money borrowed "did not . . . constitute a drain of wealth from the country" since "the borrowed capital was almost entirely used productively, with the result that in the long run returns more than covered interest payments."[27] Thus, the largest single component of the Home Charges (making up one-third in 1929–30) consisted of interest payments on the sums invested in building the Indian railway system.[28] It should also be remembered that many of the items classified as Home Charges, such as the pensions of civil servants and army personnel, or the cost of the first British-Indian telegraph cable, arose, at least in part, out of services yielded to the Indian people.

The whole Drain of Wealth controversy was, it is now apparent, conducted with a fervor hardly justified by the facts. Even if all the Home Charges are considered a pure loss to the Indian economy, they still represented less than 0.5 percent of India's national income.[29] Clearly, an investigation into the roots of India's poverty, or the tardy progress of industrialization, must begin and end elsewhere.

Let us now return to a matter touched upon in connection with the evolving pattern of trade: namely, the impact of Company government upon India's industrial sector. As we have had cause to observe, it was a staple view of critics of the effects of British rule that it led to the destruction of India's manufacturing base, with the result that India was relegated to the position of a dependent colony, reliant, very largely, upon primary industry in general and agriculture in particular. Writers within this tradition draw attention to the sophistication of manufacturing in 18th-century India. There was, they argue, a vibrant artisan culture producing a range of goods for both domestic consumption and export to Europe and Asia. India was a net exporter of manufactured goods, with the cotton industry of east India being particularly well developed. Thus in the district of Shahabad in the early 19th century Francis Buchanan, commissioned by the Company to survey the economic condition of northern and eastern India, estimated that there were 7,950 looms at work, absorbing the output of 159,500 women employed in spinning. Bhagalpur District boasted some 7,279 cotton looms, while in Gorakhpur there were thought to be around 6,114 looms and 175,000 women engaged in spinning.[30]

But it wasn't merely in such developed centers that industrial activity made a significant contribution to the lives of India's people. Industry was integrated into the domestic economies of families across India, forming a source of income to supplement farming and playing a vital part within the village communities, as artisans produced goods like utensils, tools, and pots for their fellow villagers in return for a share of the annual harvest. To quote R. C. Dutt:

> Large portions of the Indian population were engaged in various industries down to the first decade of the nineteenth century. Weaving was still the national industry of the people; millions of women eked out the family income by their earnings from spinning; and dyeing, tanning, and working in metals also gave employment to millions.[31]

Indeed some, such as Nehru, have gone so far as to suggest, "the economy of India had . . . advanced to as high a stage as it could reach prior to the Industrial Revolution" and that it was "quite possible . . . that under normal conditions it would have undergone that change."[32]

All this, it is said, was laid waste by British manufactured imports. Keen to exploit the potential of the Indian market, the East India Company and the British Parliament, writes R. C. Dutt,

> discouraged Indian manufacturers in the early years of British rule in order to encourage the rising manufactures of England. Their fixed policy, pursued during the last decades of the eighteenth century and the first decades of the nineteenth, was to make India subservient to the industries of Great Britain, and to make the Indian people grow raw produce only, in order to supply material for the looms and manufactories of Great Britain. This policy was pursued with unwavering resolution and with fatal success.[33]

By these means, concurs Digby, the British "struck down the ancient industries of India."[34] The most visible casualties were centers producing manufactured goods for export, such as Dacca and Surat, which entered into terminal decline. Where the Company had purchased 2.5 million rupees of textiles from Dacca in the 1790s, in 1807 it bought 600,000 rupees, and in 1813 only 200,000 rupees.[35] Speaking before a parliamentary inquiry of 1840, Sir Charles Trevelyan described how "Dacca, which was the Manchester of India, has fallen off from a very flourishing town to a very poor and small one . . . the jungle and malaria are fast encroaching upon the town . . . the distress there has been very great indeed."[36] Indeed, whereas in 1814, 21,631 houses in Dacca were assessed for the house tax, by 1830 the figure had dropped to 10,708.[37] It was with the example of Dacca in mind that the governor-general, Lord Bentinck, spoke of "the bones of the cotton-weavers bleaching the plains of India." Though especially traumatic, the experience of Dacca was not unique. Thus, Divekar has narrated the decline of the one flourishing textile trade of the West Indian provinces of Gujarat and Maharashtra in the face of fierce British competition. Established textile centers like Broach, Surat, Ahmedabad, Gandevi, and Poona could not match the price and quality of British machine-made goods. In Broach, "English cloth of superior quality could be obtained at half the price of the best dhoties and baftas, even at the very spot they were made." Unsurprisingly:

> The indigenous manufacture . . . decayed rapidly. By the middle of the nineteenth century almost all varieties of cloth came to be imported from England . . . and the export trade in cloth stopped almost entirely.[38]

The iron and paper trades of west India suffered a similar fate.

It was not only the urban manufacturing centers that were affected: at village level, too, the making of textiles, pottery, household utensils, and the like became unremunerative in the new conditions, undermining the delicate balance between industry and agriculture, forcing greater numbers onto the already overcrowded land, depressing living standards and increasing vulnerability to famine. As Marx famously remarked:

> The handloom and the spinning wheel were the pivots of the structure of the old Indian society . . . it was the British intruder who broke up the Indian handloom and destroyed the spinning-wheel.[39]

Even when the Company did patronize Indian producers its business practices have been widely condemned as representing an abuse of economic and political power. With its monopoly of the export trade and its ample resources yielded from tax revenue, the Company occupied a dominant position within the market for manufactures, and this it set about exploiting through its contracts with suppliers. Producers seeking to sell to the Company were forced to agree to contracts under which they could trade with no one else. Payment took the form of money advances to be used to buy raw materials and provide for consumption needs, the debts to be liquidated when the finished products were handed over to the Company's representatives. In practice, however, the selling price of the product was not sufficient to make good the loan and the artisan found himself indebted to the Company and fined for his troubles. Thus ensnared in a double bind—dealing exclusively with the Company to whom he was also indebted—the petty producer had no bargaining power and was pressed into accepting prices well below the market rate for the same goods. Everything, objected the English merchant William Bolts in 1772, "terminates in the defrauding of the poor weaver." The Company and its Indian agents "arbitrarily decide what quantities of goods each manufacturer shall deliver, and the prices he shall receive for them." These prices "are in all places at least 15 percent, and in some cases even 40 percent less than the goods so manufactured would sell in the public bazaar or market upon free sale."[40] "The whole weaving population of villages," wrote R. C. Dutt, "were thus held in subjection to the company's factories."[41] Invidious terms of this kind hardly served as an inducement to industrial activity.

It might be thought that the demise of artisanal industry at the hands of a foreign power backed by the resources of the Industrial Revolution would have been compensated for by the encouragement of modern factory production within India. Yet this was far from the case before 1858. The Company and its agents effaced little interest in the techniques of manufacturing, being more concerned to obtain goods at the cheapest rate through the manipulation of market conditions. But the Company was equally jealous of other non-Indian sources of finance entering to establish factory concerns, regarding such non-official actions as potentially disruptive of its position. In any case, British investors were very wary of doing business in India, preferring to place their funds in Company stock. Not until 1851 was the first cotton mill built in India.

It must, however, be observed that this uniformly negative account of the impact of British rule upon Indian industry has, in recent years, been qualified in important respects. The idea, for instance, that India was somehow on the verge of a breakthrough into modern economic growth at the time of the British conquest is largely discounted.[42] Indian industry, for all its vibrancy, continued to be characterized by a stagnant technique with no use of inanimate power sources or the application of modern science. Indeed, the growing surplus of labor due to population growth made a move to labor-saving technology even less likely.

While the decline of Dacca and other export centers cannot be doubted, it is now recognized that these have attracted undue attention. The great bulk of industrial production consisted of courser and cheaper cotton goods for local markets, and this did not suffer a comparable decline. Quite the reverse, local production expanded under the dual impact of rising rural incomes from midcentury, which fueled the growth in consumption demand, and cheap imports of factory-spun thread from Britain, which reduced production costs. There were 225,000 cotton looms in the Madras Presidency alone in the 1850s. By the 1890s, the output of cotton cloth in India was higher than ever, with hand-made textile products continuing to account for 25 percent of the market.[43] Despite British competition, cotton spinning itself remained a major employer, producing course thread for indigenous weavers. It was, ironically, the establishment of spinning mills within India that sounded the knell for hand spinning.[44] Thus when R. C. Dutt reported in 1902 that "weaving and spinning are practically dead," he was wide of the mark.[45] Even so late as 1951, there remained an estimated four million handloom weavers in India. M. D. Morris's summary assessment is worth quoting:

> The path of traditional handicrafts was not inexorably downward. For a long while, transport barriers offered considerable protection in many parts of the country. Even where the traditional product was directly confronted by machine-competition—cotton spinning is the obvious instance—the process of decay . . . could be quite protracted. In many cases modern factory production reduced the cost of handicraft factor inputs, thus strengthening the demand for the final handicraft products at least for a while. Handicraft systems showed considerable adaptability to available materials and market needs which enabled them to evade some of the worse impact of direct competition from factories.[46]

Outside of the textile sector, trades such as leather, metal, and woodworking experienced no significant external competition and probably, says Charlesworth, "enjoyed significant growth."[47]

Suggestions that the Company failed to encourage the establishment of factory industry in India have also been overdrawn. The mechanized production of cotton began as early as 1817, with the erection of a steam-powered mill near Calcutta. In 1854, the first Indian-owned mill was established at Bombay under the leadership of C. N. Davar, a Parsi businessman with extensive commercial links with British merchants. However, the real expansion began in the 1860s, by which time 10 cotton mills were in operation in Bombay, most of which were funded by Indian capital. Both the Company and the army were keen to see the emergence of an iron and steel industry in India and provided financial incentives to help bring this about. The most sustained effort was made at the Porto Novo works near Madras, which by the time of its closure in 1846, had received some 822,000 rupees of state funding. An attempt to resurrect the enterprise in the 1850s, with cash incentives to entice the interest of local businessmen from Madras, also ended in failure.[48]

Thus, arguments for the deindustrialization of India under British rule cannot be sustained: the share of the working population engaged in industry probably remained stable at around 10 percent.[49] By the same token, of course, it did not increase. Company tariff policy was one factor behind this stagnant industrial share, though according to Morris its effects were eclipsed by a range of structural influences including the slow growth of the market, the unequal distribution of income with the attendant bias toward luxury demand, the cost of importing foreign-made machinery and the difficulty of keeping it in repair and obtaining replacement parts, the poor quality of transport systems, and the ready availability of very cheap labor. "No single act of policy," he concludes, can explain India's tardy rate of industrial growth. It was, rather, "a web of relationships which dampened the absolute level of performance and inhibited the rate of change."[50]

Those wishing to paint a more favorable picture of the effects of British rule typically make much of the improved communications associated with British administration. Economic activity had, without doubt, long been hindered by a poor transport infrastructure. India, for instance, possessed no metaled or permanently maintained roads at all, people and goods having to make their way along dirt tracks which were narrow, uneven, and rutted at the best of times; for significant parts of the year they were totally impassable. Thus in Bengal it was estimated, in 1823, that there were no roads upon which it was possible to run a carriage for more than 20 miles all year round.[51] Carts were, accordingly, rarely utilized, their place being filled by convoys of pack horses and bullocks. In this, India was far from unusual: British roads in the early 18th century were notoriously dysfunctional. But the consequences in India were far more damaging given the greater distances between regions and market towns, the lower density of river systems, and remoteness of northern and central India from the sea.

The British took a number of measures to improve the speed and reliability of internal transport. First, they improved rivers, built canals, and introduced steam-powered boats. Steam transport speeded up communications on some crucial waterways, notably the Ganges. The 850-mile journey from Allahabad to Calcutta took 20 days in the wet season, the return upstream journey, during which boats had to be manually dragged, taking three months. In 1834, the introduction of iron-bottomed steamships reduced the downstream time to 8 days, while the upstream leg was slashed to only 24 days.[52] But this was a very expensive and selective service, not suitable for the majority of produce nor for the bulk of India. Wider improvements to the canal network were likewise minimized by the general failure to invest significantly in irrigation before the 1860s.

Second, the British began to take in hand the road system from the 1830s, the improvement of which promised military as well as commercial benefits. An improved road was constructed between Bombay and Poona in 1830, and in 1839 work began on the Grand Trunk Road, a metaled road connecting Calcutta, Delhi, and Peshawar, the construction of which cost some £1,000 per mile. It eventually stretched some 1,000 miles across north India. Further roads connected Bombay to Agra and Madras to Bombay.[53] During the 1840s, £400,000 a year was spent on road building, and by the 1850s there existed an estimated 1,600 miles of roads suitable for carts. Although a major change, it was yet only a beginning. Many thousands of miles of road awaited improvement, and in areas like the South little of note had occurred by the 1850s. Even then, in a premechanized age, road transport was slow and cumbersome and unsuitable for low-value items.

The most eye-catching and transforming technology in 19th century India was, of course, the railway, which was to become an almost totemic symbol of Britain's presence in India—and for good reason. It was the one innovation that promised to break the tyranny of distance in India. Besides the obvious fact that agricultural and industrial produce could now be shipped between markets within India, and from the interior to the ports for export (and vice versa), the railway had a deeper significance. It raised the concept of Indian unity from the level of a hypothesis to a lived reality. For the first, time it became plausible for a person to travel from one side of India to another, while the Company, now able to convey orders, administrators, troops, and supplies to the farthest reaches of its domains, could be truly held to constitute a government of India, rather than a federation of discrete centers of power located around its historic footholds of Calcutta, Bombay, and Madras. Above all, perhaps, the railway was a medium for the transmission of news, books, pamphlets, and ideas, acting as a leaven amidst even the most insular communities. Unsurprisingly, the Company came to look upon the railway as offering a fast track to the creation of a modern state in India, making up for its hesitancies, inefficiencies, and executive weakness and demonstrating that British rule was, indeed, transforming and enlightened. As early as 1846, the post office official W. P. Andrews had called for the construction of "a magnificent system of railway communications" which "would present a series of public monuments vastly surpassing in real grandeur, the aqueducts of Rome, the pyramids of Egypt, the great wall of China, the temples, palaces, and mausoleums of the Great Mogols— monuments not merely of intelligence and power, but of utility and beneficence."[54]

This said, all such exalted visions threatened to come to grief upon the basic fact that India's poverty, parochialism, and lack of technical know-how meant that it could not afford to build or run a railway network itself, and the Company's resources were not sufficient to make up the difference. This threatening logjam was broken by Lord Dalhousie, the Peelite reformer, who consciously set out to deploy the railway as a modernizing tool during his period as governor-general. He pressed his case to the Company's generally skeptical board of directors in a Minute of 1853, astutely highlighting the benefits of railway construction to Britain as well as to India:

> The commercial and social advantages which India would derive from their establishment are, I truly believe, beyond all present calculation. . . . Every increase of facilities for trade has been attended . . . with an increased demand for articles of European produce in the most distant markets of India.[55]

Not content to allow an Indian railway system to emerge ad hoc from the imperatives of local businessmen, Dalhousie sketched a plan for an all-India network of trunk lines which would connect all the chief cities and military cantonments. The funding issue was to be resolved in the manner being adopted in France and Prussia at the same time: namely, the state would offer guaranteed returns of 5 percent upon all lines, subsidizing any that fell short of this.[56]

Dalhousie's ideas found favor and the opening, in 1853, of India's first railway line, running between Bombay and Thana, was but the beginning of a program of construction that had yielded, by 1857, some 300 miles of track. British capital began to pour into Indian railway projects, and after 1869, the state itself began to pay for and build lines. By 1860, 843 miles of track were in operation, and by 1870, 4,800, by which time the railways were carrying 19 million passengers a year and 3.6 million tons of freight. The following year direct railway communications were established between Calcutta, Madras, and Bombay. By 1909, it was estimated that out of the total British investment in India of £365 million (which itself represented approximately 10 percent of the entire British overseas investments), railways accounted for £136.5 million. This compared with total investments in mining of £3.5 million and industry and commerce of £2.5 million.[57] India's railway network was by then, at over 27,000 miles, the fourth largest in the world, and it continued to expand well into the 20th century, until by 1947, it stretched over 43,000 miles, with 78 percent of India within 20 miles of a line.

Here, it might be thought, was one achievement of Company rule that would meet with general approval. Certainly, railways were faster, more reliable, and cheaper than existing forms of transport.

Table 5.3.   Expansion of the Indian Railway Network

Year	Length of track in operation (miles)
1855	200
1860	843
1869	4,000
1880	8,800
1893	18,000
1914	35,000
1932	42,000
1943	43,000

J. M. Hurd estimates that the cost of transporting a ton of freight by rail in 1930 was 94 percent cheaper than the cost of carrying the same ton by packhorse and cart in the period 1800–1840. Trade was encouraged, and this in turn helped to create a national market, with price differentials between regions reducing and regional specialization encouraged. For the first time it became popular to market significant proportions of India's agricultural output and farmers felt able to specialize in commercial crops like jute, cotton, oilseeds, and groundnuts, confident that they could market their output successfully. Hurd believes that if the railways had ceased to exist in 1900, the total output of the Indian economy would have fallen by about 9 percent.[58]

Even so, gains of this order are not sufficient to exempt the British railway program from some serious criticisms. It is argued, to begin with, that the subsidized profits granted to railway firms were excessive and came out of the already strained pockets of the Indian people. By 1900, the total subsidies paid by India to British railway operators amounted to some £40 million—a significant contributor to the drain of wealth.[59] Worse still, possessing state guarantees, the rail companies had little incentive to regulate costs and the result was a railway network that was built in a profligate fashion far beyond the modest needs of the Indian people—the first 6,000 miles costing an average £16,000 per mile—with a tendency to construct uneconomic lines requiring ongoing subsidies. Between 1879 and 1900, some 70 percent of the total length of track failed to yield the minimum profit of 5 percent and required government subsidies.[60] Appearing before a parliamentary inquiry into Indian finance in 1872, the former finance minister W. N. Massey complained:

> Enormous sums were lavished and the contractors had no motive what-ever for economy. All the money came from the English capitalist, and so long as he was guaranteed five percent on the revenues of India, it was immaterial to him whether the funds that he lent were thrown into the Hooghly or converted into bricks and mortar. . . . It seems to me that they are the most extravagant works that were ever undertaken.[61]

It is specifically alleged that the British over-invested in railways at the expense of roads and canals—the latter of which would have yielded enhanced agricultural productivity in addition to better com-munications.[62] As R. Palme Dutt pointed out, whereas by 1900 the Gov-ernment had spent a total of £225 million on railways, the total spent on canals was only £25 million.[63] Hurd concurs with this observation, concluding "it is very likely that the capital expended on much of the railway system would have yielded higher social rates of return had it been spent on other projects."[64]

On the other hand, without government subsidies, large parts of India, including most of the south, would not have been served by the railway. As it was, the subsidies paid to the railway companies after midcentury represented less than 0.3 percent of Indian national income and for this Indians gained a series of economic, social, and cultural benefits, the economic one alone, as we have seen, being in the order of 9 percent of national income.[65]

It is secondly argued that railway construction in India did not have the stimulating effect upon wider industrialization observable in Europe or America as the linkages to the domestic economy were so weak. Just about everything required for the building and initial oper-ating of the system, from the locomotives, rails, points, and sleepers to the skilled labor to run the trains, was imported from Britain. The gov-ernment made little attempt to source locally: though, for example, the first Indian steam locomotive was made in 1865, between that year and 1941 only 700 locomotives were built in India, whereas 12,000 British-made locomotives were imported. As a result, the railways could not provide the kind of leading sector in modern economic growth wit-nessed in the case of Prussia, America, or Russia.[66]

Perhaps the most damaging criticism of the British rail system is that it was built to suit the needs of the Company, not the Indian peo-ple. The motive behind the chief lines, it is often said, was to enable the Indian Army to transport troops from one place to another, so as to quell internal rebellions, or to shift troops to the frontiers in the pursuit of expansionist policies. It was not surprising, therefore, if everyday Indians benefited little from the large-scale construction works undertaken in their name. There is undoubtedly evidence that this occurred. In his Railway Minute of 1853, Dalhousie made much of the military benefits railways would bring:

> A single glance cast upon the map recalling to mind the vast extent of the empire we hold . . . the wide distances which separate the several points at which hostile attack may at any time be expected . . . will suffice to show how immeasurable are the political advantages to be derived from a system of internal communication which would admit of full intelligence of every event being transmitted to the Government . . . at a speed exceeding fivefold its present rate; and would enable the Government to bring the main bulk of its military strength to bear upon any given point, in as many days as it would now require months.[67]

In 1884, Sir John Strachey could tell an audience of Cambridge students that the railways of India "have increased, to a degree that is hardly calculable, our military strength."[68] Most prominent of the military lines were the subsidized and state-owned lines that pushed up from Delhi toward the Northwest Frontier, quickly allowing the army to reinforce a region considered troublesome and at potential risk from Russian invasion. Rail links to such remote settlements as Quetta, Peshawar, Rawalpindi, and Chaman reflected strategic, rather than commercial, imperatives. Even within cities, lines were placed away from the central business districts so they would be less vulnerable to mob attack.[69] Once again, therefore, Indians were being asked to foot the bill for their own colonial oppression.

Qualifications, however, must be made to this argument. To begin with, even if military motives were prominent in the construction of lines, this does not mean they were a pure loss for the Indian people. History shows that an independent India would have had to convey troops to its borders if it were to be secure against foreign invasion. Law and order, too, would have needed to be upheld under any system of government and yielded substantial benefits to important sections of India's population. Second, notwithstanding the military impetus behind certain lines, like those of the Northwest Frontier, most lines in fact followed existing trade and communication routes.[70] The great commercial centers of Bombay, Calcutta, and Madras were well served, as later were Delhi, the Punjab, and so forth. Third, the quest to build

an all-India network did not only reflect policing and military requirements: it was also hoped that such rail connections would allow the
transport of grain to famine-hit areas.

Clearly, pushing forward the construction of a rail system in the
context of a backward and exceedingly poor economy was bound to
be distorting and wasteful. It seems somewhat churlish, nonetheless,
to criticize the Company for over-investing in such a major infrastructure project when it is simultaneously rebuked for failing to take constructive measures to promote Indian development. In the long run,
its beneficial effects upon the Indian economy and sense of national
unity have proved inestimable. This said, it must be admitted that the
net benefits of railway construction before 1858, and indeed thereafter,
were not sufficient to offset the wider failure to promote Indian industry or defend Indian producers from the damaging effects of cheap factory goods. After all, the stability of India's industrial sector over the
19th century occurred notwithstanding any stimulus from the railway:
for better or worse, railway construction did not initiate a "take-off"
into Rostovian economic growth.

6

The Company, Class, and Caste

It was the rapidly shifting social structure of Indian society in the post-Mughal years that provided the social context for British intervention as it created class and caste groups who looked to the Company to advance their interests vis-à-vis established elites. Unsurprisingly, British rule had the effect of reinforcing the underlying dynamic of social change in India, elevating the position of those groups able to exploit new arrangements and opportunities for their benefit, and contributing to the ebbing status of those less able or willing to adapt.

Among the foremost beneficiaries of British rule was the merchant and banking class. This class had early formed close relations with the British, arranging their up-country trade and providing liquid capital to finance the activities of European merchants. It was, of course, the Jagat Sheths, most powerful of Bengal's banking houses, that encouraged and bankrolled Clive's overthrow of Siraj-ud-Daula in 1757. This, by itself, did not guarantee that such groups would uniformly prosper under Company rule. Several important commercial families lost out within the new commercial environment dominated by British commercial interests—most notably, the Sheths themselves, now subject to competition from British bankers and deprived of their customary access to the nawab's treasury.

The most debilitating influence of British rule so far as the merchant class was concerned was the restrictions it placed upon their activities and their concomitant subordination to British commercial interests. The Company dominated the trade in certain key commodities. In the case of salt, opium, and saltpeter they possessed a monopoly in the marketing of the product. Although they had no formal monopoly in the cotton textile trade, their control over the market was equally pronounced to the exclusion of Indian merchants. The Company established collection centers, known as *arangs*, to which producers in several villages were to bring their produce for purchase by British agents. Thus dependent upon one monopsony buyer, to whom they were often indebted, and under threat of sanctions if they traded with anyone else, the weavers were effectively reduced to the condition of employees. International trade and shipping was another sector overwhelmingly in British hands, forcing Indian merchants to confine themselves to inland trade. The European commercial presence was strongest in Bengal. "Virtually all the ships which handled Calcutta's greatly increased exports," observes Marshall, "were owned by Europeans."[1] The Company encouraged European banking firms to establish themselves in Calcutta and these, rather than Indian banking houses, increasingly funded the activities of European merchants. "There was," says Markovits, "no room in the Calcutta of that time for a true partnership between Indian and British businessmen."[2]

Yet, however galling these restrictions, they occurred within an overall context that provided increasing opportunities for Indian commercial groups as a whole. While Indian and British businessmen might operate within distinct spheres in a major center like Calcutta, this was less true in Bombay and far from the case up-country, where the Company and other British interests were heavily dependent upon the services provided by Indian trading networks. Europeans relied upon Indian merchants to negotiate contracts with farmers and artisans, supply liquid capital, and transport goods to market. Hence as British trade increased so did the openings for merchant groups working alongside the British. What made this necessary was the continuingly limited British presence in India. In 1852, there were only 6,000 resident adult males in India outside of the army, and the inflow of British capital was similarly limited. In these circumstances, the functioning of the Company as an economic entity was dependent upon the services of indigenous merchants and the local capital resources they were able to access. Some of the Indian businessmen who worked alongside the British became very wealthy indeed. Ramadulal Dey of Calcutta, for instance, who specialized in supplying cargoes to American ships, was said to command a fortune in excess of £300,000.[3]

Within the country districts, banking remained very much an Indian preserve, as did a large part of the trade in foodstuffs and

manufactured goods like cooking utensils, tools, and course cotton cloth, which were transported for sale in India's vibrant bazaar
economy—within which Europeans had virtually no presence. In
the flourishing hinterland around the Ganges Valley, Indian merchants, processors, and transporters all expanded their operations,
and towns that served as market and residential centers grew significantly over the first half of the 19th century: the population of
Mirzapur increased by over 50 percent between 1815 and 1850 on
the back of the cotton trade. Bareilly, Agra, Benares, Allahabad, and
Farrukhabad all grew upon the fruits of expanding trade.[4]

A particular institution that embodied this symbiosis between
European and Indian business was the Agency House. These were
holding companies which attracted funds from Europeans—notably
Company employees barred from trading on their own account—
which they then proceeded to invest on their behalf. Indians
associated with these mercantile houses prospered and the system
expanded rapidly—too rapidly, in fact, as it succumbed to collapse
in the 1830s, a collapse that left many Indian merchants indebted—
especially as they were, unlike the Europeans, personally liable for
any losses incurred.[5]

Above all, British rule in India facilitated the trading activities of
the mercantile class in two ways. First, through improvements in the
communications infrastructure. Roads, canals, and railways allowed,
as we have seen, Indians to trade more extensively over larger areas
than before. Second, by means of the protection offered to persons
and property under the law. It was an axiom of British administration that private property must be defined and protected, and in the
context of the instability following the demise of the Mughal Empire,
this represented a powerful inducement to investment in real property.
More Indians were prepared to advance loans, sink money into urban
property, buy landed estates, and tie-up liquidity in moveable stock,
far more assured that their investment would be safe and their profits realized. One indication of this newfound confidence was the rise
in urban land values—the value of landed property in Delhi, for instance, rising three-fold between 1803 and 1826.[6] An equally conspicuous consequence of the new Peace of Empire was the spread of Hindu
moneylenders through the rural communities—indeed even into the
previously remote tribal lands. Lending money at high interest and
gaining power over the produce of the farmers and artisans who found

themselves in debt, the moneylenders were among the chief beneficiaries of British rule—though also among the least popular.

The most tangible testament to the success of sections of the Indian commercial class was the growth of the new urban centers, notably Calcutta, Bombay, and Madras. All three cities grew rapidly from the 18th century and housed large and influential Indian mercantile communities occupying a milieu geographically and culturally distinct from the small British enclaves. Within these communities—referred to by the British as Black Towns—there emerged a new, and increasingly confident, Indian culture funded by profits from trade, banking, and land rental. India had, of course, possessed thriving urban centers before, but they had been more courtly than commercial, and more Muslim than Hindu. But the British ascendancy saw the eclipse of the old Mughal and Muslim elites and the rise to dominance of prosperous families of Hindu, Parsi, and Jain origin. These groups marked their new ascendancy with the overt patronage of elaborate forms of religious ritual, with large sums devoted to the construction of temples, the celebration of weddings and religious festivals, and the support of priests. Yet their growing sense of collective identity was not confined to only religious outlets; they also took up new forms of civic society inspired by British examples. Pressure groups, for instance, began to be formed, such as the Calcutta Trade Association (1830) and the Calcutta Chamber of Commerce (1834), which called upon the government to improve transport and reduce transit duties.[7]

Calcutta, indeed, boasted a large and thriving Black Town, distinct but intimately linked to the British center. By 1820, its population was some 350,000, of which Europeans made up only 3,000, confined within a secluded oasis of mansions and parks around Fort St William. Northwards ran the Black Town, itself fragmented into multiple local communities, each with its own markets and dominated, in the Bengali districts, by *dals*. These dals were multi-caste factional groups overseen by powerful families within an area that served to mediate disputes over issues such as marriage, inheritance, and caste privilege within a context of support for Bengali cultural norms. But if the dals aimed for cross-caste harmony within a locality, they generated more in the way of animosity as they competed with their neighbors for power and prestige. The leading commercial families of north Calcutta devoted far more time and energy to such rivalries than they did to improving the urban environment they inhabited, with the result that the Black Town retained something of the atmosphere of the village. Roads were left as dirt tracks and the deep mud the traveler would have to negotiate during the Monsoon was recalled by Nirad Chaudhuri:

> In Calcutta of those days tarmacadam was reserved for the so-called European quarters, and we, the Bengalis, had only rubble and earth on our streets. This mass decomposed during the rains, became thin and watery enough to be capable of being splashed head-high. . . . This mud, as it lay on the flagstones of the footpaths, converted them into grindstones for our shoes . . . those of us who cared for our shoes did wade through the streets with the precious pair in hand.[8]

But if the wealthiest residents of the Black Town showed little interest in municipal drainage, they more than made up for this in their patronage of religion and learning. They founded temples, erected sacred images, employed Brahmin pandits, devoted money to the mass feeding of sacred cows, and ensured that major Bengali festivals like the Durga Puja were celebrated in high style. And though proud of their own cultural traditions, they realized, too, the importance of coming to terms with English language and knowledge. To this end they formed the Hindu College in 1817 which, assisted by a government subsidy, soon "developed into a formidable institution at which English was the medium of instruction and English literature, western political and social thought and physics and chemistry were taught."[9]

If anything, Bombay exceeded Calcutta in the vibrancy of its urban culture. While Calcutta tended to draw wealthy Indians by virtue of its status as the capital city and *entrepot* of the empire, in Bombay they took a more leading role in the City's commercial success—working closely with European businessmen in the process. Bombay grew rapidly in the period between 1820 and 1850, its population leaping from 200,000 to half a million, by which time it was the largest city in India. This growth reflected commercial prosperity associated with the cotton trade, as raw cotton was imported from Gujarat and finished textiles were sent into the Chinese market. Meanwhile the annexation of the Maratha territories made Bombay an important administrative center as well.[10] Culturally, Bombay was less homogenous than Calcutta, with important communities of Gujaratis, Jains, Maharashtrans (who were mainly confined to more menial positions), and Parsis. The latter were highly accomplished businessmen and were especially open to western influences, building sumptuous European-style residences and taking a leading in role in the shipbuilding and cotton-manufacturing industries. It was no accident that Bombay was the site of India's first railway line.

Calcutta and Bombay were chiefly British creations. Among the most important of the native cities were Allahabad and Benares, both of which experienced strong growth in the early decades of the 19th century. Here British influence was minimal, Indian trading and banking families dominating, their prosperity underpinned by the manufacturing trades of the surrounding area—cotton textiles in the case of Allahabad and silk in the case of Benares. In Benares, traders and bankers replaced landed elites as the patrons of the Ramlila, the great festival celebrating Ram. As such, writes Markovits, the relative dynamism of these cities "testifies to the resilience of the pre-colonial urban culture."[11] But while some cities sustained the relative prosperity of pre-British days, others, including the likes of Malda, Vishnupur, and Dacca in Bengal, entered periods of steady decline. Murshidabad, once the administrative capital of Bengal, found itself eclipsed by the rise of Calcutta, its population dropping from 165,000 to 146,000 between 1815 and 1829. As a consequence, Markovits estimates that in north India the urban population as a share of the total remained stable at about 10 percent between 1810 and 1850. Still more significant for the long-term evolution of the urban experience of typical Indians was the fact that, in both the colonial and Indian cities, the British allowed expansion to occur spontaneously, making little or no attempt to plan for a new urban environment. People and businesses crowded around the narrow lanes and side roads of the city centers, while the perimeters of cities sprawled outwards in ad hoc fashion, merging imperceptibly into the surrounding countryside—pretty much, of course, as they did in Britain itself. This "insignificance of colonial achievements with regard to urbanism," concludes Markovits, reflected "both a financial prudence, justified by the chronic difficulties of the government in balancing its budget, and the absence of a true imperial vision."[12]

If there was one figure who was most widely held to encapsulate the interaction between British rule and Indian society it was the educated middle class babu. Harold Innis once observed that the British Empire was founded less upon arms than upon endless quantities of cheap pulp paper. The British administered more than they ruled, and for this they required an ever-growing army of civil servants, clerks, officials, and translators. At the head of the bureaucratic machine stood the Company's covenanted Civil Service, schooled at its Haileybury training college in Hertfordshire. But these men, by virtue of their limited numbers and generally weak grasp of local languages and customs, were dependent upon the services of a wide array of educated

Indian support staff to keep village records, collect revenue, and assemble data on land holdings and other assets. These Indians were drawn from a narrow community of ritually pure writer castes, chiefly the Brahmins and the Kayasthas, and tended to owe their appointment to family connections, learning their work by careful observation of their elder relative.[13] With their lives so closely bound up with the service of the empire, these literate babus absorbed British ways and mannerisms in a heightened fashion which made them figures of amusement and condescension in almost equal measure. This pen portrait by Evelyn Battyle displays elements of both:

> All day this good-natured, friendly little bandy-legged senior babu with the sock suspenders and the shining pumps sat on a high stool in his office. With a heavy ledger in front of him and peering short-sightedly through his rimless spectacles, he dipped and re-dipped his nib into the black ink, scratching away in meticulous script. Many were the tales of the babu's expertise with figures, and so fabulous his memory that on occasions of disasters when the books were lost or burnt, he could reconstruct whole columns from memory. He spoke in perfect English and liked nothing better than to display a use of metaphors.[14]

The value of their work was not reflected in their remuneration or their promotion prospects, and as a result, the Company's Indian employees at local level turned to a variety of stratagems to supplement their incomes, including acceptance of gifts from village headmen, failure to collect revenues on newly cultivated land, and displaying favoritism toward family members and local elites. In the Guntur District of Madras, where one-half of the senior posts occupied by Indians were held by Maratha Brahmins, the extent of defrauding activity only came to light when the revenue from the district began to dry up completely. But as Brown points out, these Indian officials operated within a social context dominated by caste and kinship loyalties and "they owed as much, and probably more, to their Indian patrons and relatives than to their British superiors: they acted accordingly."[15]

The babus employed by the Company were part of the wider emergence of a professional urban middle class in India brought forth by the expanding opportunities in professions like the law, medicine, teaching, publishing, and banking. Susan Bayly estimates that there were around 500,000 members of the intelligentsia in 1850.[16] For men of this stamp, British rule was both necessary and beneficial to India and they took up the associated virtues of British civic society with alacrity, involving themselves in the founding of newspapers, debating societies, libraries, pressure groups, religious reform movements, and colleges. Calcutta witnessed, in 1815, the formation of the Atmiya Samaj, the first society dedicated to reforming Hinduism of its more superstitious and outmoded practices, to be followed, two years later, by the Calcutta School Book Society, devoted to the production of school texts in Bengali. By 1839, there were nine vernacular newspapers in Calcutta, and a further four in Bombay.

In this manner, middle class professionals came to occupy a position of dual importance: as transmitters of British cultural values to the mass of their less-Europeanized neighbors, and as catalysts for a new public opinion within India, conveying to their British overlords the perspective of the educated Indian and raising issues to be addressed. Most intellectuals were loyal to British rule, as the events of the Mutiny were to show. This was hardly surprising: the professional class owed its rising position and urban culture to British rule and patronage. Their chief grievances primarily focused around matters of employment and promotion, in both of which they felt themselves baulked by the Company's unwillingness to appoint Indians to senior positions in the administration. In 1826, a group of intellectuals drew up a petition for consideration by the House of Commons, protesting the exclusion of the "better classes of the natives of India" from "employments of trust, dignity and emolument" and calling upon the Company to admit them to equality of status "with merchants of Calcutta or the civil servants of the Honourable Company."[17] Although the 1833 Charter Renewal Act specified that no discrimination by ethnicity or religion was to be made in Company appointments, in practice entry by Indians into the senior reaches of the civil service was almost unheard of. The British were all too ready to dismiss the babu as an inconsequential figure with a blotting paper mind. They were to pay a price for this neglect in the later 19th century as the Indian intelligentsia, its claims to equality blocked, turned to more radical demands for a say in government.

If the commercial and literary middle class were the chief gainers from British rule, the biggest losers were the existing princely and aristocratic elites. This would not necessarily strike the casual observer in pre-Mutiny India. For sure, many princely rulers had seen their states annexed by the British, forcing them to make terms and quit the scene on Company pensions, or face the consequences of resistance—to which the gory ends of Siraj-ud-Duala and Tipu Sultan bore unattractive witness. But many retained their territories and the outward forms of princely power. In 1868, there remained around 600 states outside the government of the Raj, accounting for a population of 46.2 million, compared to a total Indian population of 192 million.[18] Some of these territories were little more than landed estates—such as Lawa, with a total area of a mere 19 square miles. But others were substantial: Hyderabad, whose nizam governed an area the size of Italy with a population of around 11 million; Holkar and Sindia, remnants of the old Mahratta Federation; Marwar, the size of Ireland and the largest of the complex of Rajput states; and Mysore, with a population of 3.5 million occupying an area of 31,000 square miles.

These princely rulers enjoyed wealth and prestige and lived a life of fittingly regal splendor. In the early 19th century, several such rulers, as Chris Bayly points out, became famous for their rich patronage of art, religion, and learning. Raja Serfoji of the ancient Hindu state of Tanjore devoted 10 percent of the territory's revenue to the support of music, painting, scholarship, and religious devotion. At Mysore, Raja Krishnadevaraja (1799–1836) gave large grants of land to Hindu and Jain religious institutions, built a Mosque for his Muslim subjects, and organized splendid celebrations for the Hindu festival of Dussehra. In another southern state, Pudukottai, the ruler, Raja Rajasinha, founded temples, supported Brahmin priests, and encouraged literature and music.[19]

Ironically, this culture of princely display and munificence was a reflection, not of power and independence, but of subordination and impotence. From 1813, the British had embarked upon a policy of rendering all princely states subordinate to the imperial power by making their rulers enter into subsidiary alliances. Under the terms of these agreements, the British Raj guaranteed the territorial integrity of the state. But for this they exacted onerous terms: the rulers were to accept the stationing of Company troops on their soil, the cost of which they were to meet themselves; to admit a Resident British official to monitor their conduct; to pledge not to enter into relations with any other foreign power; and were to accept the Company as arbiter in all disputes with other states. The continued existence of the princes was, in other words, predicated upon their acceptance of the British as the paramount power such that, as John Strachey observed in 1888, "no Native State within the limits of India has any real independence."[20] Even so, it was within the power of the Company to extinguish the nominal autonomy of the princely states—and several, including Nagpur, Jaipur, Jhansi, Oudh, and Tanjore, were formally annexed by Dalhousie in the 1850s. But the majority were allowed to retain their courts, customs, laws, and even private armies. Why was this? Quite simply the Company Raj was hard pressed to govern the existing territories subject to its dominion and it made economic and political sense to retain a subordinate princely India as a buttress or firewall, serving as a loyal intermediary between the state and the Indian people. As Lord Canning commented in 1860:

> It was long ago said by Sir John Malcolm that if we made all India into Zillahs (or British Districts) it was not in the nature of things that our Empire should last fifty years; but that if we could keep up a number of Native States without political power, but as royal instruments, we should exist in India as long as our naval supremacy was maintained. Of the substantial truth of this opinion I have no doubt.[21]

If this strategy were to work, it was essential that the emasculated princes retain the respect of their people. Hence the importance attached to their splendid courts and patronage of culture and religion. As the substance of power waned, so were its outer trappings elaborated with ever more extravagance.

Such a policy brought risks, however. Courtly display came with a price to be met by the impoverished population. Protected by Company forces, the princes tended to see themselves as immune from the threat of rebellion and the result was often corruption and poor government. As John Lawrence once remarked, if there was ever a device for ensuring maladministration, it was that of a native ruler backed up by British bayonets and directed by an English Resident.[22] The case of Oudh is instructive. We have already seen how the state of Oudh entered into decline following the imposition of heavy financial charges to pay for the cost of a body of troops stationed upon its soil.[23] In 1801, the territory was forced to cede the most strategic of its territories along the Ganges and Jumna to the British. What remained of this once-great and prosperous state became an economic backwater, which under its nawab, Wajid Ali Shah (1847–56), assumed the unenviable status with the Victorians as a byword in oriental despotism. The British Resident, General Sleeman, drew up a lengthy indictment of Wajid's administration, accusing him of devoting himself almost entirely to the indulgence of his passions for music, poetry, dance, kite-flying, and women (he had a total of 359 wives), allowing the court at Lucknow to sink into corruption and misgovernment under the control of his favorites. Strachey sums up some of his allegations:

> Singers, fiddlers, poets, eunuchs, and women were his [the Nawab's] only associates. . . . The fiddlers controlled the administration of civil

justice; that of criminal justice was made over to the eunuchs; each of
the King's favourites had authority over some court or office through
which he might make a fortune for himself. . . . Every office was sold;
commands in the army were put up to auction every season, or oftener,
and the purchase money was divided among the minister, the singers,
the fiddlers, and the eunuchs.[24]

Rarely can an Indian ruler have better fitted Victorian conceptions
of the oriental voluptuary. In itself, the portrait was not inaccurate—
the nawab did have a passion for culture and sensuality, and is considered primarily responsible for the revival of the Kathak dance
form. Yet his extravagant indulgence of these preferences was both
made possible, and largely explained, by his nominal position as the
head of a state reduced to impotence by the Company. With the British Resident running the state treasury and the army, treating the
nawab as a mere cipher, it was a realistic response by Wajid to turn
to cultural expression as a means of sustaining the independence of
Oudh, gathering around his court a range of people from less privileged backgrounds whose claims to preferment were based, not upon
birth or title, but cultural performance. The "social mobility" of Oudh,
writes Chris Bayly, "accompanied by a perceptible loosening of religious, caste, and even sexual boundaries was as deeply suspicious to
the British as it was to the established Muslim oligarchy."[25] Eventually, however, the Company's patience was exhausted and Sleeman's
damning report served the crucial political purpose of vindicating
Dalhousie's decision in 1856 to annex Oudh to the empire and pension Wajid off to Metiabruz, beside the banks of the Hooghly River
near Calcutta, with an annual income of 1.2 million rupees—money
which he used to found a new court as luxurious and pleasure filled
as that he left behind at Lucknow.

THE CASTE SYSTEM

No discussion of the impact of British rule upon India's social structure can neglect to consider the changes undergone by the caste system. Unfortunately, few issues in India's history and culture are more
complex—and controversial—than that of caste. Dr J. Wilson of Bombay is reported to have written two volumes of his projected study of
Indian Caste by the time of his death without even having completed
his analysis of the Brahmin caste.[26] Let us begin with some elementary definitions. It is customary to divide Hindu society into four

caste groups: the Brahmins (the caste of priests, administrators, and writers); Kshatriyas (the caste of warriors, princes, and the landed elite); Vaishyas (the caste of merchants and bankers); and the Shudras (the caste of peasant farmers). Beyond these four caste groups were to be found the non-caste Hindus, known variously in our period as untouchables, outcastes, and pariahs. Now the four caste groups are technically known by their Sanskrit name of *varnas*. Each caste or varna is in turn subdivided into more occupationally and regionally specific groups known as *jatis*, examples of which include the Jats, Rajputs, and Chamars, within which marriage will be confined. The point about the caste system, broadly defined, is that each individual is born into a certain varna and jati, and these will determine whom he or she can marry, where they can live, which temples they can visit, what type of food they can eat, who they will be able to fraternize with, and to whom they can turn in times of hardship. These caste positions are fixed at birth and are ranked in a hierarchy, with the upper castes like the Brahmins and Kshatriyas being viewed as ritually purer and more auspicious than the lower castes, the non-caste people coming last of all.

What, then, happened to this caste system under British rule? From our definitions of the caste groups given above it will be apparent that there was a fair degree of correlation between an Indian's varna and jati status position and his social class position. In this sense, the experience of the four caste groups mirrored that of their corresponding social classes: thus, literate Brahmins gained from the greater employment opportunities for Indians within the Company administration; the Vaishyas shared in the rising prosperity of traders and financiers and assumed, as we have seen, an increasingly leading role in urban manifestations of Hinduism; the Shudras saw their overall situation remain stable, though there was significant variation as some were able to profit from the growth of commercial agriculture, while others slid ever more perilously toward the status of landless laborers; and finally Kshatryias who kept the trappings of status and authority though they were increasingly denied its substance.

However, the debate over the relationship of the British to the caste system has increasingly come to be conducted at a rather deeper level. What is at issue is not the impact of colonial rule upon this or that caste, but its effect upon the caste system as a whole. And here some unexpected themes have emerged.

For earlier writers and commentators it was taken for granted that British rule had a generally dissolving effect upon caste relationships.

While the British were careful to avoid confronting caste sensibilities, the main thrust of their modernizing project ran counter to the superstitions of caste. The British introduced to India a liberal-humanist culture that spoke of the equality of all men before God and even before the state. Such equality was conspicuously absent from India, both between Indians, and between Indians and the British, but it was assumed that over time—albeit a comfortably distant one—the Indians, exposed to British values and education, would gradually reject their caste-bound prejudices and become fitted for some degree of self-government. But it was not only British values that would work this transformation. Economic change would bring new opportunities and new types of work outside traditional caste categories. Urbanization would bring castes into close proximity so old caste rules—such as the idea that a Brahmin who passed an untouchable in the street would have to engage in elaborate purification rituals—would become unworkable. The railway in particular was seen as undermining the caste system as different castes would rub shoulders with each other on crowded carriages. "Railways," predicted Charles Trevelyan in 1853, "will be the great destroyer of caste, and the greatest missionary of all." Caste, in other words, was but one of a series of superstitions, fetishes, and irrationalities that would gradually subside as India entered modernity under British stewardship. Confirmation for this view was provided by the very popularity of the railways, and in 1894 the Orientalist Monier-Williams could write:

> It is very satisfactory to know that, although it is too true that caste is still the very life and soul of Hinduism . . . yet some of its most vexatious rules are grasdually giving way under the pressure of steam, electricity, and European influence.[27]

A. Mayhew reflected in 1941:

> Before the close of the nineteenth century ideas and aspirations that were destined to assume the compelling power of a religion had captured the mind of enlightened India, and furnished weapons against caste which were not in the armoury of refined Hinduism. It became clear that caste stood in the way of national unity, that it was an obstacle to economic advance, and that it provided strong arguments to those who opposed the grant of political self-government to India. . . . Intercourse with Europeans and social entertainment associated with political or economic conferences are bringing together men and women of all castes and no caste.[28]

This view might embody the aspirations of a class of commentators on Indian affairs. It appears, however, that reality was very different and that, far from undermining the caste system, British rule helped to entrench it—indeed, some go so far as to say that colonial rule was largely responsible for the modern caste system. British rule consolidated caste in three main ways.

First, the British routinely factored caste into their policy decisions. They made use of caste categories in their day-to-day administration. The army, for instance, was caste-conscious in its recruitment policies, tending to draw its troops initially from among high caste Bengalis. These soldiers served within a context that recognized their ritual requirements in matters like food, religion, and living arrangements. It was the move away from this rigid caste-based recruitment model from the 1840s, with the increasing employment of Sikhs from the Punjab, which helped stir up the flames of mutiny within the Indian Army. The bureaucracy, too, recruited from limited scribal caste groups like the Brahmins and Kayasthas. More widely, the British respected the old Kshatriya castes and sought to shore them up as bulwarks of their reign. We have seen this in the case of the princes, but the policy was applied to the martial castes, most notably Rajputs, whose chivalrous culture and history was celebrated in Lt. Col. James Tod's *Annals and Antiquities of Rajasthan* (1829).

The second British impact arose from the Victorian obsession with classification. The British wanted to understand India and Indians and came to the belief that the easiest and surest way was *via* the caste system. An Indian was not an individual: he was the member of a caste and jati and to know that position was to know him too. The *locus classicus* of this approach was the decennial censuses, beginning in 1871. With these censuses, Indians were not merely counted, they were categorized according to caste, jati, tribe, religion, and ethnicity. But in so doing, the British were not simply recording an objective state of affairs—they were changing it for the simple reason that in asking Indians which caste or jati they were, they forced them to label themselves and formulate an identity around caste, which often did not exist. Indians, in other words, were pushed toward caste consciousness by the state and the result was that myriad of jatis and sub-castes that came to characterize the late Victorian analysis of Indian society. It was no accident that Denzil Ibbetson's famous theories regarding the origin of the caste system—according to which caste was a social construct used by groups like the Rajputs, Jats, and Gujars in their search for political power—first appeared as a forward to the 1871 *Punjab Census Report*. Of course, as Susan Bayly is careful to emphasize, Indians were not unwilling participants in this process: the idea of categorizing society into finely graded caste and status groups was already present and Indians took up the refined British caste classifications, adopting, in particular, the pan-Indian caste tables compiled from 1891 which ranked caste groups according to their purity and occupations. With such matters as recruitment into the army or government administration depending upon caste titles, it is no wonder, she continues, that Indians took these matters seriously and skillfully manipulated census lists and communicated their perspectives to administrators.[29] Thus while several Hindu reformers, notably the Ram Mohan Roy, attacked caste distinctions as a late corruption of Hindu doctrine, other Indian writers defended caste as a uniquely Indian institution that embodied necessary moral and social virtues and stood against western tendencies toward atomistic individualism. The great Hindu popularizer Vivkananda could accordingly write:

> It is in the nature of society to form itself into groups. . . . Caste is a natural order; I can perform one duty in social life, and you another; you can govern the country, and I can mend a pair of shoes, but that is no reason why you are greater than I, for can you mend my shoes? . . . Caste is good. That is the only natural way of solving life.[30]

Finally, and most important, the British helped to produce within India a social environment within which caste concepts could thrive. The caste system encountered by the British was not a static remnant of medieval India—it was an evolving and reforming thing. We have seen how dynamic was post-Mughal India as old elites declined, new prosperous groups emerged, and adventurous rulers usurped thrones. Within this maelstrom, people turned to caste identities to protect their existing social positions or assert new claims to status. As Susan Bayly has written, the institutions and beliefs now seen as traditional to caste were only just taking shape in the 18th century, that is, in the period of rapid state building accompanying the collapse of Mughal rule and the expansion of western influence. In a context of rapid and dislocating social change, more Indians came to believe they had a stake in the traditional caste order.[31]

A notorious example was the way in which Shivaji Bhonsle (1630–80), the founder of the powerful Maratha state, though from a low-caste background, associated Brahmin priests with his court who obligingly created for him a mythical lineage under which he was descended from Rajput princes of the Kshatriya caste. His attempt to attach caste status to his dynasty culminated in a great public fire sacrifice in which his body was oiled with essences like ghee and milk and the sacred thread of the twice born was placed around him by officiating Brahmins from the holy city of Benares.[32] Shivaji's example proved a potent one, and by the end of the 18th century, says Susan Bayly, virtually every realm had aspiring Kshatriyas with money to spend on initiation ceremonies.[33] At a more mundane level, communities under pressure from economic change and urbanization began to emphasize caste distinctions so as to maintain and defend their positions from interlopers from the countryside who were often associated with ritually unclean trades like leatherworking, pottery, and metalworking. This migrant labor was accordingly pushed toward menial service and laboring work in the docks, construction sites, rubbish collecting, and household cleaning with the result that the concept of untouchability, far from declining under the impact of modernizing change, assumed a new and prominent reality.[34]

This, then, was the situation encountered by the British. The social impact of the Company was twofold. Initially, western intrusion only intensified the sense of social disequilibrium in India. The British overthrew some dynasties, patronized others, made extensive use of educated Brahmins and other writer castes, did business with merchants, disbanded landlord armies, recruited mercenary soldiers, confiscated zamindari estates, and so on. In such a fluid environment, existing social groups turned to caste symbols and status to preserve their local standing and press their claims under the new dispensation. After all, if a social group failed to successfully assert caste status, it risked being lumped within the non-caste menials—with disastrous results for their economic and social standing.

But once the Company Raj had stabilized, a new dynamic began. For it was one consequence of British rule to bring greater stability and order to India and, through their land reforms especially, promote the spread of more settled cultivation. As we have seen, a basic effect of this was to extend conventional Hindu society into areas where it had hardly impacted before—such as tribal, mountain-dwelling, and nomadic communities. And with Hinduism came caste. As social systems became more stratified and rigid, as India became more rural and more village-centered, so did it become more caste-bound. Sometime pastoralist and martial groups who had existed outside the Hindu caste system now formed themselves into jati groups like the Ahirs, Jats, and Goalas—a process welcomed by the British who were disturbed and suspicious of nomadic and tribal groups.[35]

Caste, therefore, became part of a package by which groups under colonial government identified themselves in relation to the state and each other. More and more people became conscious of caste rules and their caste position and used it to secure objectives, such as protection, promotion, work, self-respect, and so on. This was not intended by the British, who had a genuine distaste for some aspects of caste prejudice and were always wary of the conspiratorial and superior manner of the Brahmin. But their mental attitudes, governing style, and policies helped to produce this outcome—and in truth, it was one they found quite congruent with their own Victorian obsession with class and precedent. Far from subverting caste, the British themselves fit into the system until they came to constitute, with their civil service hierarchies, British-only clubs and hill stations, and rejection of mixed-race marriages, but another caste within the Indian scene.

7

The Experience of the State

It is sometimes said, usually by those seeking to mollify critics of British rule, that most Indians barely ever encountered a white man. Though the proposition reads peculiarly as a justification of British rule, it contains much truth. "The Englishman proceeding to India," reflected Lord Curzon in 1909, "except in the great cities, will rarely come across an Englishman at all. I once visited a city of 80,000 people in which there were only two official Englishmen—both of whom happened to be away."[1] The basic unit of British administration was the district, the average size of which in 1893 was 3,859 square miles, with a typical population of 876,242, all of which was overseen by four British representatives: the district collector, two assistants, and a judge. In 1903, the total number of Europeans employed in the entire civil government of India was 6,500, of which only 1,200 were members of the prestigious Indian Civil Service.[2] Yet, though the average Indian may have rarely encountered the human face of the British state (at least in its British form—there were in 1903 some three million Indians working for the government), he was to become ever more familiar with its policies and actions. This chapter reviews these points of contact in three main areas: taxing and spending; law and order; and the legal system.

Robb has written that by 1850 the British government in India conceived of itself as operating according to a modern agenda.[3] This claim to modernity rested upon such features as a rational system of administration, an emphasis upon data gathering and processing, impartiality in its relations with its subjects, a strategic promotion of communication technologies like railways and telegraphs, and an ethos of national as opposed to sectional advantage. Yet, Robb continues, this modernism was far from complete. In reality it was checked, transformed, and compromised as a result of executive weakness on the one hand, and the complexity, variability, and resilience of Indian social practice on the other. A foremost example of this was public finance.

An indictment of British rule traditionally found in the pages of Indian critics like R. C. Dutt and Naoroji was that the government, unchecked by the force of Indian public opinion, spent too much and spent it wastefully. All the members of the Governor-General's Council, complained Dutt, are heads of spending departments and are "driven by the duties of their office to seek for more money for the working of their departments; there are no Indian Members to represent the interests of the people. The forces are all arrayed on the side of expenditure, there are none on the side of retrenchment."[4] Paradoxically, more recent critics have argued the opposite. The Indian state, they say, failed to spend the kind of sums necessary to reform and improve Indian conditions. The budget was small, often tending to deficit, and inadequate to the task of delivering the wider modernizing agenda.[5]

What government spending there was directed primarily to the costs of defense and administration, leaving little for social improvement projects like irrigation, road building, drainage, hospitals, and schools. Thus, in 1852–53, the government's income was £20.4 million. Of this, one half was spent on the military, and by the time administrative costs, pensions, and interest payments on debts had been covered, a mere £424,000 was left for public works of all kinds.[6] Although the breakdown of total government expenditure for 1868–69 (Table 7.1) shows a significant advance in the share given over to public works and railways, they still accounted for only a fifth of government spending compared to the one half devoted to the military and administration, with education still languishing at less than 1 percent.

To be sure, the culture of government in the first half of the 19th century, in Britain as much as India, gave little recognition to the idea that the public sector had a role to play in directly promoting social and economic development. This was the age of laissez faire, and this general reluctance to interfere in matters considered best left to private enterprise was compounded, in the Indian case, by a wariness of upsetting the equilibrium of Indian society. For a small, alien, group of men were well advised to collect what money they required to sustain their rule and remit some profit and keep themselves as clear as possible from the day-to-day workings of a society and culture they barely understood.

Table 7.1. Indian Government Expenditure 1868–69

Expenditure	Total (£)	Percentage
Interest on public debt	6,208,476	11
Cost of tax collection	5,442,583	10
Mint, post office, and telegraphs	1,493,360	3
Law and justice	2,845,447	5
Civil services	2,172,519	4
Police	2,476,580	5
Education	599,858	1
Stationary and printing	397,704	1
Political agencies	349,855	1
Allowances under treaties	1,778,358	3
Miscellaneous	831,083	2
Pensions	1,669,968	3
Army and Marine	17,410,211	32
Public works	6,272,334	12
Railways	4,483,352	8
Total	**54,431,688**	**100**

Source: G. Chesney, *Indian Polity*, p. 456.

Even if they had wished to do more, British administrators would have found themselves coming up against the powerful constraint of finance. India's poverty meant that its tax-generating capacity was naturally limited, and the British then proceeded to box themselves in still further owing to their ideological and self-interested opposition to traditional sources of revenue like customs duties. This left the land tax—which, as we have seen, placed a heavy burden upon the cultivators, and one that, it was realized, needed to be reduced if agriculture were to develop. India's agricultural economy, comments Chris Bayly, never performed well enough to underwrite the costs of European dominion.[7] In addition to the land tax, there were a handful of taxes that, if wide in application, fell most heavily upon the poor causing much resentment. The prime example was the salt tax, a duty imposed per unit of weight sold of what was obviously a basic necessity of life. As such, it was a lucrative source of revenue, accounting for 10 percent of all receipts in 1850. Prior to 1883, the duty was levied in different ways and at different rates between the provinces of India, and the result was an endemic problem of smuggling. This was especially acute on the border of the Bengal Presidency, which had a higher salt tax than the rest of India. How was the movement of lower-taxed salt into Bengal to be stopped? Somewhat bizarrely, the solution arrived at in 1843 was to plant a densely packed and particularly thorny hedge running from the banks of the Indus in the north to the border of Madras in the south—a distance of 2,500 miles, equivalent to the distance between Moscow and Gibraltar. It was patrolled by 12,000 men day and night operating out of 1,700 guard posts. "It may easily be imagined," wrote the hedge's chief critic, Sir John Strachey, "what obstruction to trade, what abuses and oppression, what annoyance and harassment to individuals, took place . . . for extraordinary folly, it would be hard to find a parallel."[8] Strachey, indeed, was to be the architect of the Great Hedge's demise as he oversaw, in the early 1880s, a move to standardize the rates for the salt tax across India—thereby rendering India's Great Hedge redundant.

The government never felt secure enough to impose new taxes or increase old ones: quite the reverse, as the land and salt taxes were lowered gradually. As a result, the company's finances were perennially shaky—over the 45 years 1814–59 the budget was in deficit for 33—and it was forced to operate imperialism on the cheap.[9] It simply never had the funds to embark upon serious reconstruction work, as Lord Bentinck was to find in the early 1830s when his projected schemes for improving irrigation and communications had to be shelved. Hence the overall tax burden upon Indians was quite low, at around 5–7 percent of national income. It was this low tax rate that was the key to the state's failure to pursue a more active modernizing project. Yes, military spending did consume the largest part of the budget, but at 2–3 percent of national income, it was still low by contemporary and subsequent standards. What made it seem so disproportionate was the generally low level of spending. Of course, this didn't prevent government taxes representing a heavy burden upon the poor of India: Digby calculated in the 1890s that the average Indian incurred a tax burden three times heavier than the average Englishman.[10] Quite simply the poverty of India was matched by the poverty of the government.[11]

If asked to justify its spending on the armed forces, the Indian government could point to the defense of India from foreign attack on the one hand, and the maintenance of internal peace on the other. The internal peace and stability yielded by British rule—the so-called *Pax Britannica*—remains today the chief advantage credited by most writers to the account of British administration. The British, it is claimed, inherited an India racked by internal conflict and destabilized by predatory bands that made life precarious and fraught with danger for the humble peasant. The Marathas intimidated and exhorted produce from large swathes of India. In the Deccan, Pindari bands looted and terrorized as they went, while across India armed robbers, known as *dacoits*, attacked homesteads at night, torturing their occupants until they disclosed the whereabouts of their valuables. In Oudh in 1840, there were estimated to be up to 2,000 active dacoits, often operating with the complicity of local chiefs and village watchmen, who received a share of the spoils. Most notorious were the Thugs, a highly secretive sect devoted to the goddess Kali who befriended travelers in country districts before strangling them with long strips of red cloth and burying their bodies in out-of-the-way locations so no trace of their work was ever discoverable.[12]

One by one, these threats to settled life were removed, and in so doing, the British made trade more profitable, cultivation more worthwhile, and travel safer. The Pindaris were scattered in 1817 as an offshoot of the British campaign against the Marathas, while the reign of the Thugs was ended during the 1830s by the government's use of informers—suspected Thugs were offered the chance to escape execution by implicating their fellow gang members. Between 1831 and 1837, 3,000 Thugs were convicted in this way, the informers being set usefully to work making carpets in Jabalpur. Despotic British rule may have been, but to the peasant and merchant this was a small price to pay for the chance to sleep safely in their beds and to be able to plant a crop they had every expectation of harvesting.[13]

However, important reservations must be entered against this optimistic narrative. First, British hegemony was won and sustained by the sword. If the Company eventually ended internecine conflict, it did so through a series of wars—with Mysore, Nepal, the Marathas, the Sikhs, Sind, and so on. In the decade 1813 to 1823 alone, the Company fought 28 battles and captured 128 fortresses.[14] "Progress was impossible without peace," reflects James, "and peace could only be obtained through war."[15] Second, the lawlessness and instability of pre-British India has been exaggerated. Maratha rule was not one of mere rape and plunder. The threat from the Thugs, too, was probably exaggerated by British officials who became increasingly preoccupied with the idea that India was riddled by irrational and ungodly conspiracies, of which the Thugs seemed to represent the tip of a submerged and murky iceberg. If India were, indeed, as sunk in lawlessness and conflict as is sometimes suggested, it would be hard to account for the prosperity, trading networks, and flourishing cities that drew Europeans to the subcontinent in the first place.

But if the disturbed condition of India prior to the establishment of the Raj has been overemphasized, so too, has been the success of British pacification policy. Crime and unrest remained endemic in areas governed by the company—within, even, Bengal itself. When the British annexed a territory, their understandable wish to remove potential sources of resistance saw them disband the armed retinues of zamindars and local chieftains. The problem was that it was these martial-elites who had upheld local order and the British signally failed to fill the vacuum with an alternative policing system. Though the Indian Army earned respect for its discipline and fighting prowess, this was hardly true of the police. Police work enjoyed a low status in the Company hierarchy. Few British officers were employed, and these relied upon a body of Indian recruits who were overworked, underpaid, and widely believed to be corrupt and oppressive. In the Bengal of the 1850s, for instance, when the population was some 30 million, there was only 1 British Superintendent of Police, 400 Indian inspectors (*darogas*), and 10,000 regular policemen. With such limited staffing, they had, necessarily, to rely upon an informal network of village watchmen or *chowkidars*, whose loyalty and probity was far from certain and who were often in league with local criminals. Allegations of police misconduct were frequent: in the Madras Presidency in 1848, 551 such complaints were received, of which 191 were upheld; the corresponding figures for 1849 were 726 and 128.[16] With so many Indians disempowered for reasons of literacy, poverty, and caste inequalities, the numbers of unreported abuses must have been substantially higher. In one year alone, notes James, in the Hooghly district of Bengal 13 out of the 18 darogas "were sacked for misdemeanours, including neglect of duty, suppressing evidence of a crime, bribery, and torture."[17] Not without reason did Bentinck complain that "police management" is "beyond measure oppressive." Everyone "in or out of authority, admits fully the extent of their exactions and most tormenting and exacting conduct."[18]

In view of these circumstances, it is hardly surprising that crime remained high and conviction rates low. Dacoity was believed to be increasing in early 19th century Bengal, with some 1,500 offences being recorded each year between 1803 and 1807.[19] According to R. C. Dutt:

> Daring robberies were committed in large towns and centres of trade, and villages remained in a continuous state of terror, and often paid blackmail to renowned heads of robbers. From 1800 to 1810 the country was kept in a perpetual alarm; the deeds of Bengal Rob Roys were narrated in bazaars and market places; the Magistrate and the Police were powerless; the people accepted their fate.[20]

In response, the governor-general Lord Minto initiated a wave of oppressive measures that saw thousands arrested upon the testimony of informers, justifying his actions in a Minute of 1810:

> A monstrous and disorganised state of society existed under the eye of the Supreme British authorities, and almost at the very seat of the Government to which the country might justly look for safety and protection. The mischief could not wait for a slow remedy; the people were perishing almost in our sight; every week's delay was a doom of slaughter and torture against the defenceless inhabitants of very populous countries.[21]

Although violent crime was reduced under Company surveillance, burglary proved beyond the powers of the police to handle and continued at high levels, with dacoits increasingly operating out of Native States outside of British jurisdiction. Behind the phenomenon of crime lay economic conditions. The economic dislocation of Bengal under Company rule fuelled the upsurge in dacoity witnessed there, and harvest failures and economic recessions helped to spark urban riots in protest at high grain prices or industrial competition, such as that witnessed in Benares (1809–18 and 1830s), Delhi (1833–38), and Madras (1803, 1833, 1854).[22]

When it came to law and order, the bias of the British, in India as in Britain itself, was upon the mechanism of the law. The impact of British rule on India's legal system was perhaps the most direct and lasting of all its areas of action, for it was here, says Spear, that the interaction of western and eastern ideas and minds was most widespread, penetrating, and sustained.[23]

The British found a state of law in India that was complex and alien to many of their basic assumptions. Indeed, it would be misleading to talk of a legal system or even systems as such in 18th-century India. With the demise of Mughal power, more formal judicial procedures had broken down and the law was formed and enforced at community level by a range of authorities. These were often powerful landowners and chiefs, who made personal decisions in civil cases and enforced their rulings through the use of their armed followers. Another center of community authority at village level were the Hindu caste councils or *panchayats* who regulated the conduct of caste and jati groups. In both cases, the main purpose was not to inquire into the guilt and innocence of the parties involved, but rather to settle disputes and prevent social disorder. In either case, procedures and sanctions were informal, traditional, and often ad hoc. In so far as there were more formal legal systems, these were divided along communal grounds. The basic form of criminal law, evolved under the succession of Muslim rulers since the 12th century, was *Sharia* law. But Muslim law had never applied to Hindus in civil or personal cases, and in any case was more a formal body of doctrine derived by Muslim jurists on the basis of the Koran and the traditions of the Prophet, than a working set of practical procedures.[24]

The question was how to proceed: a problematic one as legal reform threatened to carry the state into areas of indigenous life it otherwise wished to avoid. But a British state so wedded to ideas of consistency, legal procedure, and the upholding of contracts and property rights could hardly do nothing. The first move was, in fact, taken by the British Parliament that, concerned by reports of abuses committed by British subjects in India in the wake of the Battle of Plassey, sought to bring British settlers within the pale of British law. To this end, the Regulating Act of 1773 provided for the establishment of three Supreme or King's Courts in the cities of Calcutta, Madras, and Bombay. Indians could, however, appeal to them too and they were instructed to apply Muslim or Hindu personal law according to the religion of the litigant.

While the British government was establishing courts in the presidency cities, the Company was proceeding to put in place its own network of courts in the surrounding districts, known as the Mufassal courts. The issue naturally arose as to what law to administer? Besides lacking the resources, personnel, and authority required to impose an alien British system of law upon the Indians, the view was taken that law in India was closely bound up with religious sensibilities and that these must be taken into account when formulating legal policy. Accordingly, it was decided to work with, rather than against, existing legal conventions. What this meant in most cases was the implementation of Islamic law or Sharia in criminal cases, with British judges working alongside Muslim learned men—variously designated as *kazi*, *mufti*, and *kotwal*—who assisted them in forming judgments, a practice that continued until 1864. This decision to engage the services of Muslim jurists had an additional benefit, namely that British rule was associated with the maintenance of elements of Muslim life, so lifting from Muslims any obligation to engage in a holy war against British rule.[25] Of course, the British judges actively amended Muslim law when it too obviously clashed with western tradition. Thus the Muslim principle that a blood price could be paid in settlement for a murder was discarded, as was the rule that a Muslim could not be prosecuted on the evidence of a non-Muslim, while the idea—alien to Muslim tradition—was introduced that a crime against a person was also a crime against the state.

In cases of domestic and religious issues, such as marriage, adoption, and inheritance, communal laws were applied according to whether Hindus or Muslims were involved. This posed relatively few problems in the case of Muslim personal law, where the principles derived from the Koran equally applied and were set down in precise and accessible terms. It was quite another matter when it came to Hindus. Here no legal textbooks were at hand, and to find written authorities for their pronouncements the courts were led to undertake research in the ancient legal texts of India, such as the Laws of Manu, Yajnavalkya, and Narada, which mainly dated back before A.D. 600. In such inquiries, the British judges were assisted by a Hindu pundit attached to the court, who effectively decided which laws were to be applied in a given instance. Unfortunately, this procedure was based upon a misconception. Hindu law was not fixed in ancient texts. There were differing interpretations that had evolved over time and the customs prevalent within the India of the early 19th century were often not those contained within the early texts. In fact, as Benjamin Lindsay observed, Hindu law "was pure customary law made up of a volume of local usages which varied from place to place."[26] Only in 1868 was it finally resolved by the Privy Council that clear proof of usage would supersede written Hindu law. In this manner, attempts by the courts to discover principles of Hindu personal law under the guidance of the pundits had the effect of stabilizing, fixing, and—importantly—extending the reach of this law, which now had the formal sanction and authority of the British courts. As such, the law provides another instance of that tendency, already observed, for British rule to consolidate the hold and reach of Brahmanistic Hinduism upon India as a whole.

In reality, the law of British India was not purely Hindu or Muslim as it was administered by British judges, whose own legal perspectives inevitably crept in. There remained, too, the question of which law to apply to the other religious groups of which India abounded—the Jews, Jains, Parsis, Armenians, Sikhs, and so forth. Here again, custom provided a guide, but the judges had much more flexibility in these cases, frequently basing judgments on the personal application of British legal ideas.

What emerged from this process was a hybrid legal system that combined, in varying degrees, Islamic, Hindu, and British legal conceptions. This had everything to recommend it but the one thing that British jurors most wished to see: consistency. The diversities and anomalies of legal practice, which meant that the same offence would attract different punishments in different parts of the country, were highlighted by an enquiry into the state of Indian justice preparatory to the Company's charter in 1833. Speaking before Parliament that year Thomas Macaulay condemned a situation in which "in our Eastern empire Hindoo law, Mahometan law, Parsee law, English law, perpetually mingling with each other and disturbing each other, varying with the person, varying with the place." In its place he called for a regular code of laws to be established that, while it would not seek to trespass upon the sensibilities associated with religion and caste, would uphold the central principle: "uniformity where you can have it; diversity where you must have it; but in all cases certainty."[27] When, accordingly, the Charter Renewal Act of 1833 provided for the appointment of a Law Member to the Governor-General's Council who was, in conjunction with a Law Commission, to draw up a body of law for British India, the first occupant of the position was Macaulay himself. Arriving in India in 1834, Macaulay applied himself for four years with his characteristic single-mindedness of purpose to produce a legal code that would synthesize the best of both traditions. His resulting Code of the Criminal Law of India exhibited the precision and consistency that he had called for, such that Sir James Stephens could write in the 1880s that, though it had been in daily use for more than 20 years "in every part of India by all sorts of courts . . . no obscurity or ambiguity worth speaking of has been discovered in it."[28]

However, the results of Macaulay's labors were not finally introduced into India until 1860, and till that time the criminal law administered by the Company courts continued to be based upon Muslim law, prompting Sir George Campbell to comment, "the

hidden structure on which the whole building rests is this Maham-
meden law; take this away, and we should have no definition of, or
authority for punishing, many of the most common crimes."[29] Fur-
thermore, private law remained specific to religious communities, a
suggestion to codify this being finally dropped in 1853, mainly out of
a wish to avoid intruding in the religious practices of the Hindu and
Muslim communities.

Still, the British court and legal system had a big impact in India. At
first, Indians were highly wary of the new procedures, in particular their
insistence upon the importance of written documentation that Indians
often lacked, but shortly sections of Indian society began to see how they
could work in their favor and recourse to law became more and more
common. Within the years 1795 to 1802, some 328,064 cases were heard
before the Company's Bengal courts alone. Overwhelmed by business,
backlogs soon developed: in Bengal 130,000 suits were in arrears by the
early 1800s.[30] Within the courts, Indians learned to manipulate judicial
procedures to suit their own interests. What proved especially alien was
the idea of objective testimony. An individual was located within a particular family, tribe, caste, class structure with attendant loyalties, and
as a result, when called upon to bear witness these claims of loyalty
took precedence over obligations to a fair trial. The plaintiffs themselves
turned to the services of special pleaders or *vakils* who, through connections and bribes to court officials, got cases to be considered and who
could, for the small sum of two annas a day, find witnesses prepared to
"testify to anything under the sun."[31] The judge therefore had to steer his
way through a labyrinth of false and subjective testimony that clashed
with British models of impartial justice. Metcalfe complained in 1820:

> Our courts are scenes of great corruption. The European judge is the
> only part of them that is untainted. He sits on a bench in the midst of a
> general conspiracy, and knows that he cannot trust any one of the Of-
> ficers of the Court. Everyone is labouring to deceive him and to thwart
> his desire for justice. The pleaders have no regard for the truth.[32]

In case this picture is considered overdrawn, compare it with the
following account of the experiences of a young district magistrate in
the 1930s, fictionally named Greenlane, as described by the former Indian civil servant, and later historian of India, Penderel Moon:

> In Indian conditions the whole elaborate machinery of English law,
> which Englishmen tended to think so perfect, simply didn't work and

had been completely perverted. Greenlane and myriads of Indian magistrates daily spent hours in their Courts solemnly recording word for
word the evidence of illiterate peasants, knowing full well that 90 percent of it was false. Even if the events described had actually occurred,
the alleged eye-witnesses had not seen them. Even if the accused were
guilty, it was perjury that proved their guilt. . . . Litigation had become a
national pastime and the criminal law a recognised and well-tried means
of harassing, imprisoning, and even hanging one's enemies.[33]

In reality, then, the introduction of the rule of law was not the un-
questionable boon it has often been depicted. A system of legal practice,
evolved in Western Europe, could not be straightforwardly applied to
a society working along very different lines. With British judges and
magistrates small in number, often ignorant of local customs and mores,
and applying a hybrid law through the advice of people learned in the
more arcane traditions of Hindu and Islamic jurists and pundits, it was
only to be expected that the law should work, in practice, in ways ut-
terly at variance with the ideals of the colonial elite. For those Indians
with the skill and resources to operate the Court system in their favor,
it yielded substantial benefits. This was most obviously true of the Indians who took up the law as a profession. Educated Indians from
both Muslim and Hindu backgrounds were essential to the working of
the court system, and the law provided the first arena in which Indians could build careers within the British Raj—first as pundits, clerks,
translators, and interpreters, later as magistrates, judges, and barristers. As early as the 1820s, Indian judges were being appointed in
Bombay and Madras, and in 1831 the governor-general, Lord William
Bentinck, introduced a regulation allowing Indians to serve as judges
in *zila* and city courts, which operated across the districts under the
superintendence of the Civil and Session Judge. These Indian judges,
known as *munsiffs*, were empowered to try cases involving non-
Europeans and were in receipt of salaries of up to 750 rupees. Within
the Supreme Courts in the Presidency Towns (Calcutta, Madras, and
Bombay), Indians served in the ranks of the barristers and were eventually able to win promotion to the highest offices—two Indians having
been appointed to the bench of the Calcutta High Court by the 1870s.
By the 1880s, Strachey was able to say, "Native judges preside over the
great majority of the courts; excepting the higher appellate tribunals,
almost the whole administration of civil justice is in their hands." The
Lord Chancellor paid tribute to their work in 1883: "in respect of integrity, of learning, of knowledge, of the soundness and satisfactory

character of the judgements arrived at, the judgements of the Native judges were quite as good as those of the English."[34]

Yet for the majority of Indians, the new legal system represented but a new form of oppression, a forum in which the illiterate, those without a clear legal status, lacking proof of land ownership, unable to travel the great distances to court or sustain the costs of lengthy court cases or the funds to buy the favors of a witness or official, were at the mercy of the privileged and well-to-do. For this majority of Indians the court system was something they sought to remain as far away from as possible. But even acknowledging all these deficiencies, the reformed law of the 19th century did establish one principle that was revolutionary in the Indian context: namely, the idea of equality of all men before the law. No longer could a Brahmin not be punished on the evidence of a Shudra, or a Muslim not be subject to the testimony of a non-Muslim. In theory, all Indians (though not all persons, Europeans still possessing legal privileges over Indians) had equal standing in law. The reality of this equality might be characterized as a work in progress.

The last of the major institutions affecting the lives of the people was the Indian Army. This was, by some way, the most intense point of interaction between the British and the Indians. Here the two races served, lived, fought, and died together. British rule was founded upon military power, and military strength underpinned its continuance. It was, ultimately, a military despotism.[35] It was all the more ironic, then, that this military power primarily resided with the Indians themselves. That is to say, beneath a veneer of British officers and regiments of soldiers on tour of duty from Britain itself, the bulk of rank and file troops were recruited within India. Thus in 1830, out of a total Indian Army of 223,400 men, 187,000 were Indians. "Orators, we know," declared an officer in the Bengal Army in 1829, "love to call British India, the 'Empire of Opinion'; but it is the Empire of the Sepoys; and woe to its rulers, when they shall venture to neglect this mainspring, this too crucial secret of its mechanism."[36] By reasons of culture and history, the British were too alien ever to ingratiate themselves with Indian elites as previous foreign rulers had done. They did not evoke sentiments of affection or seek to build dynastic alliances. Their status was founded upon respect born of fear. It was correspondingly vital that the British deploy their military supremacy effectively. And for the most part they did.

It was widely recognized that the sepoys had confidence in their officers and pride in their regiments—showing themselves time and again prepared, says Mason, to "give their lives for a flag they could hardly call their own."[37] How was this sustained? Partly by brave and bold leadership by the Europeans. White soldiers were, writes James, the cutting edge of the army and had, by the 19th century, won a reputation for invincibility, and this self belief infused itself into the esprit de corps of the wider ranks of the army. Yet this high morale was underpinned by the inculcation of a belief that the Indian Army offered to the sepoy a career in which he would be rewarded during his service and provided for in his retirement. The pay, at 7 rupees a month for a regular soldier, was good and, equally important, was paid regularly—something that could never be taken for granted in the various militias and princely retinues of post-Mughal India. After 16 years service, his pay rose to 8 rupees, and after 20 years reached 9 rupees. Twenty years service also brought with it a pension on retirement of 3 rupees, a figure raised in 1836 to 4 rupees after 16 years.[38] Such regular remuneration was unprecedented in India and ensured that the sepoy was a man commanding respect in his village. The vast majority of soldiers came from rural backgrounds where money was scarce, and the 3 rupees or so they could afford to remit to their villages each month was highly prized. And with recruitment running in families through generations, service under the British was a highly attractive and honorable option.

A third element in the effective unity of the Indian Army was the vital role played by the Indian NCOs or *suadars*. Although no Indians were allowed to serve as commissioned officers, these senior sepoys fulfilled an inestimable service as intermediaries between the white officers and their Indian men. Living alongside the Indian troops, they were, says Mason, rather like foremen, acting as the eyes and ears of the more distant British officers, passing on intelligence, representing the views and grievances of the men, and generally providing a pivotal link in the chain of command.

The last factor acting to bind the sepoy to his alien masters was the distinctive patterns of recruitment that were operated. Recruitment into the Indian Army was very far from random as the British actively engaged troops from communities that they considered had a tradition of martial service. In the case of Bengal, as the army was built up in the wake of Clive's seizure of power, the Company drew the bulk of its troops from the ranks of the soldiers who had previously found service in the armies of the Mughals and local military chieftains-cum-landlords. Most conspicuous were the high-caste Rajputs and Bhumihars of Oudh and Benares, regions that, by the early 19th century, were providing some 80 percent of the Bengal troops.[39]

The Bengal Army was, indeed, largely composed of men from high caste backgrounds and allowance was made for caste sensibilities of diet, living arrangements, and travel. This was not true of the armies of Madras and Bombay, where Indian troops of diverse caste backgrounds served together. In either case, recruitment into the army was along closely prescribed lines. The British, ready as ever to categorise Indians in essentialist ways, constructed the idea of hereditary martial classes that had an inbuilt capacity for soldiering. As with the wider process of caste classification, this had a self-fulfilling consequence in that social and regional groups identified themselves in terms of their martial employments. What made this a reality was the method of recruitment, whereby existing soldiers were permitted to serve as recruiting sergeants, returning to their own villages to gather new sepoys. The result was an army compounded out of a series of tight-knit communities, where soldiers were bound by family, jati, and village ties in a manner that sustained camaraderie and added powerful social pressures to regular military discipline. A soldier who behaved badly would bring disgrace upon his family and village—while one exhibiting bravery and securing promotion would yield valuable status. They visited their native villages every two or three years and, wrote Sleeman, the "good feelings of their families continue through the whole period of their service to exercise a salutary influence over their conduct as men and as soldiers."[40]

The result was a cohesive and interdependent military system that proved a reliable basis for British power throughout nearly all the period of British rule. Given the divergences of race, culture, status, and power that characterized the Indian Army, disciplinary incidents were remarkably few in number. Philip Mason comments that between 1825 and 1833 there were, among the 50,000–60,000 sepoys of the Bengal infantry, only 35 serious cases tried: "of these, 16 were for desertion . . . six for mutiny, one for absence, one for embezzlement, one for sleeping on duty and eight for miscellaneous offences. None were for drunkenness or malingering."[41] But there were exceptions and we should not allow our image of the Indian Army be overly colored by the sentimental recollections of old British officers. One sepoy reflected bitterly upon his lot in the early years of the 19th century:

> Horses, palanquins, carriages, lofty houses, ample tents, couches, pleasure and enjoyment, gratification and delight, whatever yields joy is the portion of the European Officer; pain, wind, cold and heat, fatigue and

hardship, trouble and pain and the sacrifice of life itself is the portion of the Sepoy.[42]

Frustrations like these could fuel unrest, especially when compounded by disputes over pay or terms of service or, more dangerously, perceived insults to caste or religious status. Thus at Vellore in the Madras Presidency in 1806, the decision by the commander in chief to forbid the wearing of all marks of religion and caste and force the sepoys to shave their beards, remove jewelry and wear only European headgear, helped to provoke an uprising against British officers. Several were killed and homes attacked before the mutiny was crushed by British reinforcements. Subsequent investigations revealed the extent of disillusionment among the Indian troops—and especially amidst the ranks of the jemaders and NCOs, who conspired to hide the gathering plot from their British superiors.[43] It is generally argued that relations between British officers and their men deteriorated over the early decades of the 19th century. Newly arrived officers took for granted British power and, to the general indifference toward Indian cultural traditions, was added the hardening factor of Christian Evangelicalism which increasingly imbued the officer class and promoted a contempt for the vicious superstitions of Hinduism. Mason relates cases of young officers abusing the Indian troops as niggers and black brutes and of one party shooting dead a monkey within the precincts of a temple.[44] In terms of cultural sensibilities, it was the Bengal Army that caused the most concern. Not only was it by far the biggest of the Company armies, it was explicitly recruited from higher caste groups who were very watchful of their caste status. In November 1824, a mutiny broke out among a regiment of the Bengal Army at Barrackpore, near Calcutta, when rumors spread that it was to be sent across the sea by boat to fight in the First Burma War—an act that had come to be seen as breaking caste rules. Although the revolt was suppressed by a force of British infantry and artillery, with 12 sepoys being executed after court martial, the events at Barrackpore proved a prelude to the far more explosive Mutiny of 1857—though even then it should be remembered that the bulk of the Indian Army remained loyal to its officers and took an active part in restoring British power.

Thus, while ordinary Indians had little face-to-face contact with their white rulers, they inhabited a world increasingly structured around British values and interests: in the taxes they paid, the land tenure they enjoyed, the legal system they turned to or shunned, the army they might join or whose presence they felt. The British were more powerful than previous rulers, insisting on total authority and constructing a state apparatus "more powerful than any previous one."[45] Yet still, the limitations of the British presence must be continually recalled. The British came to see themselves as implementing a modernist agenda and their formal procedures and rhetoric supported this. But deficiencies of men and resources, combined with the complexity and depth of traditional Indian attitudes, meant that there were powerful limits to the reach of the state into many areas of social life.

8

Cultural and Religious Life under Company Rule

It would have surprised the early British settlers in India to have learned that the most discernable long-run effects of the British encounter with India were to be in the sphere of cultural life. It wasn't merely that they went to India to exchange goods, not ideas; it was that they evinced little interest in Indian society and culture and had no wish to engage with it, let alone change it. But economic, and still less political, activity cannot exist in a vacuum. Intended or not, the British found themselves governing Indians and this meant engaging with them in numerous ways, not simply as administrative units, but on the level of law, education, religious practice, and ideas. However much the British aspired to operate only upon the surface of Indian life, governing just so far as was necessary to realize the revenue to pay for their activities and remit a tidy profit home, they could not avoid constituting a dynamic catalyst for change within the Indian body politic, producing responses unexpected, unpredictable, and ultimately constructive. British India was an observably new India—however much continuity accompanied and obscured difference.

The key axis of change was mental. The Indian mind was quick, subtle, reactive, imitative, and resilient. As the old Mughal order subsided, new forms of mental life awoke and found new vehicles amidst the emerging groups that filled the space left by the Muslim elites. This new India was more Hindu than Muslim and more middle than upper class—an India of scribes and Brahmins, moneylenders and merchants. It was these men who were most willing to cooperate with the Company, and out of this collaboration came new opportunities and status. This openness extended beyond a mere willingness to profit from the possibilities the company provided. It took, also, the form of a preparedness to learn from the evidently potent civilization that underpinned British power—the civilization that brought new business strategies, access to distant and lucrative markets, new types of technology, military organization and tactics, new approaches to law and property, taxation, government administration, unfamiliar languages, new literary forms and themes, religious ideas, and varieties of civic life. India's literate classes wanted to understand the western civilization that the British, however imperfectly, embodied and sought to reconcile these new insights and practices with their own established beliefs. The result was a civilization that combined powerful elements of both in a dynamic and ever-shifting equilibrium.

What the British essentially introduced to educated Indians was a new spirit of rational inquiry. Indians had very complex systems of thought elaborated over many centuries. But these systems had tended toward rigidity and closure. Rather like medieval scholasticism, they had evolved ever more subtle permutations upon established themes. The British did not shatter this worldview; but they did unlock it and push it into innovative directions and modes of expression. It was the British themselves who pioneered critical approaches to Hinduism itself as a few of the early settlers took up research into the history and meaning of the religion. Their motives were partly utilitarian. To understand the Hindu law they were seeking to implement, scholars like the famous jurist and linguist William Jones turned to ancient Sanskrit texts, which were translated, printed, and analyzed in ways hitherto associated with classical scholarship. But intellectually, too, the British had an historical consciousness previously lacking in India. For the first time the real history of India was recovered: the origins of Buddhism were revealed, forgotten scripts deciphered, ancient coins catalogued, the evolution of temple architecture traced, lost artistic masterpieces like the cave paintings of Ajanta rediscovered, the chronology of dynasties—all were revealed for the first time and discussed in the pages of learned journals like the publications of the Asiatic Society, founded in 1784 under the patronage of Warren Hastings. Delhi saw the formation of an Archaeological Society to study the city's abundant monuments and ruins, which drew its membership both from British officials and prominent Indians such as the mathematician Ram Chandra and Arabic scholar Maulvi Ziauddin.[1] In this manner, educated Indians were exposed, for the first time in a millennium, to the richness of their own history and civilization.

The attempts of these early British scholars to understand Hinduism prompted Indians to rationalize their own beliefs in new ways.[2] Macaulay and other British reformers complacently believed that once

Indians were exposed to western ideas and scientific discoveries, they would turn their backs upon traditional Indian beliefs as so much superstitious nonsense. "From the beginning," writes James, "the ultimate goal of all programmes for spreading Western education throughout India was the conversion of the Hindus."[3] Yet this was not what happened. Rather, Indian intellectuals sought to use the new thinking to show that Hinduism was not a mass of unthinking custom or dogma, but something that could be explained and justified on European rational terms. Thus, comments Robb, Vedic texts were held to expound a monotheistic religion, Ayurvedic medicine was founded upon proven science, and yoga was a health-giving form of exercise.[4] The influence of Christian theological and ethical teaching was important here. Few Indians actually embraced Christianity as a faith, but they were impressed by the teachings of Jesus Christ and were keen to show that Hinduism contained within it many of the aspects of Christian doctrine that they came to respect. The result was a wave of Hindu reform movements.

The most famous were those associated with Ram Mohan Roy and his Hindu reform organization, Brahmo Sabha. Roy (1772–1833), a Bengali Brahmin who had worked for the Company before retiring to devote himself to his intellectual, social, and religious interests, was well versed in the teachings of Buddhism, Christianity, and Islam. Though he remained a Hindu, he was impressed by the teachings of other faiths and used the reasoning of the West to reassess Hinduism and purge it of its more unthinking, idolatrous, and superstitious aspects that, he believed, had corrupted the original Vedic teachings over the centuries. This purer Hinduism was, he argued, quite compatible with the findings of modern science and was more than capable of holding its own in the company of Christianity. A key element was the idea of God itself. Turning away from the idol worship of popular Hinduism, he extracted from the Upanishads a more ethereal concept of the deity, according to which, God, as Brahma or supreme being, was abstract, monotheistic, and transcendental and to be approached through the medium of rational inquiry. Similarly, he promoted the idea of the equality of all Hindus before God, denouncing the caste system as an alien product of oppression and prejudice. In 1828, Roy founded the Brahmo Sabha organization to propagate his ideas. A temple was opened in Calcutta dedicated to the Eternal Being and open to men of all religions, being devoid of all pictures and statues. Roy's work was carried forward by members of the wealthy business Tagore family. Debendranath Tagore (1817–1905) had, as a result of a religious experience, turned his back on his father's business and devoted his life to propagating the truths that he believed had been vouchsafed to him, inculcating the love of, and obedience to, the Supreme Being, the sole font of wisdom, goodness, power, and truth. Like Roy, Debendranath believed that such a faith was consistent with classical Hinduism and he opposed the attempts of Christian missionaries to proselytize within India. In 1845, he merged his own organization with Roy's Brahmo Sabha to form the Brahma Samaj, a movement promoting a reformed Hinduism free from the worship of idols and accepting members irrespective of caste or religious background.

Of course, those reassessing their beliefs in the light of Western thought were a tiny minority, and even here there were differences. Where some used the new techniques of rational argument to press for a version of Hinduism more akin to Christian concepts of God, others, such as the Dharma Sabha association (1830), defended orthodox views upon matters such as caste and sati (widow burning) against the attacks of the reformers. The Dharma Sabha, which was based in Bengal, attracted support from Hindu zamindars and was prepared to use the techniques of the West in order to counter its ideas, publishing its own newspaper, the *Samachar Chandrika*, whose editor Bhawani Charan Banerji was the organization's secretary.

Roy and the reformers were part of a wider body of Indians who wanted greater access to western education. For most, this was desired for utilitarian reasons—western education seemed to offer greater opportunities to progress under the Raj, whether in business or government service, and in Calcutta, private academies for the teaching of English had been established in the late 18th centuries. But in either case, it was the Indians who wanted more western education than was being provided. This was important as the British themselves were very uncertain how to proceed in this area. The basic wish of the majority of the leading Company administrators in the late 18th and early 19th centuries was, as we have seen, to disturb traditional India as little as possible, in some cases out of genuine respect for venerable Indian practice, more commonly because of a fear of the consequences of disturbing the settled waters of Indian life. Men such as Hastings, Munro, Elphinstone, and Malcolm believed that by governing so far as possible in accordance with traditional conditions, they could secure the acquiescence of the elite groups whose cooperation was necessary if Company rule was to be sustainable. From this perspective, the state was best employed patronizing established forms of Indian

learning, which consisted of instruction in Sanskrit for the Brahmin
castes and Arabic and Persian among Muslims. To this end Hastings
founded a Muslim madrasa in Calcutta in 1781 to be conducted by a
notable Muslim scholar or *maulvi*, Majid-ud-Din. "The establishment
of the maulvi in suitable quarters, with forty stipendiary students and
a sweeper on 3 rupees a month, begins the history of educational action in India as a concern of the British government."[5] A decade later
the religious balance was restored when Lord Cornwallis sanctioned
the foundation of a Sanskrit College in Benares with a view to "the
preservation and cultivation of the laws, literature and religion" of the
Hindus "at this centre of their faith and common resort of all their
tribes." This so-called Orientalist practice of publicly supporting the
indigenous learning of India dominated attitudes toward educational
provision through the 1820s. Thus although, under the terms of the
renewal of the Company's Charter in 1813, some £10,000 per annum
was to be set aside for the encouragement of modern scientific learning
among Indians, the government, still reluctant to interfere with educational provision, failed to disperse the monies. Eventually in 1823,
a Committee of Public Instruction was set up to consider what to do
with the money but, with Orientalist and conservative attitudes yet in
the ascendant, it decided to use the money to encourage the formation
of a further series of Sanskrit and Persian colleges—stating, "tuition in
European sciences [is] neither among the sensible wants of the people
nor in the power of Government to bestow."[6] Roy, predictably, was an-
gered by the loss of this opportunity to promote western learning, arguing in a letter to the Company directors that it would merely ensure
more teaching of Sanskrit subtleties of no use to students or society,
keeping India in darkness.[7]

But in truth, the Orientalist approach was destined to be eclipsed by
those wishing to introduce western ideas and knowledge into India.
The test issue was the language of instruction—and indeed of government in general. Should the British patronize the established educated
languages of India—primarily Sanskrit and Persian—or should it make
English the basic medium of official communication? Notwithstanding the opinions of the Committee of Public Instruction, the pressures
pointing toward English were obvious: utilitarian reformers, businessmen, merchants, Company employees, missionaries wanting to introduce Christian teachings to the Indian heathen, and, of course, the rising
middle class of India itself all favored, and pressed with ever more insistence, for the use and teaching of English. It was, indeed, the Indians of
Calcutta who took matters into their own hands in 1817, raising, through

local subscription, 10,000 rupees to found a Hindu College to teach the new western ideas to Indians through English. The initial objective was to use western learning as a means to reform Hinduism itself, but the college soon became a vehicle for Hindus seeking social advancement through education. With the lead thus provided, the Company began to subsidize the venture, and by the 1820s the College had developed, says Marshall, "into a formidable institution at which English was the medium of instruction and English literature, western political and social thought, and physics and chemistry were taught."[8] It was supported in its endeavors by the Calcutta Book Society, also formed in 1817, which had sold over 30,000 books in English in two years.

The issue was finally settled during the governorship of Bentinck, who moved to adopt English as the official language of government, the law, and higher education as part of his wider reform initiatives. Again, the loud and confident voice of Macaulay made itself felt via his notorious Minute of 1835, penned in his role as president of the Committee of Public Instruction, which dismissed traditional Indian beliefs as so much fantastical nonsense and trenchantly argued for the promotion of English.

> The question now before us is simply whether, when it is in our power to teach [English], we shall teach languages which, by universal confession, there are no books on any subject which deserve to be compared to our own; whether, when we can teach European science, we shall teach systems which, by universal confession, whenever they differ from those of Europe, differ for the worse; and whether, when we can patronise sound philosophy and true history, we shall countenance, at the public expense, medical doctrines, which would disgrace an English farrier, astronomy, which would move laughter in the girls at an English boarding-school, history, abounding with kings thirty feet high, and reigns thirty thousand years long, and geography, made up of seas of treacle and seas of butter.[9]

Only then, believed Macaulay, would the British create within India a class of persons able to share in the business of government, instruct a wider Indian public in the virtues of English knowledge, develop a taste for the products of English manufactures, and ultimately, be fitted one day for a measure of self-government.

Whatever the merits of Macaulay's heavily rhetorical prose, there is no doubt that he captured the rising tide of mid-19th-century British cultural self-confidence and it came as small surprise when, in March 1835, Bentinck announced, "the great object of the British Government ought to be the promotion of European literature and science among the natives of India." The funds available, however, were nowhere near sufficient to construct a national system of elementary education in English, and it was decided to concentrate government support upon the promotion of higher education in English, in the belief that this would not only create the kind of service class the British required, but would lead to a trickle down of the benefits of English instruction to the wider Indian masses. The medium for this transmission in Bengal was a series of English or Anglo-vernacular schools at the headquarters of each district.

With English education thus encouraged there were, by midcentury, some 200 English educational establishments with 30,000 students.[10] The most influential center of English-inspired education was Calcutta. Here there emerged a class of students, centered around the Hindu (later Presidency) College and designated by the appellate Young India, who openly embraced western thinking and culture and explicitly rejected older Indian models. Their first leading figure was the charismatic Henry Derozio (1809–31), an Anglo-Indian iconoclast who wrote Romantic poetry in the manner of Byron and Shelley. Though born a Protestant and educated by Scot missionaries, he criticized religion in all its forms, calling upon the Bengali students at the Hindu College—where he was a lecturer—to read skeptical empiricists like Hume, Pain, Locke, and Francis Bacon. In 1828, he founded his academic association for the discussion of advanced social and political ideas, like freewill, the nature of patriotism, and the existence of God, hoping to reawaken the mind of India which, he believed, had been bound in what Blake called "mind-forged manacles" for too long. As he wrote in a poem, "The Harp of India":

Why hang'st thou lonely on yon withered bough?
Unstrung forever, must thou there remain;
Thy music once was sweet—who hears it now?
Why doth the breeze sigh over thee in vain?
Silence hath bound thee with her fatal chain;
Neglected, mute, and desolate art thou,
Like ruined monument on desert plain:
O! many a hand more worthy far than mine
Once thy harmonious chords to sweetness gave,
And many a wreath for them did Fame entwine
Of flowers still blooming on the minstrel's grave:
Those hands are cold—but if thy notes divine
May be by mortal wakened once again,
Harp of my country, let me strike the strain!

Unfortunately, Derozio's views were too radical for an institution established to reform—not reject—Hindu teaching, and he was expelled from the faculty. Sunk into poverty, he died shortly afterwards of cholera aged only 22.

Although Derozio and his followers understandably attracted much attention, the number of students who had access to western ideas was very small. The promotion of education was a low priority for the government, receiving less than 1 percent of government spending—or below 0.2 percent of GDP. In 1828, the Hindu College had 436 students, and even in the years 1845–49, only 36 students passed the rigorous examinations in literature, math, history, natural history, moral philosophy, and economics—leading to that distinctive designation of academic attainment in India, the M.A. (Failed). These students came almost wholly from the ranks of the traditional literate and scribal castes who aspired to careers in government service. The traditional ruling elites and the very wealthy were little involved, neither were the poor or women.[11]

Outside Bengal, the provision of English education was still slower to develop. In Bombay there were, in 1850, only 10 government-funded schools with 2,000 pupils, while the Madras Presidency was still tardier, with only three government-aided institutions in 1854. The main providers of English-based education were, in fact, the missionaries, who at mid-century were educating about 30,000 pupils, compared to the 17,360 pupils in government-supported schools. The Company did make some effort to encourage learning in the local vernaculars. Here it was Bombay that took the lead, the Board of Education adopting a policy of establishing a vernacular school in every village of more than 2,000 people, provided they bear a share of cost. By 1842, there were 120 such schools. A similar scheme initiated in Bengal had more limited success: of the 101 vernacular schools established in 1844, only 33 remained 10 years later. What the people wanted, one district collector was told, was not Company schools to teach them their own language, but schools to teach them English.[12] More important than the state in providing elementary education in Bengal were various missionary bodies. The London Missionary Society, the Baptist Missionary Society, and the Church Missionary Society all opened schools teaching basic literacy in Bengali and after 1813 were in receipt of some government funding. The Baptist Society claimed 10,000 pupils were being educated in its schools in 1818.[13] Also receiving Company grants was the Calcutta School Book Society, which produced textbooks in Bengali.

Notwithstanding the efforts of the Company, missionaries, and Indians themselves, access to education of all kinds remained very limited in India. A survey of Bombay district in 1832 showed that out of a population of 5 million, only 35,143 students were attending schools.[14] In the south, it has been suggested that access to education among 5–10 year olds actually declined between 1822 and 1852.[15] In 1854, Sir Charles Wood wrote an Educational Dispatch reviewing the government's policy. Although, like Macaulay, he saw English education as the key to unlocking the economic potential of India, continuing constraints on funding meant Wood eschewed any new departures, merely reiterating the existing strategy under which the government provided education in English at university level (with new universities proposed for Bombay and Madras) and granted subsidies to assist private and missionary schools at the elementary level. For the mass of the population, Wood looked for English knowledge to be imparted via schools teaching in the vernaculars, but, as Monier-Williams regretted in 1879, this aspect of his recommendations was not pursued.[16] Unsurprisingly, the overall expansion of basic literacy in India remained painfully slow: in 1881 it was estimated that only 8 percent of men were literate, a figure that had crept up to 12 percent in 1921.[17]

Yet, despite the failure to create anything like mass literacy in India in the 19th century, British rule was associated with an awakening of cultural and intellectual life. For the among the educated elite, which had always been tiny in the context of India as a whole, contact with the west provided a myriad of new ideas and literary forms to explore, and, crucially, the example of new types of institutions and media within which to develop and disseminate them. We have noted already the willingness of Indians like Mohan Roy and Derozio to embrace English as a medium of expression. But equally notable developments occurred within the vernacular languages of India— hitherto submerged under the dominating presence of Sanskrit and Persian. Bengali was the first to come into its own. J. C. Ghosh dates the beginning of the modern period in the development of Bengali to the formation of Fort William College in Calcutta in 1800.[18] The College was intended to introduce British administrators to the language, law, and customs of India and thereby brought "within the pale of official recognition" the emerging work of British and Indian scholars operating within vernaculars—and Bengali especially. One of its first lecturers was the Baptist missionary and linguist William Carey, who published a Bengali translation of the *New Testament* in 1801. Aided by the introduction of the printing press, writings in Bengali circulated with a rapidity and reach previously unknown, replacing the Bengali oral tradition with a written one. The formative figure in this Bengali Renaissance was Madhu Dutt, a highly westernized convert to Christianity. Madhu Dutt began his literary career writing in English, but crucially took the decision to switch to Bengali, to which he introduced—under the influence of Milton—the poetic forms of blank verse and the sonnet. He also wrote the first Bengali epic poem, the *Meghnadbadh*, in which he steered clear of all religious content and incorporated ideas from the *Odyssey*. Other writers and literary forms soon followed, such as the modern drama, continuous prose, and the novel—in which latter Bankim Chatterji was the seminal figure, earning the title of the father of Indian fiction.

But Bengali was not the only language to feel the effects of the new spirit of the west. In the 1830s and 1840s, Swami Sarawati introduced a purer and more direct form of Hindi prose as part of a wider attempt, in the manner of Mohan Roy, to purify Hinduism of its dogmas and idolatry.[19] The early 19th century saw, too, the emergence of a written prose tradition in Urdu, the impetus again coming from the College of Fort William, whose principal, Dr. John Gilchrist, compiled a dictionary and grammar in Urdu for use by British officials. The center of activity soon switched to Urdu's natural home of Delhi, where the poet Ghalib and Sir Saiyid Khan (who had served as a judicial officer under the British government) established a flourishing tradition of Urdu poetry and prose. At Delhi College instruction in all subjects took place in both English and Urdu and the "joint efforts of Indians and Europeans," says Narayani Gupta, "led to Urdu transforming itself from a language of poetry to the transmitter of western knowledge."[20] In the south, the ancient Dravidian language of Tamil had already undergone significant changes under the earlier impact of the Portuguese, and the main effect of Company rule occurred via the establishment of the printing press that led, for the first time, to an outpouring of texts on secular subjects, ranging from novels and poetry, to geometry and history.

Besides its role in the dissemination of books, pamphlets, and textbooks, printing exerted a distinct, and ultimately transforming, effect upon Indian political and intellectual life through the medium of the newspaper press, which expanded exponentially over the course of the 19th century. The British introduced journalism to India and the first papers—beginning with Hickey's *Bengal Gazette* of 1780—were produced for the British community. However, with the appearance of the *Samachar Durpan* or "Mirror of the News," a Bengali paper edited by the missionary Joshua Marshman, there began a quickly expanding sphere of vernacular papers. Mohan Roy occupies a typically prominent place in the story, founding, in 1821, a weekly paper entitled *Moon of Intelligence*, its purpose being to further the public good through the discussion of Roy's reformist Hindu views. This was, writes Wordsworth, "the first Bengali paper edited and conducted by Bengalis."[21] Orthodox Hindus promptly responded with their own paper, *Samachar Chandrika*, to defend what they took to be traditional religious practices. Bombay got its first paper in Gujarati in 1822—the *Bombay News*, and by 1839, it had four vernacular papers alongside Calcutta's nine.

Besides the costs of establishing Indian papers, and the limited market represented by those with the money and literacy to buy them, the main hindrance upon press activity was the Company, which viewed the press—British as well as Indian—as a threat to its authority. In a Minute of 1822, Munro argued that India, with a foreign government necessarily ruling despotically a politically backward people, was not yet ready for a free press which might stir up aspirations for liberty which could not be satisfied, threatening, thereby, the very rule that was in India's best interest. Others were less high minded in their opposition to the actions of journalists: Wellesley denounced "the whole tribe of editors" and told his officials to tranquilize them if they could—and if not "suppress their papers by force and send their persons to Europe." In 1823, the government promulgated a press ordinance, under which all papers were required to possess a license and could print only such matter as the government approved of. Mohan Roy composed a petition of protest, supported by five other leading Bengalis, for submission to the Supreme Court in Calcutta that argued that the ordinance unjustly deprived Indians of the civil liberties that Britons in England enjoyed. When the appeal failed, Roy closed down his Persian-language paper, the *Mirut-ul-Akhbar* (Mirror of News), in disgust at the restrictions on press freedom. Only in 1835 were the controls on the press lifted under the reforming hand of Macaulay—though they were periodically reintroduced, for example during the Mutiny year of 1857.

Notwithstanding the difficulties under which it labored, the vernacular press steadily grew in numbers and quality, until by 1875, some 254 papers were in existence. This press exerted a profound influence, providing a forum for debate and instruction, quickening the spread of new ideas, and helping the development of a style of prose punchier, simpler, and better able to capture and comment upon the rapidly changing social life of 19th-century India. As such, the press contributed to the wider emergence of a new kind of civic society in key Indian centers. Indians formed debating, literary, religious, political, and cultural societies of their own—mirroring western models but existing in a genuinely Indian context and reinforcing the new urban Hindu culture of the cities that the rise of the service and commercial classes was encouraging. Roy's *Brahma Sabha* was one of the first pressure groups in India, while the joint petition he organized in 1823 against the restrictive press laws has been described as the beginning of the agitation for constitutional rights in India. The first distinctly political association was the Zamindari Association of Calcutta (1837)—which became the Bengal Landholders Association the following year—the chief object of which was to resist the government's perceived pro-peasant bias. Less important than the particular ends of such bodies was the methods they deployed to achieve them. As Robb explains:

> All these societies were influenced in form and behaviour by the public and civic bodies set up by the Europeans . . . they do mark the beginnings of "modern" politics in India. This was because they were in large part the product of, and attempted to further, exchanges with a foreign government, and therefore were shaped by its procedures and expectations . . . they did so, at first, by holding meetings, electing chairmen, passing resolutions, and presenting petitions. Thus the forms and procedures expected by the state began to shape civic and even private as well as public life.[22]

Typically, then, no neat summary of the impact of British rule is possible. Yes, there was the emergence of the kind of Anglophile elite service class that liberal reformers looked to. But there was also a growth in vernacular literature, the emergence of an Indian civil society, and a reawakening of interest in Indian religions. Even when Indians did evolve organizations that were superficially wholly western in inspiration, like trade unions, political parties, clubs, etc., they retained religious and caste affiliations—though, of course this was true in the west also. And still, we must enter the caveat that, whether English or vernacular, the new literate India was a wholly minority affair. The example of the Indian press is indicative. There were, it is true, a multiplicity of vernacular publications. But the circulations of these papers were exceedingly limited. It was estimated, in 1843, that the eight Bengali titles produced in Calcutta had a combined sale of 1,300, with only 195 being sent into the interior of the country each month. And of the total 4,000 circulation of the English language papers, as few as 125 were received by Indian subscribers.[23] Literacy in India was very low and slow to increase. For the mass of the population, traditional cultural values and attitudes continued to structure their world.

A good example of the patchy influence of western ideas is provided by the career of Christianity. The rise of the Company to preeminence in India coincided with the growth of Christian Evangelicalism in Britain, and it might be thought that India provided unparalleled opportunities to spread the Christian message among a people sunk in every variety of religious error. So indeed, it appeared to Evangelicals like the Company employee, Charles Grant:

> Upon the whole we cannot avoid recognising in the people of Hindostan, a race lamentably degenerate and base; retaining but a feeble sense of moral obligation; yet obstinate in their disregard of what they know to be right, governed by malevolent and licentious passions, strongly exemplifying the effects produced on society by a great and general corruption of manners, and sunk in misery by their vices.[24]

However, this was not at all how matters were perceived by the Company as a whole. Conscious of the exposed and alien nature of the British presence, and only too aware of the acute sensitivities aroused by religious matters, the Company had no wish to provoke unrest through the leaven of Christian religious activity. Accordingly, missionaries were barred from operating in India from 1793 until 1813. Those that did, like the Baptist William Carey, did so unofficially, usually operating out of non-Company territories—in Carey's case, the Danish enclave of Serampore. In fact, the Company, following the custom of Indian rulers, actually patronized indigenous religious institutions, supporting temples, participating in Hindu festivals, and collecting pilgrim taxes. This was notably the case in the south, where the Madras Board of Revenue was responsible for financing and regulating Hindu temples and festivals and respected the tradition that lands set aside for the support of Brahmin priests should be exempt from land taxes.[25]

While this policy made evident sense within India, viewed from Britain it was perverse and ungodly. How could Britain conquer and profit from the Indians and yet withhold from them the greatest gift Britain could bestow—the teachings of Jesus Christ? Accordingly, the Company came under mounting pressure to lift its bar on Christian missionaries, and the periodic renewals of the Company's Charter provided the opportunity for these demands to be made effective. Under the terms of the Charter renewal of 1813, missionaries were to be allowed to enter India under license. From 1833, the need to have a license was dropped altogether. Christian missionaries started to arrive in significant numbers, including the notable figure Alexander Duff, who sought to use the provision of western education in Calcutta to break down, brick by brick, "the huge and hideous fabric of Hinduism." By 1846, the chief missionary societies operating in India had a combined budget of £425,000, using their funds to translate the Bible and other religious works like the *Pilgrim's Progress* into the vernaculars, and establish church schools teaching English and Christian principles. During the 1830s, the Company was also forced to end its patronage of the Hindu religion—a decision which, observes Chris Bayly, provoked popular protest in the south, with riots in some towns and mass petitions demanding reconsideration.[26] In 1850, evangelical pressure also yielded a change in the law under which converts to Christianity were no longer to be required to relinquish their ownership of land.

Yet despite this activity and more favorable institutional climate, Christianity made little headway in India. Hindus attended Christian schools and learned English. Not a few were impressed by Christ's teaching. But the number actually converting to Christianity was miniscule. In 1851, there were only 200,000 Christians in India, of which just 90,000 were Protestant. By 1881, Christians made up a mere 0.7 percent of the Indian population. The fact of the matter was that for the typical Indian, conversion represented a radical and irreversible step, bringing with it ostracism from their community, the loss of caste, an association with an impure western lifestyle, and very often the adoption of non-Indian names and styles of dress. Hardly any Indians were prepared to make this change, and besides, had not religious reformers like Mohan Roy demonstrated that it was possible to find Christian precepts within the still broader church of Hinduism? "Virtually no Hindu of any consequence," writes Marshall, "was converted to Christianity."[27] Only among Anglo-Indians, some untouchables and tribal groups, and traditional centers of Portuguese-inspired Catholicism such as Goa, did Christianity make any real headway. The vast bulk of India's population, Hindu, Muslim, Jain, Sikh, or other, remained wholly outside of the Christian faith. The downside of Christian activity was that it increased the distance between rulers and ruled and encouraged, among Indians, the belief that it was a long-term goal of British conquest to destroy Indian religion—a perspective that fuelled the suspicions that were to surface so graphically in the Indian Mutiny.

The attitude of the state to religion was mirrored in its approach to Indian family and communal life. Once again, the company was loath to interfere in the day-to-day life of Indians in ways that could only risk stirring a backlash against British rule. In any case, the widening social gulf between the British and Indian people meant that most Europeans were wholly ignorant of the private lives of the Indians. One Mrs. Graham, visiting Calcutta in 1810, complained, "the distance kept up between the Europeans and the natives, both here and at Madras, is such that I have not been able to get acquainted with any native family."[28] Indicative was the position of women. Formally, the position of women in India was one which attracted much censure from British observers: they lacked rights in property; they were, among more elite groups, often confined within *purdha*; female babies were regularly put to death in parts of India as they brought with them the burden of providing dowries; they were married while still children; and windowed Hindus were expected to become domestic servants and not allowed to remarry. Most notoriously, among some groups like the Rajputs and high caste Bengalis, the custom of *sati* existed, whereby a widowed Hindu woman was under pressure to cast herself upon her husband's funeral pyre—an act bringing great spiritual benefits to herself (sati means virtuous one) and her family.

In the matters of female infanticide and sati, British sensibilities found it increasingly hard to remain detached from Indian custom. Certain district officers—such as John Campbell in Orissa—led campaigns to stop female infanticide, and it was declared illegal in Bengal territories in 1795—though enforcing the prohibition was exceedingly difficult as it usually took place immediately after birth, and was, besides, especially prevalent within the Princely State of Rajasthan where the British writ did not run. Sati was still more controversial. Even according to official statistics, some 1,000 widows were burned each year in the early 19th century and the British came to believe that many were forced into committing sati from families eager for the religious benefits or the material utility of having an unproductive widow out of the way. Ramabai Pandita, a Brahmin from Maharashtra who was herself widowed at 24 and later converted to Christianity during a visit to England (where, curiously enough, she became instructress in Sanskrit at Cheltenham Ladies College), described the pressures to which a bereaved Hindu wife was subject in her 1887 book, *The High-Caste Hindu Woman*:

> The act was supposed to be altogether a voluntary one, and no doubt, it was so in many cases. Some died for the love . . . which they cherished for their husbands. Some died . . . because they believed with all the heart that they should be made happy hereafter. Some to obtain great renown, for tombstones and monuments were erected to those who thus died, and afterwards the names were inscribed on the long list of family gods; others again, to escape the thousand temptations, and sins and miseries which they knew would fall to their lot as widows. Those who from pure ambition or from momentary impulse, declared their intentions thus to die, very often shrank from the fearful altar; no sooner did they feel the heat of the flames than they tried to leap down and escape the terrible fate; but it was too late. They had taken the solemn oath which must never he broken, priests and other men were at hand to force them to re-mount the pyre.

In 1803, Wellesley tried to abolish sati in Company territories, but the Calcutta Supreme Court ruled that on a matter such as this the government should follow "the religious opinions and prejudices of the natives." But some restrictions were introduced: from 1812, British officials were to attend at a sati to ensure that the woman was over 16, not pregnant, and was committing a voluntary act.

Witnessing these scenes added to pressure for change, yet the impetus was not from the British alone. Indian reformers like Mohan Roy also condemned the practice as a corruption of Hindu teaching, pointing to the *Laws of Manu*, where sati was not endorsed, it being instead prescribed that the Hindu widow should "emaciate her body, by living voluntarily on pure flowers, roots, and fruits. . . . Let her continue till death forgiving all injuries, performing harsh duties, avoiding every sensual pleasure, and cheerfully practicing the incomparable rules of virtue which have been followed by such women as were devoted to one only husband." It indeed appears to be the case that sati was in important respects an invented tradition, growing in prevalence among newly caste-conscious Hindus in areas like Calcutta.[29] In 1785, there were 378 cases of sati in Bengal, in 1818, 839.[30]

Debate raged as to whether it would be acceptable for the British to outlaw this religious practice, with some Indians, such as the members of the *Dharma Sabha*, seeing the attack on sati as part of a Christianizing agenda. A petition in defense of sati was presented in

1830 by "the Orthodox Hindu community of Calcutta," in which it was argued, "Hindoo widows perform, of their own accord and pleasure, and for the benefit of their husbands' souls and for their own, the sacrifice of self-immolation called suttee" and "any interference with a persuasion of so high and self-annihilating a nature, is . . . an unjust and intolerant dictation in matters of conscience" and would be viewed with "dismay throughout the Company's dominions, as the signal of an universal attack upon all we revere." The dilemma for the British in how to proceed was well captured by Bentinck in a Minute of November 1829:

> Whether the question be to continue or to discontinue the practice of suttee, the decision is equally surrounded by an awful responsibility. To consent to the consignment . . . of hundreds of innocent victims to a cruel and untimely end, when the power exists of preventing it, is a predicament which no conscience can contemplate without horror. But on the other hand . . . to put to hazard, by a contrary course, the very safety of the British empire in India, and to extinguish at once all hopes of those great improvements affecting the condition . . . of millions, which can only be expected from the continuance of our supremacy, is an alternative which . . . may be considered as a still greater evil.[31]

It was the board of directors in London who eventually settled the issue, instructing Bentinck to abolish the practice. This he did in company territories in 1829 and 1830, declaring in a Regulation of December 1829 that reflected the reforming ideas of Roy:

> The practice of suttee . . . is revolting to the feelings of human nature; it is nowhere enjoined by the religion of the Hindus as an imperative duty; on the contrary a life of purity and retirement on the part of the widow is more especially and preferably inculcated, and by a vast majority of that people throughout India the practice is not . . . observed. . . . Actuated by these considerations the governor-general in council, without intending to depart from one of the . . . most important principles of the system of British government in India, that all classes of the people be secure in the observance of their religious usages, so long as that system can be adhered to without violation of the paramount dictates of justice and humanity, has deemed it right to establish the following rules. . . . The practice of suttee, or of burning or burying alive the widows of Hindus, is hereby declared illegal, and punishable by the criminal courts.[32]

The decision provoked outcry among the religiously orthodox in Bengal and the *Dharma Sabha*'s petition to reverse the decision was taken as far as the Privy Council in London. However, Roy, among others, pressed the Council to uphold the ban, which it did. Although cases of sati continued until late into the 19th century, it ceased to be a regular practice.

Other measures to enhance the position of women followed. They became a legal category in matters of marriage and property and, in 1856, prompted by a vigorous campaign by the Bengali Hindu reformer, Iswar Vidyasagar, Hindu widows were given the right to remarry. Vidyasagar also campaigned for the introduction of a female minimum age of sexual consent and again his work bore some fruit when an Act of 1860 introduced a legal minimum of 10. However, missionary pressure for a legal minimum age of marriage was not acted upon, the Company reverting to its traditional reluctance to interfere in anything that could be considered of religious significance. Some women did gain more positively from British rule. Though still tiny, the numbers of women gaining access to education and training increased—mostly under the auspices of the missionaries. In Calcutta in 1823, the Church of England Society was conducting 23 girls' schools with some 500 pupils. Interestingly, the girls attending were from the lower social classes. In 1849, Bethune School was founded for girls of higher social backgrounds. Initially it did so poorly that it had to be personally subsidized by the governor-general, Lord Dalhousie, but in 1856, it was taken over by the government and became the first institute of higher education for women in India. Women also began to train as nurses and midwives and even as doctors from the 1880s.

However, the practical importance of most of these changes was minimal. Widow remarriage, though legal, was still viewed with repugnance by most Hindus and hardly occurred; infanticide was very hard to detect and even harder to prevent; child marriage continued and in this context the law on sexual consent was effectively unenforceable; for a girl to attend any kind of school remained very much the exception: in 1872, out of the 1,100,000 children in government and non-government schools of all kinds, only 50,000 were girls.[33] Indeed, in some ways the position of women deteriorated under the British presence. The influx of British cotton goods meant that female spinners lost an important source of family income, while among the emerging prosperous commercial classes of the major cities there was a move to confine more women to purdha as a mark of social status. In short, notwithstanding the conspicuous official initiatives in areas like sati and remarriage, for the typical woman—and above all the woman dwelling in village India—the impact of British rule was close to non-existent. Monier-Williams reviewed the situation in the 1870s in the most pessimistic terms:

> One hundred millions of women, supposed to be the actual subjects of the British Empire, are, with few exceptions, sunk in ignorance. They are unable to read a syllable of their mother-tongue, they are never taught the rules of life and health, the law of God, or the most rudimentary truths of science. . . . The women of India are the victims of the worst form of social tyranny.[34]

Some women had more direct and intimate experience of the Raj. In the earlier part of the Company's history officers, administrators, and merchants established relatively formal and permanent relationships with Indian women—though marriage was rare and most left their mistresses behind when they returned to Britain. A striking exemplar of this more liberal attitude to Anglo-Indian relations was provided by the military leader and Company official, David Ochterlony, who had 13 Indian wives, being known by the Delhi locals during his period as Resident as Loony Akhtar.[35] British troops turned regularly to prostitutes for sexual activity and one result was high rates of infection with syphilis. In the first half of the 19th century between one-eighth and one-third of British troops were so infected. In an attempt to reduce this debilitating ailment, soldiers were encouraged to establish regular Indian mistresses, which they would abandon when moving from one part of the country to another. One result was an expanding population of Anglo-Indian or Eurasian children: it was estimated, in 1784, that 700 Eurasians were born annually in Madras and the Coromandel Coast.[36] They occupied an awkward position within the Indian social system, being looked down upon by Indians and British alike, forming almost a sub-caste of their own.[37] Those fathered by regular troops would drift into the ranks of the urban poor. Those with wealthier fathers were better educated and some—especially the fairer ones—were sent to England for their education. Even so, their life prospects were limited. Eurasian sons were, from 1792, barred from government service and sought work as clerks and businessmen. For Eurasian daughters the best prospect lay in marriage to British soldiers—though this became rarer as British prejudice against mixed marriages increased during the 19th century.

Much of what has so far been said of the Indian reaction to the cultural and moral values of the west applies more especially to the Hindu community. In the case of the Muslims, the 19th century experience of British rule registered some important differences.

Muslims constituted approximately 20 percent of India's population, most of which had converted to Islam over the centuries of Muslim rule and were Sunni in their allegiance—though in the Northwest, the Shia branch of the religion prevailed. Muslims were very unevenly distributed across the subcontinent: the most Islamicized province was Sind, where 75 percent of the people were Muslim; by contrast, in the Central Provinces, Muslims made up only 3 percent of the people. Bengal was another province with a strong Muslim presence, but it was primarily focused in the rural areas of the east rather than the towns and the west. Thus, although the British were much in the habit of considering the Muslims to be an homogenous group, they were in fact divided by location, religious affiliation, and class background—there being a wide distance separating the descendants of the Mughal elites from the peasants who had converted under their rule.

The 19th-century Indian administrator and historian, W. W. Hunter, famously considered the Muslims to be "a race ruined under British rule." This was certainly true of previous ruling dynasties that lost prestige, position, and social function. The Mughal court lingered melancholically within the Red Fort at Delhi. The Muslim military gentry, who had made up the cavalry in the armies of the Mughals and the nawabs, found themselves discarded as the Company extended its rule and the humble infantryman armed with a musket superseded the previous preeminence of the mounted soldier in warfare. After Plassey, 80,000 troops in Siraj-ud-Daula's army were disbanded.[38] Opportunities for adventurous and martial Muslims to found dynasties, which had been striking in the flux of 18th-century India, dried up under the rigidity of Company rule. Unlike the Hindus, few Muslims became zamindari landlords since, even under the Mughals, most tax gatherers had been Hindu. In making these tax gatherers hereditary landlords the route to landlordism was closed to the Muslims of Bengal, 90 percent of that province's zamindars being Hindu.[39] Outside Bengal, Muslim elites faired better. In the Northwest provinces, existing Muslim landholdings were respected, and in Sind, Napier treated the Muslim *Jagidars* as an aristocracy and confirmed them in their revenues and privileges.

The Muslim service class also lost out as jobs increasingly went to Hindus. The displacement of Persian by English as the court language opened the way to a greater role for Hindus who were quicker to take up the language. The process was not rapid—the British continued to rely upon educated Muslims for administering the law—but it was inexorable: by 1856, of the 366 persons holding appointments in the judicial and revenue service of Bengal, only 54 were Muslim.[40] Among the wider population, Muslims did lose out in some ways—such as the Muslim cotton weavers of Dacca who succumbed to British factory competition, or the poorer peasants of Bengal burdened by heavy revenue assessments, but it is the opinion of Hardy that they suffered because of their class, not their faith.

Yet even when the problems confronting Muslims were primarily economic in character, communal tensions made themselves felt. The reason for this is evident when it is recalled that, not only were the zamindari landlords overwhelmingly Hindu, but this was equally true of the moneylenders who stepped in to advance money to peasants unable to pay their rent demands. The potentiality for communal discord was exacerbated by the activities of Muslim groups that emphasized the duty to resist Hindu moneylenders and landlords. As Hardy notes, Muslim revivalist movements in Bengal emerged within the context of peasant revolts against Hindu landlords and creditors.[41] In the west of Bengal, Titu Mir (1782–1831), a Muslim who had travelled to Mecca and had come under the influence of radical *Wahabi* teachers, proclaimed a policy of resistance toward the zamindari landlords and their British backers. Gathering a total of approximately 5,000 followers, he organized guerrilla raids against the zamindari's armed henchmen as well as conducting particular operations against the Hindus, killing cows and smearing blood in Hindu temples. He built a bamboo fort at Barasat, from which he declared independence from British rule. A Company army was accordingly dispatched, and in 1831, Titu's revolt was crushed, its leader dying when his fort was stormed. East Bengal saw a comparable movement in the shape of the *faraizi*, founded by Hajj Shariat-Allah (1781–1840), who went among the peasants urging a return to religious purity according to the teachings of the Koran. Under his son, Dahdu Miyan, the movement took a more militant form. He organized resistance to Hindu landlords and moneylenders, boycotting the payment of taxes and interest charges. He also formed an armed force of cudgel bearers to attack the zamindars and their followers and then went one stage further by attempting to form a parallel Muslim government within East Bengal. District Commissioners called *khalifas* were appointed to each village, their role being to raise funds, carry out propaganda, and settle disputes between villagers who were forbidden from taking their cases to the British courts without permission. The British made persistent attempts to prosecute Miyan for crimes ranging from theft to murder, but all such allegations foundered from a lack of witnesses prepared to give evidence—though he was placed under arrest during the Mutiny. However, the faraizi "state within a state" went into decline following Miyan's death in 1860.

Thus, Muslim reaction to the British presence in India sometimes took quite radical forms. At one extreme, it could involve declaring British rule anti-Islamic, with the implication that a state of Holy War existed within the subcontinent. This was the view taken by those associated with the Wahabi sect, notably Saiyyid Ahmed who, protesting at the adulteration of Sharia law by legal precepts of western origin, established himself with his Ghazi followers at Peshawar from whence he declared a jihad against the Sikhs, whom he engaged in several battles. But as an Indian interloper, Ahmed was always viewed suspiciously by the Pathan tribesmen and when, in 1830, he tried to regulate the marriages of their daughters they rose against him and expelled him from Peshawar, and he was murdered shortly afterwards.

However, the view that India was a "land of conflict" was far from typical among Muslims; for most, British governance exhibited sufficient Islamic elements, most notably, of course, a legal system that continued to be based upon Sharia law.[42] Attempts to politicize Islam as a basis for joint action made little headway in the 19th century, support being mainly confined to the small class of clerks, teachers, and petty landlords.[43] This said, it remained the case that in their general response to the British presence, Muslims were less receptive and responsive to western ideas. Islamic belief was more rigidly prescribed and there was less scope for the kind of redefinition of the faith in the way that occurred among Hindu reformers. To Muslims, notes Hardy, the British were boorish, arrogant, scandalous infidels—eating pork, drinking wine, exposing their women's flesh, and ignorant of true religion. From such people, Muslims had nothing to learn and the appropriate response was simply to close ranks and purify their own religion.[44] "The British historian of British India," he concludes, "often fails to appreciate how little British rule had touched the minds and still less the hearts of Muslims in India before 1857."[45]

But as with the Hindus, encouragement from printing and the spread of education did encourage the emergence of a more distinct Muslim identity. As Robb observes, where in the 18th century there had been a tendency for Muslim and Hindu elite cultures to merge, during the 19th century they grew ever further apart, Muslim and Hindu alike becoming ever more conscious of a distinct cultural and religious identity—something to have a weighty political legacy.[46] Muslim reformers emphasized the differences between Hindus and Muslims and denounced Muslims who patronized Hindu shrines or practiced vegetarianism. The British, perceiving the Muslims as a counterweight to the numerical strength of the Hindus, encouraged this tendency toward communal differentiation, patronizing religious and community leaders as a means of exerting influence over their followers. The result was an India evermore watchful of religious identity and sensitive to perceived threats to status and custom.

It is apparent, therefore, that there was, among the more articulate sections of Indian society, a definite quickening in the pace of cultural change in the first half of the 19th century. This was far from being merely a reflex response to the British presence. India, as we have often observed, was a dynamic and evolving society in the 18th century. The decline of Mughal power opened the way for more vigorous debate within urban centers and courts like Lucknow, Delhi, Benares, and Hyderabad, while there was an increasingly self-confident and conscious Hindu society underpinned by trading wealth. Within this context, the British added a powerful new force for change—by attraction and repulsion. No educated Indian could ignore the British presence and all were forced to consider what it meant for their own beliefs and practices. In the main, Indians did not jettison their traditional culture as liberal reformers like Macaulay anticipated. Rather they reinvented and reinvigorated it, producing new approaches and syntheses. Western ideas and social models didn't just happen to Indians: they were appropriated and adapted by a people operating within their own powerful cultural traditions who yet found in the new technologies and institutional systems brought by the British powerful media through which their ideas could be formed and popularized. Yet still, we are talking about the literate classes. The great majority of Indians were unaffected by these surface disturbances and continued to live and worship in traditional ways. This was, after all, the age in which the classical Hinduism of caste and community extended and entrenched itself more powerfully in India than ever before.

9

Resistance to British Rule

It must not be inferred from the ability of the Company to govern India with so limited a number of European administrators and troops that the Indians did not openly question or resist British rule. The British had to fight their way to supremacy, defeating a series of rival powers of varying degrees of military capacity. Having conquered large parts of India, they had to uphold their rule with a large standing army and an extensive network of police and intelligence officers. The *Pax Britannica* had to be imposed and upheld against a range of challenges since, as Chris Bayly observes, "armed revolt was endemic in early colonial India."[1] Even though these revolts were all contained, India was never truly pacified, and British rule was never regarded as truly legitimate—it was too alien, too at odds with Indian expectations to be that. This state of affairs was admitted frankly by Lord Metcalfe in the 1830s:

> All India is at all times looking out for our downfall. The people everywhere would rejoice, or fancy they would rejoice, at our destruction. And numbers are not wanting who would promote it by all means in their power.

Resistance to British rule was of two types: that which arose out of a desire to maintain aspects of the old India and that which reflected the rising trends encouraged by the British presence. It was the former that was dominant before midcentury and produced the greatest of all challenges to British hegemony: the Mutiny of 1857–58.

The first kind of resistance tended to be centered around figures wielding traditional forms of authority and often carried with it the use or threat of violence. It also increasingly had a religious dimension, in many cases being linked to the message of some religious leader or millenarian prophet. Geographically, this was characteristically an agrarian phenomenon. The countryside was peopled by significant numbers who felt they had a grievance either with the British, or with the social systems or elites sustained by British rule. According to Markovits, agrarian resistance remained a chronic problem during the entire period and every year witnessed agrarian disturbances somewhere in India.[2]

Landlord and military elites were key groups to take up armed resistance against the British in defense of their traditional power structures. These elite groups, such as the Maratha chiefs of the Deccan, the Rajputs of central India, the Poligars of the Tamil South, and the Nayars of Kerala, were able to command peasant followers on the basis of caste and clan ties.[3] Although the British generally respected the position of the so-called Native Princes, they were not so tender toward more local village and district elites, who found themselves subject to direct imperial rule, and either liable to new forms of taxation and control, or replaced by new zamindari families who had secured revenue and land rights. Open resistance to these British policies did occur—as in peasant conflicts with Company revenue agents in the Birbhum, Rangpur, and Dinajpur districts of Bengal between 1779 and 1781, or the eight-year guerrilla war waged by Kerala Varma, the displaced Raja of Kottayam, who successfully mobilized popular support in his campaign against the Company until his death in 1806.[4] Metcalfe described how, upon his arrival as assistant to the British Resident in Delhi in 1806, British authority was "openly defied within a few miles of that city" and "a company of infantry was necessary to attend the officer making the revenue settlement." Such resistance was invariably crushed by the Company's superior military forces—Metcalfe himself beginning the process around Delhi when in 1807 he toured the region making a settlement mounted on an elephant and surrounded by soldiers.[5]

More frequent were attacks directed, not against the British themselves, but those associated with their policies or who carried forward their modernizing agenda. Thus there were frequent peasant revolts against zamindars, which, as we have seen, could have a Hindu-Muslim component. Pre-dating the movements of the faraizi and Titu Mir was that led by Abdul Rahman of Gujarat, who sought to unite Muslim weavers and agriculturalists in opposition to Hindu landlords as well as the British. Moneylenders were another target.

In a report to the Bombay Government in 1852, Sir George Wingate described how:

> These two cases of village moneylenders, murdered by their debtors . . . must, I apprehend, be viewed not as the results of isolated instances of oppression on the part of creditors, but as examples in an aggravated form of the general relations subsisting between the class of money lenders and our agricultural population.

Perhaps the most successful of the agrarian opposition movements was that of the indigo cultivators of Bengal in the years 1858 to 1860. British planters persuaded local farmers to take up the growing of indigo, which was used to make blue dye, by advancing them loans to pay for their initial production and subsistence costs. The amounts the cultivators received upon delivering the crop were rarely sufficient to cover the initial loan and debts steadily mounted which, passed from generation to generation, rendered the farmers effectively bonded labor with no prospect of escaping from the clutches of the planters. Peasant discontent found a voice in 1858 when two brothers, Charan and Digambar Biswas, organized a boycott of indigo cultivation within their village. The boycott spread across the indigo-growing region, and the Blue Mutiny attracted the support of Indian journalists and political reformers, the Bengal dramatist Dinabandhu Mitra producing a popular play on the subject entitled *The Mirror of Indigo*. As the characters complained:

> We have nearly abandoned all the ploughs; still we have to cultivate indigo. We have no chance in a dispute with the Sahebs. They bind and beat us, it is for us to suffer. We are consequently obliged to work.
>   What shall we eat; and how shall I pass the year? Ah, our land was bright as the golden champah. By the produce of only one corner of the field we satisfied the mahajans. . . . This large family may die without food. Every morning two recas [nearly 5 lb.] of rice are necessary. What shall we eat then? Oh, my ill-fortune! . . . what has the indigo of this white man done?[6]

The efforts of the planters to enforce a recommencement of cultivation failed, with the Bengal colonial authorities sympathizing with the plight of the farmers, and by 1860, the indigo had largely ceased to be grown in Bengal—the planters shifting their operations to the Champaran district of Bihar.

We have already noted the resistance of tribal peoples to the incursion of the paraphernalia of 19th century modernity into their hitherto closed communities: settled agriculture, commercial logging, money-lenders, missionaries, and government administrators. The Bhils of central India, the tribes of Chota Nagpur, and the Santhals of Bengal all provide examples of this phenomenon. In the latter case, the San-thal tribes retreated before the advance of zamindari landlordism into the hills of Rajmahal, where they soon found themselves becoming embroiled in debt to aggressive moneylenders. In 1855, they rose in rebellion against the British state that, they had come to believe, lay at the root of their deteriorating condition. Poorly armed, they were soon crushed by the Company's forces, their act of resistance quickly being eclipsed by the far greater challenge of the Mutiny. Nomadic pastoral-ists like the Bhattis of Hissar and the Gujars of the Doab also clashed with settled farmers, such as the Jats, to whom the British apportioned land in the belief that they represented a more productive and compli-ant class than the less-tractable nomads, whom they came to perceive as manifesting a tendency to criminality.[7]

Violent protest was not, however, a monopoly of the rural areas. Towns and cities also witnessed periodic unrest—usually provoked by rising food prices and associated transgressions of what histori-ans label the "moral economy of the crowd." Thus periods of scar-city and high prices led to attacks on grain and rice merchants who were accused of hoarding supplies in the hope of profiting from a ris-ing market. Madras saw notable "rice riots" in 1806, 1833, and 1854. Government tax demands could also generate protests, as when, in Surat in 1844, a crowd of 30,000 demanded that the magistrate reverse a recent rise in the salt tax.[8] According to Chris Bayly, the most com-mon cause of urban unrest in the early 19th century was the attempts by influential residents to resist official moves to tax real estate—such men being able to mobilize the growing underclass of underemployed and unskilled labor draining into the cities from the surrounding rural districts.[9]

If it is important to recognize the prevalence of active protest against British rule and its associated effects, it is equally important to appre-ciate its essentially reactive and fragmentary character. Most of the disturbances, whether agrarian or urban, had a conservative agenda, representing an attempt to resist some challenge to custom and usage and focused around established tribal, religious, caste, and village lead-ers. Rural revolt in India, as Stokes was always at pains to emphasize, was an elite phenomenon, associated with the minority of landowners and clan leaders. Scattered between different localities and communal groups, and lacking a coherent program or organization, these protest movements represented little threat to the Company, which was able to suppress them without too much difficulty. Yet before 1857, there were signs of a new and ultimately more dangerous form of opposition: political opposition by the articulate middle class. While in most cases this, as yet, took the form of pressure for some reform in Company administration, it could, in the hands of a figure like Derozio, involve a questioning of British rule as such.

The essential element at work here was a basic dissonance between rhetoric and reality. The British appeared to offer a new range of opportunities to the educated Indian, and reformers like Macaulay explicitly looked to the day when an Anglicized elite would cooperate as equals in the government of the country. Crucially, however, the higher reaches of Company administration remained in British hands. This not only blocked channels for promotion but meant that in composition British rule was always alien—something that had not been true under previous conquering regimes like the Mughals. The situation of the middle class was not yet such as would provoke real anger or discontent. To educated Hindus especially, the British were opening wholly new prospects for service in the state and professions, whether it be employment in the expanding court system, the lower reaches of administration, education, or the commercial houses of Bombay or Calcutta, and to such people the settled order of British rule appeared preferable to a return to the militaristic free-booting of the post-Mughal kind. Even so, the literate classes had grievances and looked to the newly emerging civil society of pressure groups, public meetings, and reform societies to press them before their English masters. The renewal of the Company's charter in 1853 provided a focus for Indian political activity, and 1851 saw the formation of the British India Association to press for land reform and greater access for Indians to senior government positions. In 1852, it organized a high-profile meeting in Bombay that attracted representatives from across the Hindu, Muslim, and Parsi communities. One delegate uttered a warning that events were seemingly to vindicate:

> The British government professes to educate the Natives to an equality with Europeans, an object worthy of the age and of Britain. But if Englishmen after educating Natives to be their equals continue to treat them as inferiors—if they deny the stimulus to honourable ambition, and show the Natives that there is a barrier over which the superior Native merit and ambition can never hope to pass . . . are they not in

effect undoing all that they have done ... and pursuing a suicidal policy, which will inevitably array all the talent, honour and intelligence of the country ultimately in irreconcilable hostility to the ruling power?[10]

The British response to such demands was variable. Some administrators, such as Munro and Colonel Walker, repeatedly insisted upon the importance of admitting Indians to responsible positions within the state. Writing as early as 1822, Mountstuart Elphinstone, the governor of Bombay, was emphatic upon the dangers consequent upon a failure to act:

Besides the necessity for having good native advisers in governing natives, it is necessary that we should pave the way for the introduction of the natives to some share in the government of their own country. It may be half a century before we are obliged to do so; but the system of government and education which we have already established must some time or other work such a change in the people of this country that it will be impossible to confine them to subordinate employment; and if we have not previously opened vents for their ambition and ability, we may expect an explosion which will overturn our Government.[11]

Yet such views were always those of a minority and were less and less often aired as the Raj consolidated itself over the 19th century. The British attitude to even the best-educated Indians was essentially condescending and inflexible. However much liberals like Macaulay might rhapsodize about a future in which Britain would gladly relinquish the reins of Indian government to an elite Anglicized in sensibility, religion, understanding, and culture, the typical Britisher in the cantonments, clubs, and hill stations was unwavering in his conviction that India had been won by the sword and that the unquestioned superiority of British ways and character rendered any talk of transferring power toward the Indians naïve nonsense.

Before midcentury, the disjuncture between Indian aspirations and British unwillingness to share power was more a tendency than a fact. India was yet too disparate, too compartmentalized along lines of caste, class, locality, language, and religion, for the idea of Indian nationalism—of India for the Indians for good or ill—to take root beyond a tiny minority of Bengali graduates. Even so an explosion against British rule of the magnitude, if not the kind, Elphinstone had anticipated did occur in 1857 to shake, if only for a time, the complacent Victorian assumption of Britain's God-ordained right to rule India.

THE INDIAN MUTINY 1857–58

The Mutiny represented the culmination of a series of discrete tendencies, each of which could threaten unrest, but which together brought a conflagration. Was there a common theme? Yes: the impact of British rule. It was the British who were seen to lie behind a diverse range of changes to Indian society and ways of life that provoked a pervasive sense of alienation and anger; and it was British rule, which correspondingly, provided a focus for discontent, ensuring that groups with otherwise little in common made common cause in their fight against the foreigners or *furinghi*. The Mutiny was not *motivated* by a political will to overthrow British power; but anti-British sentiment supplied whatever dynamism and unity of purpose the rebels displayed.

The Mutiny began at Meerut on May 19, 1857, when three sepoy regiments of the Bengal Army, objecting to the arrest of 85 of their number for refusing to use the new Enfield rifle on the grounds that the grease used to lubricate the cartridges was made from unclean beef and pork fat, killed their officers and marched on Delhi. A series of grievances had been agitating the Bengal Army for some time—there had been nascent mutinies at Dum-Dum in January 1857 and Barrackpore in March—yet the military authorities had failed to respond by reinforcing their position. Complacently, the ratio of European to Indian troops had been allowed to steadily decline, until there were just 23,000 European soldiers to 128,000 Indians. More ominously, 14 of the army's 19 British regiments were stationed in the recently conquered Punjab and the adjacent Meerut, and with two also in Calcutta, there were virtually no British troops in the north-central districts of India between Bengal and Delhi.

What made the Meerut incident decisive was the immediate decision of the Muslim Third Native Cavalry to march for Delhi where, in the virtual absence of British troops, they had little difficulty in spreading their revolt among the sepoys and townspeople. Joined by the urban poor, a wave of attacks were unleashed, not only on the British residents, but on all people and things associated with British rule: Anglicized Indians, Christians, moneylenders, bankers, law courts, churches, civil servants. They also got themselves a leader by pressuring the 82-year-old Bahadur Shah II, a pensioner of the East India Company living a twilight existence amid the fading splendor of the Red Fort, to proclaim a refounded Mughal Empire. In practice, Bahadur Shah's leadership was only ever nominal, and authority came to reside with the Administrative Court, a committee of 10 members—6 drawn from the military and 4 from civilian backgrounds—and whose decisions were subject to the approval of Shah and Muhammed Bakht Khan of Bareilly, who had been appointed governor-general. From Delhi, the revolt spread to other historic centers of central-north India, like Lucknow, Cawnpore, Allahabad, Jhansi, and Mathura. Within a few weeks, most of the major military stations in the Northwestern provinces and Oudh were in rebel hands. Military mutiny became the spur to civilian rebellion, and the fragility of British rule in the countryside was quickly exposed as colonial administration was swept away across large tracts of village India. One ICS officer described the events in Oudh:

> When . . . the troops at the capital had set the example, all the rest soon followed, and the fabric of civil government fell to pieces like a house made out of cards. As the regiments mutinied at each station, the civilians fled, or were destroyed: the offices were burnt; the police and revenue out-stations, and officials left without a head, broke up; the people were left to themselves, and anarchy ensued.[12]

Crucially, however, the rebel leadership never formulated a clear strategy—either for how to defeat the British or what to put in their place. By default, they fell back upon consolidating their grip on Delhi, full as it was of historic and symbolic associations. By August 1857, there was an army of 40,000 encamped within its perimeters. What they failed to realize was its limited strategic value: by digging in, they effectively dug their own grave for the simple reason that they lost the momentum surprise had given them. Even more culpably, they neglected to sever the British supply lines running northwest from Calcutta. The Grand Trunk Road was held effectively by the British and, says Stokes, "British military formations moved along it with the sureness of destroyers passing over a dark and turbulent ocean."[13] The Jumna and Ganges Rivers similarly remained under British control. In the long run, this sealed the Mutineers' fates since they were doomed to lose the numbers and resources game once the British had recovered from their initially exposed position. "Delhi," says Chris Bayly, "was the greatest victory and the ultimate undoing of the revolt."[14]

The foundations of a British fight back were soon discernable. Notwithstanding the speed at which the Mutiny spread, it remained the case that the bulk of India did not join in. The Punjab, though having only recently been forcibly annexed by the British, remained calm and was, in fact, to play a vital role in the resurgence of British power. Since their defeat, 16,000 Sikhs had enrolled into the Bengal Army—and these men had an intense dislike for the Bengalis and Biharis that had traditionally made up its core and who had entered their state as conquerors. The armies of the Bombay and Madras Presidencies did not rebel, and even Bengal itself remained calm. There were many more British troops in Bengal, but even so the old Muslim elite who might have turned to revolt to recover their old position had been thoroughly marginalized, the new elite of zamindars owing their privileges and incomes to the British. Bengal's distinctive middle class of merchants and literate professionals viewed the revolt as backward looking, the British India Association passing a motion condemning the uprising. As Brown notes, those areas where British power had been longest established did not join the revolt.[15] This gave the colonial authorities access to ample tax revenues—unlike the mutineers, who were unable to construct a tax raising system and were forced to extract supplies and loans from bankers and merchants by compulsion. From this basis, the British were able to reinforce their position gradually as the 39,000 additional European troops Governor-General Canning had requested from London began to arrive—and that, by 1858, were to take the combined European military presence in India to 80,000.[16]

From the middle of 1857, the British began to drive back into the rebel heartlands. This was no quick or clean business. The British, too, made tactical mistakes, dispersing forces and making for symbolic centers like Lucknow, where some 1,000 British soldiers and civilians were besieged behind the walls of the Resident's palace. Militarily little could be done for Lucknow; politically, it could not be left to its fate. But gradually the weight of the British advance made itself felt. A British force of 3,800 from the Punjab reappeared at Delhi on June 9. Unable to retake the city, it occupied a position on the ridge overlooking the city from which it repelled repeated assaults by the Mutineers. On September 4, British artillery arrived and began bombarding the walls, opening the way to an assault on September 14. The city was finally recaptured after six days of intense fighting, with the Mughal Emperor being sent into exile in Rangoon and three of his sons summarily executed.

The loss of Delhi was a decisive blow to the Mutineers. The next major center was Lucknow, which after several inconclusive relief efforts, was captured in March 1858. Jhansi also fell in March—the rani of Jhansi famously escaping dressed as a soldier, only to be shot shortly afterwards. In the process of reconquering lost territory, the British administered violent retribution upon those they considered implicated or complicit in the deaths of British people. At Delhi, the Urdu poet Ghalib lamented, "Here there is a vast ocean of blood before me, God alone knows what more I shall have to behold."[17] "No man's life was safe," reported Main-ud-Din, "all able-bodied men who were seen were taken for rebels and shot."[18] The city's entire population was expelled into the countryside and only allowed to return on payment of a fine. What especially fired the British to vengeance were the lurid accounts—often exaggerated—of massacres of women and children, most notably the slaughtering at knifepoint of the women of the Cawnpore garrison. Colonel Neil, who led the first force to enter Cawnpore, gave orders that guilty villages "are to be destroyed; all men in them to be slaughtered. All sepoys not giving a good account of themselves are to be hanged at once; all heads of insurgents to be hanged."[19] Upon entering the town, and visiting the room in which the massacre of the women took place, Neil ordered:

> Each miscreant after sentence of death is pronounced on him . . . will be forced into cleaning up a small portion of the bloodstains; the task will be made as revolting to his feelings as possible and the Provost-Marshall will use the lash in forcing anyone objecting to complete his task. After properly cleaning up his portion, the culprit is to be immediately hanged.[20]

Despite the loss of the main strongholds of the Mutiny, resistance to the British was sustained by bands of guerrillas operating in districts like Gwalior and Nagpur, where Tantia Topi emerged as an effective insurgent leader. However, by the late summer of 1858, most of these opposition forces had been banished, symbolized by the death of the rani of Jhansi at Gwalior in June 1858 and the eventual capture and execution of Topi in April 1859. The Mutiny-cum-rebellion of 1857–58 was over.

The Mutiny stands out as the single most dramatic event in the history of Britain's engagement with India, and the question as to what caused it must be addressed. There are two issues to be considered: first, what prompted the initial breakdown of discipline in the Bengal Army; and second, why did this military mutiny evoke such a wide-ranging and popular response?

It is generally recognized that the Bengal Army was becoming an increasingly unstable entity owing to mounting grievances among the sepoys. What were these grievances? One factor was the ramifications of the occupation of the Punjab. The Bengalis did not like the Sikhs, whom they regarded unclean and uncouth, and resented their deployment to the Punjab. These feelings were exacerbated, first, by the formal British annexation of the Punjab, which meant that the soldiers lost their previous wage bonuses for serving outside the Company territories, and second, by the increasing recruitment of Sikhs and Gurkhas into a Bengal Army, previously the preserve of Brahmins, Rajputs, and Muslims. Further concerns over terms and conditions were aroused by the General Service Enlistment Act of 1856 that removed the exemption most of the Bengal Army had previously enjoyed of not having to serve anywhere that necessitated a sea-voyage—this being held to be against caste rules. The problem was that the Bengal Army was required for military operations in Burma, and for this, the sea-transportation of men was essential. The Bengal Army had always been acutely conscious of caste distinctions, and the changes to service rules and the recruitment of non-caste Sikhs seemed to prefigure a wider assault upon caste status within its ranks. Fears to this end were already being awakened by a tendency toward more aggressive Christian proselytizing by missionaries and some officers. Colonel Wheler, who commanded the 34th Native Infantry, was quite frank about his ambition:

> As to the question whether I have endeavoured to convert Sepoys and others to Christianity, I would humbly reply that this has been my object, and I conceive is the aim . . . of every Christian . . . that the Lord would make him the happy instrument of converting his neighbour to God, or, in other words, of rescuing him from eternal destruction.[21]

Attitudes such as this were indicative of that widening distance in sympathies between officers and men that had been developing since the early decades of the 19th century and were reflected in the complacent willingness of the officer class to leave the day-to-day running of the army to poorly paid and undervalued sabadars.

It wasn't just the annexation of the Punjab that created problems; the annexation of Oudh in 1856 was the source of still more tension. Oudh was traditionally a strong recruiting ground for the Bengal Army, with 75,000 of the sepoys having links to the landed and farming families of the princely state. Having assumed control, the British set about reforming the land and revenue systems in high-handed fashion, depriving the established *taluqdars* of their landlord rights and imposing heavy tax burdens on the cultivators. The grievances of the people of Oudh fed readily through to the Bengal Army that was, as has often been observed, a peasant army. From this perspective, the bungled handling of the Enfield cartridge issue merely ignited a compound primed to explode. Thus when, on March 29, 1857, Mangal Pande ran around the Barrackpore parade ground with a gun shouting "from biting these cartridges you will become infidels;" the sepoys who heard him, if they did not respond to his lead, knew full well the import of his words. That same month Major Edwards, who was commanding the 43rd Regiment at Barrackpore, received a letter that captured the fevered sense of unease and rumor that was running rife through the ranks by this time:

> We will not give up our religion. We serve for honour and religion. . . . The Lord Sahib has given orders, which he has received from the Company, to all commanding officers to destroy the religion of the country. We know this. . . . The officers in the Salt Department mix up bones with the salt. The officer in charge of ghee [butter] mixes up fat with it; this is well known . . . the Sahib in charge of sugar burns up bones and mixes them in the syrup the sugar is made of; this is well known . . . the senior officers have ordered rajas, noblemen, landowners, money-lenders and peasants all to eat together and English bread has been sent to them; this is well known . . . throughout the country, the wives of . . . all classes of Hindus, on becoming widows are to be married again; this is known. Therefore we consider ourselves killed.[22]

As James summarizes, "every examination of the events of 1857 comes back to this fact: that the rank and file of the Bengal army imagined that they were about to be made Christians."[23]

What, then, about the rapid spread of the Mutiny beyond the ranks of the aggrieved soldiers? A series of factors were relevant, none of which were uniform in their action. For every generalization that is made, a host of exceptions immediately intrudes itself. It is for this reason that the whole issue continues to provoke such debate. Three elements may be singled out for particular emphasis.

In the first place, there stands this matter of religion. The Bengal Army, in giving voice to its religious fears, was only reflecting a wider set of concerns provoked by an accelerating set of policies promoted by the Company which seemed to prefigure a conspiracy against India's traditional belief systems. Governor-General Dalhousie was a convinced modernizer, and his administration in the years preceding the Mutiny had seen a range of unsettling reforms: the lifting of the

ban on the remarriage of Hindu widows; the removal of the traditional prohibition under which Hindu sons who converted from their
faith were not allowed to inherit family lands; the encouragement of
western educational provision which appeared to question orthodox
Hindu and Muslim beliefs directly; the aggressive promotion of railway building, which intruded western progress into conservative rural
communities and made no allowance for caste distinctions in its pas-
senger provision; and the Doctrine of Lapse, which unilaterally cast to
one side Hindu adoption law. For the orthodox Hindu, it was not hard
to deduce from these changes that the Company was abandoning its
previously neutral stance toward the faith of Indians and was meditat-
ing the kind of mass Christian conversions that had always been the
dream of missionaries and aggressive Anglicizers. And when the kind
of rumors encapsulated in the Barrackpore letter are recalled, it is easy
to understand the dread that these changes might have given rise to.
One of the earliest proclamations issued by the rebels in Delhi testifies
to the prevalence of this alarm, if only because the Mutineers turned to
this issue to legitimize their actions:

> It is well known that in these days all the English have entertained these
> evil designs—first, to destroy the religion of the whole Hindustani Army,
> and then to make the people by compulsion Christians. Therefore, we,
> solely on account of our religion, have combined with the people, and
> have not spared alive one infidel, and have re-established the Delhi dy-
> nasty on these terms.[24]

However, several observations bring into question the notion that
the Mutiny was a religious reaction preceding British policies. The fact
that Hindus and Muslims were jointly engaged in the struggle suggests
a motivating role for factors besides religion as a post-British India
under Muslim Mughal rule was not one that would have been equally
sensitive to the religious privileges of both religions—Muslims, for instance, being resolved upon the re-establishment of Sharia Law, which
the British had been amending in recognition of the legal equality
of Hindus. Second, the idea that it was the progressive modernizing
agenda of the Company that was the disturbing factor, challenging orthodox social attitudes, is seemingly contradicted by the circumstance
that those areas where modernization had been most systematically
pursued—such as Bengal and Bombay—remained quiet, while the
central areas of unrest were comparatively untouched by westerniza-
tion. As Eric Stokes writes: "So far from the main rebellion zone being

situated in the seabound regions longest exposed to advanced influences, the North-Western Provinces, still less Oudh and Central India, had only tardy and limited contact with modernity."[25]

An alternative version of the religious interpretation holds that the revolt was, in its essentials, a Muslim uprising or Holy War into which the Hindus were more or less unwittingly drawn. This was a view commonly held by British officers in the field. A young Alfred Lyall, who served in the Bulandshahr district, wrote to his father, "The whole insurrection is a great Mohomedan conspiracy, and the sepoys are merely the tools of the Mussulmans."[26] The commissioner of the Meerut Division similarly observed, in his official narrative of events, "the real movers were the Mahomedans" who endeavored to "make the mass of the population join them," the Hindus later complaining, "they have been bitterly deceived."[27]

Muslims certainly took a prominent role in the rebellion. It was, as we have seen, the Muslims of the Third Native Light Cavalry who took the fateful decision to ride for Delhi and place the Mughal Emperor at the head of the movement—who accordingly declared that he was going to restore the rule of the house of Akbar and Shah Jahan and appointing a Mughal prince, Mirza Mughal, Commander in Chief of the rebel forces. Muslim holy men spread the idea that the uprising was a Holy War or jihad aimed at restoring Muslim rule to India, the religious teacher Mohammed Husain seeking to spread the Mutiny into the Bombay Army. Two spiritual leaders, Liaquat Ali and Ahmad Ullah Shah, took the lead among the rebels at Lucknow, with Ullah Shah speaking of annihilating the British presence in India and even taking the war to London.[28] Hardy notes that in the Doab and Aligarh districts, Muslims were fierce for the uprising, while in Rohilkhand, Khan Bahadur Khan, grandson of the territory's last Muslim ruler, assembled a large force of Muslim Pathans, and pledged his allegiance to Bahadur Shah.[29]

Yet the idea that the Mutiny was an essentially Islamic revolt cannot be sustained. It was, for one thing, high caste Hindus of the Bengal Army who initiated it, and Hindus were represented strongly at all levels of the rebellion, including such prominent figures as the rani of Jhansi and Nana Sahib. When Nana Sayyid sought to raise the standard of jihad in the Jama Masjid mosque in May 1857, he was promptly told to remove it by the emperor, who added that Hindus and Muslims were alike to him.[30] Nor were Muslims unanimous in their support for the uprising. In the later 19th century, the Muslim Saiyid Ahmad Khan, seeking to lift the view that it was the Muslims who were the driving force behind the Mutiny, wrote a pamphlet, *Who were the Loyal Mussulmanns?*, in which he cited numerous examples of Muslims who had collaborated with, rather than resisted, the British. These included the nizam of Hyderabad, the leading Muslim ruler, as well as the nawabs of Rampur, Karnal, Muradabad, and Dacca. Mathura, a mainly Hindu district, was held in the British interest by a Muslim deputy collector, while the "Muslims of Bengal," writes Hardy, "who had certainly suffered most, economically, from British rule, did not stir."[31] Although well-placed British observers highlighted the Muslim contribution, others, no less well informed, drew very different conclusions. Sir George Campbell, writing in 1857, commented:

> The Mahomedans have, I think, behaved better than might have been expected, considering their antecedents and position; and that the result, far from bringing to light a chronic Mahomedan conspiracy, has been to show that we have not in that class of subjects that formidable danger that has sometimes been apprehended.

And in an 1859 assessment of the causes of the Mutiny, L. Bowring concluded that, while all Muslims would like to see their religion once more ruling India, "the facts . . . show that the Mahommedans only took a partial share in the mutiny and that after its development."[32]

A second explanation for the rapid spread of the Mutiny, which again has a pedigree stretching back to the events themselves, sees the uprising as primarily an attempt by various traditional elites to recover the status and position they had enjoyed prior to British rule. This was the interpretation favored by the first major historian of the revolt, J. W. Kaye, who traced its roots to the steady alienation of the old aristocratic elite by British policy.[33] Foremost among those who might be motivated to join the rebellion by a wish to regain past glories were, of course, the various princely rulers who had seen their states annexed, or their hereditary dynastic rights cast aside, by the British. Bahadur Shah himself, though still technically the head of a Mughal Empire which included Bengal among its provinces, had been reduced to a condition of impotence within the court in Delhi and had been told by Canning only months before that, upon his death, the British would cease to recognize his imperial line. Another prominent figure in the revolt, Khan Bahadur Khan, was the grandson of the last independent ruler of Rohilkhand, which had been annexed by the Company in 1801. He gathered a force of 40,000 at Bareilly and pledged himself the nizam to the Mughal Emperor. Dalhousie's expansionist ambitions played a key role in pushing princely families into rebellion. Under the terms of the Doctrine of Lapse it was seen, says James, that henceforward "there would be no dynastic security for any prince, however loyal and accommodating."[34] The rani of Jhansi, the widow of the raja, repeatedly implored the British to allow their adopted son to succeed to the title—to no avail. For her, revolt was the only route by which she could recover her autonomy and status. Another leading figure in the uprising was Nana Sahib, the adopted son of the peshwa, Baji Rao II, who had seen his claim to the peshwaship taken away by the Doctrine of Lapse. The strongest center of the revolt outside Delhi was Oudh, which had been annexed by the British in the preceding year, who terminated the rule of the nawab, Wajid Ali Shah, and disbanded 50,000 of the state's troops.

Yet again no simple correlation can be drawn between Princely India and support for the revolt. The old Mughal himself had been taken wholly unawares by the uprising—initially ordering the gates of the Red Fort to be closed against the Mutineers—and had to be pushed into accepting its leadership. Bahadur Khan of Rohilkhand was another reluctant convert: he was receiving a comfortable pension from the British and had earlier warned the British of impending unrest.[35] In fact, the likes of Khan, Jhansi, and Oudh were very much the exceptions. As Masani observes:

> The princes . . . in general refrained from lending their support to the rebels and rendered memorable assistance in suppressing the revolt. Had the Sikh, Maratha, and Rajput states, particularly Hyderabad, been disloyal, or had they espoused the cause of the deposed descendant of the Moguls, Bahadur Shah, the whole country would have been overrun and dominated by the mutineers. It was the loyalty of these states that turned the scale in favour of the British.[36]

More relevant, perhaps, was the contribution of disaffected elites at district and village level. Whereas most princes had been treated with some sensitivity by the British, conscious of their potential power, this had not been true of traditional landowning and martial elites and clan leaders, many of whom had seen their rights to land, military service, and community leadership disregarded by the colonial authorities. It is now recognized that the deteriorating economic and social position of this local elite class forms one of the key explanatory variables of the events of 1857–58. The "critical factor in rural reactions," remarks Stokes, "was the presence or absence of a thriving magnate element heavily committed by interest to British rule."[37] Where these elites stood firm for the British they were usually able to maintain peace within their sphere of influence. This was true, for example, of those occupying lands along the main communication routes like the Ganges and Jumna Rivers and the Grand Trunk Road. These men had prospered from the opportunities to grow cash crops for market and saw their interests as being bound up with British rule. In eastern Mazaffarnagar, where many peasant proprietors had found themselves forced to sell their lands after becoming indebted to urban moneylenders, a revolt was headed off by a few leading Sayyid families who had built up estates and accumulated offices under the British.[38] Their loyalty was an important factor in the Company's ability to keep its main supply lines open. Local rivalries could also play a role: even in Oudh, where support for the Mutiny was strong, the landed magnates in the south, who traditionally resented the domineering manner of the landlord elite centered around Lucknow, favored the British. Similarly the failure of the Muslim nobles of Hyderabad to back the revolt arose partly out of their associating it with activities of their historic enemies, the Marathas—Gwalior and Jhansi being indeed Maratha states.[39]

By contrast, local magnates who had seen their position deteriorate with the rise of British rule were only too pleased to take the chance to settle old scores and were able to use customary allegiances to mobilize the peasantry and coordinate outbreaks of unrest into a serious force. As Sir George Campbell observed in 1857, the rebellion was not generally Muslim or Hindu, it was a rebellion of the previously dominant classes in the Northwestern Provinces who had been rejected by the British. Oudh provides the classic example of this phenomenon. Here the taluqdar landlords, who had customarily collected revenues from groups of villages, were treated in cavalier fashion by the British after annexation, some 21,000 finding their estates confiscated and redistributed. Unsurprisingly, they entered into revolt with alacrity, and successfully mobilized the local peasants in their interest—themselves smarting from increased revenue assessments. Even so, a simple economic-determinist model of elite responses doesn't account for all the facts: in Rohilkhand, for instance, the Rohilla landlords were active for the revolt—yet this was the very group that had done best out of British revenue reforms in the area and had successfully branched out into commercial moneylending.[40]

A third perspective upon the course of the revolt, which has attracted increasing interest in recent years, focuses on the contribution of the peasantry. For some, notably S. B. Chaudhuri, 1857 was a "rising of the people"[41] which he traced to the disruption of agrarian communities under the British land revenue and property reforms. It was the disposition of traditional landed groups, and the heavy burdens upon indebted peasants, that fuelled the uprising: "both the orders being the victims of British civil law were united in the revolutionary epoch of 1857–58 in a common effort to recover what they had lost."[42] In this he has been supported by Thomas Metcalfe, who believes that it was agrarian grievances which lay behind the rebellion, which was directed at the new landlord class created by the British, with both peasants and traditional landed elites joining in the attack with a view to restoring "'the *status quo ante*." Peasants thus played a dual role: they could be mobilized by ties to local elites, as well as having their own grievances and agenda. The foundations of peasant rebellion ran deep. As Chris Bayly notes, the years of population growth, heavy taxation, and low prices during the first decades of the 19th century left most in a state of profound poverty. Although there has been some improvement from the 1840s, it was too slow and piecemeal to alleviate peasant suffering seriously.[43] Peasants struggling to make revenue payments found themselves embroiled in the clutches of moneylenders, and these formed a prime target for popular anger: many moneylenders were attacked and their records destroyed. The peasant leader Devi Singh of Tappa Raya forced moneylenders to cancel debts and encouraged his followers to loot shops and houses. Other peasant targets were zamindars and princely rulers. In 1857, the peasant activist Udwant Singh sought to break away from the rule of the raja of Benares—who captured him and handed him over to the British.

Pastoralists and nomads were another section of the rural population joining in the unrest of 1857. As we have noted, groups like the Gujars and Bhattis had been subject to deteriorating conditions under British rule as traditional grazing routes were partitioned and assigned to settled cultivators, like the Jats around Delhi and Haryana. Accordingly, they were keen to exploit the breakdown in law and order to exact retribution upon settled villages and farmers—though in the process they attacked supporters and well as opponents of the Mutiny, including the Mughal Emperor's supply lines.[44] It was, for instance, the Gujars who plundered the Company's vital gunpowder stores at Wazirabad, three miles from Delhi, before the Mutineers could take possession of them. Interestingly, although the Jat farming caste had, overall, benefited economically from British rule—being precisely the kind of sturdy cultivators administrators favored—there were important variations and many supported the Mutiny. Chris Bayly notes that those Jats opting for the rebels tended to be those who occupied dry land and who, despite not yet been given access to the irrigation works associated with the East Jumna and Ganges canal works, still found themselves subject to the higher revenue assessments that improved irrigation invariably brought with it.[45]

Still, as authors such as Stokes and Chris Bayly have emphasized, the rebellion of 1857 cannot be considered a purely peasant revolt. Though peasants played an active role in unrest in many areas, they rarely occupied leadership positions and were often subordinate to landlord and clan leaders whose agenda was very different. "During the revolt," writes Chris Bayly, "no rhetoric of land redistribution or cry for the modification of the rental system took hold" and "anti-landlordism or conflict with an emerging class of rich peasants hardly figures in the evidence."[46] As a class, the peasants were no more united than other key social groups and these divisions were not wholly reducible to varying economic fortunes. While the farmers of the Punjab had been won over to the British by low revenue assessments and the first stages of irrigation provision, the prosperous peasantry of the Muzaffarnagar and Meerut districts split in response to the revolt in ways that appear to reflect old factional alignments as much as differential affluence.[47] The same was true in the district of Mainpuri where the breakdown of order in 1857 was the signal for a clash between two landowning castes, the Chauhon Rajputs and the Ahirs, each of which had been rivals for local mastery.[48]

Considering the rebellion as a whole, the safest generalizations would appear to run as follows. There was no all-India revolt and no clear strategy or ideology united the insurgents. Essentially, the revolt was dominated by Indians who felt undermined and damaged by Company policy and who saw the removal of colonial rule as the key to their recovery of status and position. What did they want to replace it with? They had no new program: what they looked to was some reversion to a previous state of affairs. The precise details of this desired *status quo ante* depended upon the position and history of the individual and the social group with which he most closely identified. Within this context, the aspiration to restore the Great Mughal to his empire provided merely a symbolic center for a movement more characterized by pluralism and parochialism than unity of purpose or design. As such, the rebels could be princes or landlords, peasants or nomads, sepoys or the urban poor. Where these disaffected groups were strong, or those backing British power weak or indecisive, the revolt took hold and the rebels able to settle accounts with those whom they considered the agents of degrading change— whether it be the British, educated babus, zamindars, bankers, moneylenders, or tradesmen. In localities where the balance of loyalties favored the British, the revolt met with little response. Thus, whereas in Aligarh and Mathura, local landed elites felt they had prospered under British rule and rallied to the *Pax Britannica*; in Oudh they considered themselves ruined by the British presence and took the lead in breaking it down. And it was this differential response among the influential elites that was crucial: for it was the loyalty of social groups who conceived of themselves as having done well out of the British which meant that the rebels never had complete control over even northern India, and these loyal Indians provided the basis from which British rule could be reestablished.

To trace the character of the revolt's support is also to delineate the reasons for its failure. Fragmented and localized, it never mobilized the majority of Indians or spread its work across the greater part of the subcontinent. Quickly restricted to its heartland around Delhi it was exposed to a resurgent Company power, richer in resources, manpower, and leadership. Holding, already, a weak hand, the Mutineers proceeded to play their cards badly, failing to take strategic initiatives and exhibiting, in military engagements, a lack of decisive command so that even advantageous positions—such as that occupied by the rebels in Delhi when the initial British assault faltered, the men turned to drink, and their commander wept. As John Lawrence confessed: "had a single leader of ability arisen among them [the rebels], we must have been lost beyond redemption."

But while the revolt failed, its consequences were no less profound for that. It extinguished, of course, any lingering hope of restoring a pre-British Mughal-Muslim India. The Mughal dynasty itself was stripped of all official recognition, and its last representative sent into exile in Rangoon. The associated martial elites suffered a permanent loss of prestige as Indians of succeeding generations, reflects Spear, came to look for leadership to the westernized middle class.[49] Yet, paradoxically, the British also emerged losers from a war they had seemingly won. For the Mutiny marked the end of British, just as much as Mughal, strategies of rule. The most visible casualty was the East India Company itself, which ceased to rule India altogether, being replaced by direct political control from the British government in the name of the queen. And rather than taking the defeat of the Mutiny as a vindication of their rule and a green-light for accelerated modernization, they elected, instead, to treat it as a morality tale as to the dangers of pressing an alien liberal philosophy upon a people immersed in ancient cultural practices which, once unpicked, would unravel in unpredictable and disastrous ways. This revived Orientalism was first propounded, appropriately enough, by Benjamin Disraeli, the Conservative-Jewish devotee of the "Asiatic Mystery" who, as early as 1857, was blaming the Mutiny upon the meddling liberal reforms of the likes of Bentinck and Dalhousie and calling for the queen to assume a sovereignty of India predicated upon the maintenance of the customs and religions of its people. This interpretation soon became conventional, and the British set themselves to bolstering precisely those traditional landed and princely elites whom they had apparently banished in 1857–58. They recognized that the fate of British rule had depended, ultimately, upon whether a local chief or magnate considered his interests lay with being pro- or anti-British and they now set about shifting the balance in their favor. Annexations and the Doctrine of Lapse ceased. Local landed elites, including the taluqdars of Oudh, were patronized, and their traditional rights respected. The burden of taxation was shifted from the land to the towns—a peculiarly misjudged move in that it occurred when rural incomes were rising and increased urban taxes alienated the very groups who had been loyal during the conflict. They reformed the army and targeted recruitment away from the caste-conscious groups of Bengal, Bihar, and Oudh and toward the newly designated martial races like the Sikhs, Dogras, Jats, Pathans, and Gurkhas—each of which were kept, so far as possible, in separate units.

In this sense, neither modernity nor tradition triumphed as a result of the Mutiny. Superficially, British power had never been more entrenched, more splendid. Yet behind the façade, the self-confidence of the colonial power had been dealt a crushing blow. Optimistic talk of transforming India into a nation of Christianized Anglophile liberals was abandoned as the British elected to found their rule, not upon a culturally superior western rationality, but on the maintenance of established Indian interests. British rule became still more what it had always been: a mechanism for administering India so as to yield sufficient revenue to fund a minimalist state. The Raj was, after all, not a means to an end; it *was* the end.

Notes

Chapter 1: First Impressions

1. P. J. Marshall, *Bengal: The British Bridgehead in Eastern India 1740–1828* (Cambridge: Cambridge University Press, 1987), p. 24.
2. C. Markovits, ed., *A History of Modern India 1480–1950* (London: Anthem Press, 2004), p. 317; D. Kumar, ed., *The Cambridge Economic History of India*, vol. 2, *c. 1757–c. 1970* (Cambridge: Cambridge University Press, 1982), p. 246.
3. Markovits, *History of Modern India*, p. 317.
4. Quoted in R. P. Dutt, *India To-Day* (London: Gollancz, 1940), p. 40.
5. Quoted in M. Chamberlain, *Britain and India: The Interaction of Two Peoples* (Newton Abbot: David and Charles, 1974), p. 26.
6. Kumar, *Economic History of India*, 2:243.
7. This was the burden of the pioneering research of Henry Sumner Maine; cf. *Village Communities in the East and West* (London: John Murray, 1881).
8. R. C. Dutt *The Economic History of India* (London: Kegan Paul, Trench, Trubner, 1902), 1:386–87.
9. Marshall, *Bengal*, p. 13.
10. Kumar, *Economic History of India*, 2:18.
11. Cf. B. Stein, *A History of India* (Oxford: Blackwell, 1998), p. 202; C. A. Bayly, *Indian Society and the Making of the Indian Empire* (Cambridge: Cambridge University Press, 1988), p. 8.
12. P. Spear, *A History of India* (Middlesex: Penguin Books, 1970), 2:116–17.
13. Markovits, *History of Modern India*, p. 295.
14. C. A. Bayly, *Indian Society*, p. 35.

Chapter 2: Indians and the Making of the Raj

1. M. Edwardes, *Raj: The Story of British India* (London: Pan Books, 1967), p. 31.

2. Marshall, *Bengal*, pp. 160, 162.
3. Ibid.; C. A. Bayly, *Indian Society*, p. 46.
4. Ibid., p. 48.
5. L. James, *Raj: The Making and Unmaking of British India* (London: Little, Brown, 1997), p. 20.
6. Ibid., pp. 24–26. He was recalled to France in 1753, where he died in poverty.
7. Marshall, *Bengal*, p. 71.
8. Ibid., p. 64.
9. Ibid., p. 65.
10. P. Mason, *A Matter of Honour: An Account of the Indian Army, Its Officers and Men* (Basingstoke: Macmillan, 1974), p. 77.
11. T. B. Macaulay, "Lord Clive" in *Critical and Historical Essays* (London: Methuen, 1903), p. 420 .
12. Markovits, *History of Modern India*, p. 233.
13. K. M. Pannikar, *Asia and Western Dominance* (London: Allen and Unwin, 1953), p. 99.
14. Marshall, *Bengal*, p. 85.
15. James, *Raj*, p. 80.

Chapter 3: Bengal and Beyond

1. Markovits, *History of Modern India*, p. 245.
2. R. P. Dutt, *India To-Day*, p. 114.
3. Cited in R. C. Dutt, *Economic History of India*, 1:23.
4. Ibid., pp. 114–15.
5. Marshall, *Bengal*, p. 135.
6. J. Brown, *Modern India* (Oxford: Oxford University Press, 1985), p. 51.
7. P. Spear, *The Nabobs* (Oxford: Oxford University Press, 1963), pp. 137–39.
8. Brown, *Modern India*, p. 56.
9. W. W. Hunter, *The Indian Empire* (London: Smith, Elder, 1893), p. 471.
10. E. Eden, *Up the Country* (London: Virago Press, 1983), p. 209.
11. James, *Raj*, p. 109.
12. Quoted in ibid., p. 110.
13. C. A. Bayly, *Indian Society*, p. 135.
14. Quoted in P. J. Griffiths, *The British in India* (London: Robert Hale, 1946), p. 92.
15. Quoted in C. A. Bayly, *Indian Society*, p. 103.
16. Ibid., pp. 90–92.
17. Quoted in V. Mahajan, *Modern Indian History* (New Delhi: S. Chand, 1990), pp. 173–74.
18. Mason, *Matter of Honour*, p. 56; H. Kulke and D. Rothermund, *A History of India* (London: Croom Helm, 1986), p. 225.
19. Stein, *History of India*, p. 211.
20. Ibid., pp. 210–11.

Chapter 4: Landed Society and British Rule

1. K. Marx, "The Future Results of British Rule in India," quoted in R. P. Dutt, *India To-Day*, p. 102.
2. J. Nehru, *The Discovery of India* (Calcutta: Signet Press, 1946), p. 306.
3. Brown, *Modern India*, p. 58.
4. Ibid., p. 61.
5. R. Coupland, *India: A Re-statement* (Oxford: Oxford University Press, 1945), p. 59.
6. Stein, *A History of India*, p. 213.
7. Kumar, *Cambridge Economic History of India*, 2:86.
8. P. Hardy, *The Muslims of British India* (Cambridge: Cambridge University Press, 1972), p. 42.
9. Dutt, *Economic History of India*, 1:56.
10. James, *Raj*, p. 188.
11. Kumar, *Cambridge Economic History of India*, 2:211.
12. Marshall, *Bengal*, p. 8.
13. Ibid.
14. Ibid., p. 55.
15. Ibid., p. 121.
16. Hardy, *Muslims of British India*, p. 43.
17. Ibid., p. 46.
18. R. P. Dutt, *India To-Day*, p. 211.
19. C. Bayly, *Indian Society*, p. 109; Robb, *History of India* (Basingstoke: Palgrave), pp. 126–27.
20. B. Chaudhuri, in Kumar, *Cambridge Economic History of India*, 2:89.
21. Brown, *Modern India*, p. 62; Robb, *History of India*, p. 127.
22. Cf. Stein, *History of India*, p. 212.
23. Nehru, *Discovery of India*, p. 304.
24. Robb, *History of India*, p. 128.
25. Quoted in Marshall, *Bengal*, p. 118.
26. R. C. Dutt, *Economic History of India*, 1:94–96.
27. Marshall, *Bengal*, pp. 141, 144. Bayly concurs that the increases in tax demands were "significant but not massive." C. Bayly, *Origins of Nationality in South Asia* (Oxford: Oxford University Press, 1998), p. 257.
28. Kumar, *Cambridge Economic History of India*, 2:94.
29. Ibid., p. 89.
30. Marshall, *Bengal*, p. 146.
31. Kumar, *Cambridge Economic History of India*, 2:96.
32. R. P. Dutt, *India To-Day*, p. 209.
33. Robb, *History of India*, p. 273.
34. Marshall, *Bengal*, p. 147.
35. Ibid., p. 152.
36. Quoted ibid., p. 150.
37. Kumar, *Cambridge Economic History of India*, 2:217.
38. P. Kendall, *India and the British: A Quest for Truth* (London: Charles Scribner's Sons, 1931), p. 186.

39. L.S.S. O'Malley, ed., *Modern India and the West* (Oxford: Oxford University Press, 1941), pp. 281–82.
40. C. Bayly, *Indian Society*, p. 63.
41. Robb, *History of India*, p. 128.
42. C. Bayly, *Indian Society*, p. 109.
43. Cited in R. P. Dutt, *India To-Day*, p. 213.
44. For the debates over the Madras settlement, see R. C. Dutt, *Economic History of India*, vol. 1, chap. 8.
45. Brown, *Modern India*, p. 63.
46. E. Stokes, *The Peasant and the Raj* (Cambridge: Cambridge University Press, 1978), p. 187.
47. Brown, *Modern India*, p. 72.
48. Stokes, *Peasant and the Raj*, pp. 185, 187.
49. Kumar, *Cambridge Economic History of India*, 2:221.
50. W. Digby, *Prosperous British India* (London: Fisher Unwin, 1901), p. 35.
51. Kumar, *Cambridge Economic History of India*, 2:312–13.
52. Ibid., p. 310.
53. Marshall, *Bengal*. p. 171.
54. Stokes, *Peasant and the Raj*, p. 245.
55. Cited ibid., p. 155.
56. Robb, *History of India*, pp. 276–77.
57. J. C. Jack, *The Economic Life of a Bengal District* (Oxford: Oxford University Press, 1916), p. 100.
58. James, *Raj*, p. 193.
59. Markovits, *History of Modern India*, p. 309.
60. Edwardes, *Raj*, p. 115; C. Bayly, *Indian Society*, p. 130.
61. Edwardes, *Raj*, p. 115.
62. For this, see C. Bayly, *Indian Society*, p. 139.
63. Ibid.
64. Kumar, *Cambridge Economic History of India*, 2:297.
65. H. H. Mann, *Land and Labour in a Deccan Village,* vol. 1 (Oxford: Oxford University Press, 1917), p. 46.
66. In his 1927 *Essentials of Indian Economics*, G. Sapre estimated that 20–25 acres of dry land and 5–7 acres of wet land were required to support a family.
67. Cf. Robb, *History of India*, p. 273.
68. C. Bayly, *Indian Society*, pp. 143–44.
69. Cf. www.struggleindia.com.
70. James, *Raj*, p. 200; Hunter, *Indian Empire*, p. 114; C. Bayly, *Indian Society*, p. 142.
71. James, *Raj*, p. 200.
72. C. Bayly, *Indian Society*, p. 144.
73. Marshall, *Bengal*, p. 62; Kumar, *Cambridge Economic History of India*, 2:214.
74. Ibid., p. 182.
75. Chamberlain, *Britain and India*, p. 125.
76. Digby, *Prosperous British India*, p. 439.
77. Marshall, *Bengal*, p. 142.

78. N. Charlesworth, *British Rule and the Indian Economy* (Basingstoke: Macmillan, 1982), p. 16.

79. P. Spear, *Twilight of the Mughuls* (Cambridge: Cambridge University Press, 1951), pp. 108–9.

80. Marshall, *Bengal*, p. 185.

81. Ibid., p. 334.

82. Quoted in Digby, *Prosperous British India*, p. 50.

83. Markovits, *History of Modern India*, p. 358.

84. Cf. Kumar, *Cambridge Economic History*, 2:345; C. Bayly, *Indian Society*, p. 147.

85. Charlesworth, *British Rule and the Indian Economy*, p. 23.

86. Digby, *Prosperous British India*, pp. 127–30.

87. Edwardes, *Raj*, p. 105.

88. Markovits, *History of Modern India*, p. 310.

89. Marshall, *Bengal*, p. 153.

90. C. Bayly, *Indian Society*, p. 152.

91. R. P. Dutt, *India To-Day*, p. 218; Markovits, *History of Modern India*, p. 313; C. Bayly, *Indian Society*, p. 146.

92. Brown, *Modern India*, p. 72.

Chapter 5: Commerce and Industry under Company Rule

1. Kumar, *Cambridge Economic History of India*, 2:814.

2. Marshall, *Bengal*, p. 104.

3. Brown, *Modern India*, p. 59.

4. Marshall, *Bengal*, pp. 113, 158.

5. Brown, *Modern India*, p. 40.

6. Markovits, *History of Modern India*, p. 315.

7. C. A. Bayly, *Indian Society*, p. 108.

8. Kumar, *Cambridge Economic History of India*, 2:272.

9. Ibid., p. 764.

10. C. A. Bayly, *Indian Society*, p. 124.

11. Kumar, *Cambridge Economic History of India*, 2:306–7

12. Ibid., p. 276.

13. Ibid., p. 307.

14. Ibid., p. 277.

15. Quoted in R. C. Dutt, *Economic History of India*, 1:289.

16. H. H. Wilson, *The History of British India from 1805 to 1835* (London: James Madden, 1858), 1:385.

17. Kumar, *Cambridge Economic History of India*, 2:842.

18. Robb, *History of India*, p. 131.

19. R. C. Dutt, *Economic History of India*, 1:295, 299.

20. Ibid., p. 50.

21. Brown, *Modern India*, p. 39.

22. Kumar, *Cambridge Economic History of India*, 2:870.

23. C. A. Bayly, *Indian Society*, p. 116.

24. Quoted in Mahajan, *Modern Indian History* (New Delhi: S. Chand, 1990), pp. 601–2. For the view that monies remitted from India actually made the Industrial Revolution possible, see Digby, *Prosperous British India?*, pp. 31–33.

25. Cf. Chamberlain, *Britain and India*, p. 130.

26. Coupland, *India: a Re-Statement*, p. 58.

27. V. Anstey, "Economic Development" in O'Malley, *Modern India and the West*, p. 272.

28. J. Cumming, ed., *Modern India* (Oxford: Oxford University Press, 1931), p. 264.

29. Charlesworth, *British Rule and the Indian Economy*, pp. 53–54.

30. Quoted in R. C. Dutt, *Economic History of India*, 1:238, 242, 245.

31. Ibid., 1:256.

32. Nehru, *Discovery of India*, p. 285.

33. R. C. Dutt, *Economic History of India*, 1:x.

34. Digby, *Prosperous British India?*, p. 36.

35. Kumar, *Cambridge Economic History of India*, 2:279.

36. Quoted in R. P. Dutt, *India To-Day*, p. 127.

37. Kumar, *Cambridge Economic History of India*, 2:278.

38. Ibid., pp. 347–48.

39. Cited in R. P. Dutt, *India To-Day*, p. 100.

40. Ibid., p. 110.

41. R. C. Dutt, *Economic History of India*, 1:264.

42. Cf. Charlesworth who writes, "the sub-continent in 1800 was undoubtedly far from any spontaneous industrial take-off." *British Rule and the Indian Economy*, p. 14.

43. Kumar, *Cambridge Economic History of India*, 2:670.

44. Ibid., 2:669.

45. R. C. Dutt, *Economic History of India*, 1:236.

46. M.D. Morris, "The Growth of Large-Scale Industry," in Kumar, *Cambridge Economic History of India*, 2:673.

47. Charlesworth, *British Rule and the Indian Economy*, p. 34.

48. For details of the Porto Novo scheme, see Kumar, *Cambridge Economic History of India*, 2:584–85.

49. Cf. Charlesworth, *British Rule and the Indian Economy*, p. 35.

50. Kumar, *Cambridge Economic History of India*, 2:558.

51. Marshall, *Bengal*, p. 162.

52. Kumar, *Cambridge Economic History of India*, 2:257.

53. Edwardes, *Raj*, p. 114.

54. Quoted in James, *Raj*, p. 175.

55. Quoted in R. P. Dutt, *India To-Day*, pp. 138–39.

56. Hunter, *Indian Empire*, p. 648.

57. R. P. Dutt, *India To-Day*, p. 143.

58. Kumar, *Cambridge Economic History of India*, 2:740–41.

59. Ibid., pp. 142, 741.

60. Ibid., p. 742.

61. Quoted ibid., p. 142.

62. Digby, *Prosperous British India?*, p. 144.

63. R. P. Dutt, *India To-Day*, p. 195.
64. Kumar, *Cambridge Economic History of India*, 2:743.
65. Ibid.
66. Ibid., 2:749.
67. Quoted in P. Griffiths, *The British Impact on India* (London: Robert Hale, 1952), p. 423.
68. J. Strachey, *India* (London: Kegan Paul, Trench, Trubner, 1894), p. 171.
69. Kumar, *Cambridge Economic History of India*, 2:742.
70. Chamberlain, *Britain and India*, p. 121.

Chapter 6: The Company, Class, and Caste

1. Marshall, *Bengal*, p. 259.
2. Markovits, *History of Modern India*, p. 325.
3. Marshall, *Bengal*, p. 167.
4. Kumar, *Cambridge Economic History of India*, 2:266.
5. Markovits, *History of Modern India*, p. 323.
6. C. A. Bayly, *Indian Society*, p. 107.
7. Edwardes, *Raj*, p. 110.
8. N. Chaudhuri, *The Autobiography of an Unknown Indian* (Basingstoke: Macmillan, 1951), pp. 272–73.
9. Marshall, *Bengal*, p. 174.
10. Markovits, *History of Modern India*, pp. 366–67.
11. Ibid., p. 328.
12. Ibid.
13. Brown, *Modern India*, p. 57.
14. E. Battye, *Costumes and Characters of the British Raj* (Exeter: Webb and Bower, 1982), p. 24.
15. Brown, *Modern India*, pp. 57–58.
16. S. Bayly, *Caste, Society and Politics in India* (Cambridge: Cambridge University Press, 1999), p. 149.
17. Marshall, *Bengal*, p. 177.
18. G. Chesney, *Indian Polity* (London: Longmans, Green, 1870), p. 57.
19. C. A. Bayly, *Indian Society*, pp. 112–13.
20. Strachey, *India*, p. 357.
21. Quoted in R. P. Dutt, *India To-Day*, p. 394.
22. Strachey, *India*, p. 367.
23. See above, p. 41.
24. Strachey, *India*, pp. 369–70.
25. C. A. Bayly, *Origins of Nationality in South Asia*, pp. 53–54.
26. Hunter, *Indian Empire*, p. 243.
27. M. Monier-Williams, *Hinduism* (London: Society for Promoting Christian Knowledge, 1894), p. 164.
28. O'Malley, *Modern India and the West*, p. 310.
29. Ibid., p. 126.
30. Quoted ibid., p. 166.

31. S. Bayly, *Caste, Society and Politics in India*, pp. 4–5.
32. Ibid., pp. 56–60.
33. Ibid., p. 67.
34. Ibid., pp. 126–27.
35. Ibid., p. 84.

Chapter 7: The Experience of the State

1. Quoted in Cumming, *Modern India*, p. 89.
2. T. W. Holderness, *Peoples and Problems of India* (London: Williams and Norgate, 1912), p. 177.
3. Robb, *History of India*, p. 151.
4. R. C. Dutt, *Economic History of India*, 1:xvii.
5. Cf. Robb, *History of India*, p. 168.
6. James, *Raj*, p. 180.
7. C. A. Bayly, *Indian Society*, p. 106.
8. Strachey, *India*, pp. 134–35.
9. Brown, *Modern India*, p. 64.
10. Digby, *Prosperous British India*, p. 5.
11. Kumar, *Cambridge Economic History of India*, 2:905.
12. For an influential and lurid account of the Thugs, see P. Meadows Taylor, *Confessions of a Thug* (London: Folio Society, 1974).
13. Cf. Coupland, *India: A Re-Statement*, p. 48.
14. F. Yeats-Brown, *Martial India* (London: Eyre and Spottiswoode, 1945), p. 64.
15. James, *Raj*, p. 73.
16. Ibid., p. 204.
17. Ibid.
18. Spear, *Twilight of the Mughuls*, p. 112.
19. Marshall, *Bengal*, p. 98.
20. R. C. Dutt, *Economic History of British India*, 1:314.
21. Quoted in ibid., pp. 314–15.
22. Markovits, *History of Modern India*, p. 281.
23. Spear, *History of India*, 2:127.
24. B. Lindsay, "Law," in O'Malley, *Modern India and the West*, p. 131.
25. C. A. Bayly, *Indian Society*, p. 114.
26. O'Malley, *Modern India and the West*, p. 128.
27. Lord Macaulay, *Miscellaneous Writings and Speeches* (London: Longmans, Green, Reader, and Dyer, 1878), pp. 569–70.
28. Quoted in Strachey, *India*, p. 77.
29. Quoted in Edwardes, *Raj*, p. 92.
30. R. C. Dutt, *Economic History of British India*, 1:322.
31. Spear, *Twilight of the Mughuls*, p. 111.
32. Quoted in Edwardes, *Raj*, p. 130.
33. P. Moon, *Strangers in India* (New York: Reynal and Hitchcock, 1945), pp. 38–39.

34. Strachey, *India*, pp. 88–89.
35. C. A. Bayly, *Indian Society*, p. 81.
36. Quoted in James, *Raj*, p. 119.
37. Mason, *A Matter of Honour*, p. 15.
38. Ibid., p. 200.
39. C. A. Bayly, *Indian Society*, p. 81.
40. Mason, *A Matter of Honour*, p. 166.
41. Ibid., p. 202.
42. Quoted in James, *Raj*, pp. 134–35.
43. Ibid., pp. 133–34.
44. Mason, *Matter of Honour*, p. 169.
45. Marshall, *Bengal*, p. 180.

Chapter 8: Cultural and Religious Life under Company Rule

1. N. Gupta, *Delhi Between Two Empires 1803–1931* (Delhi: Oxford University Press, 1981), p. 8.
2. Cf. D. Kopf, *British Orientalism and the Bengal Renaissance* (Berkeley: University of California Press, 1969).
3. James, *Raj*, p. 175.
4. Robb, *History of India*, p. 297.
5. J. R. Cunningham, "Education," in O'Malley, *Modern India and the West*, p. 140.
6. Ibid., p. 146.
7. Edwardes, *Raj*, p. 137.
8. Marshall, *Bengal*, p. 174.
9. G. O. Trevelyan, *Life and Letters of Lord Macaulay* (London: Longmans, Green, 1876), 1:401–4.
10. Brown, *Modern India*, p. 76.
11. Ibid., p. 77.
12. O'Malley, *Modern India and the West*, p. 152.
13. Marshall, *Bengal*, p. 129.
14. R. C. Dutt, *Economic History of India*, 1:336.
15. Kumar, *Cambridge Economic History of India*, 2:374.
16. M. Monier-Williams, *Modern India and the Indians* (London: Kegan Paul, Trench, Trubner, 1891), p. 300.
17. Kendall, *India and the British*, p. 252.
18. J. C. Ghosh, "Bengali Literature and Drama," in O'Malley, *Modern India and the West*, p. 484.
19. Ibid., p. 495.
20. Gupta, *Delhi Between Two Empires*, p. 7.
21. O'Malley, *Modern India and the West*, p. 202.
22. Robb, *History of India*, p. 145.
23. O'Malley, *Modern India and the West*, p. 191.
24. Quoted in Chamberlain, *Britain and India*, pp. 55–56.
25. Brown, *Modern India*, p. 68.

26. C. A. Bayly, *Indian Society*, p. 114.
27. Marshall, *Bengal*, p. 177.
28. Spear, *Nabobs*, p. 139.
29. C. A. Bayly, *Indian Society*, p. 122.
30. Edwardes, *Raj*, p. 125.
31. "William Bentinck: On Ritual Murder in India, 1829," Modern History Sourcebook, http://www.fordham.edu/halsall/mod/1829bentinck.asp.
32. "Primary Sources: Official Documents, Lord William Cavendish Bentinck," Women in World History, http://chnm.gmu.edu/wwh/modules/lesson5/lesson5.php?s=6.
33. Monier-Williams, *Modern India and the Indians*, p. 326.
34. Ibid., p. 316.
35. Gupta, *Delhi Between Two Empires*, p. 10.
36. Spear, *Nabobs*, p. 63.
37. James, *Raj*, p. 216.
38. Hardy, *Muslims of British India*, p. 35.
39. Ibid., p. 43–44.
40. Ibid., p. 37.
41. Ibid., p. 45.
42. C. A. Bayly, *Indian Society*, p. 114.
43. Hardy, *Muslims*, p. 59.
44. Ibid., p. 61.
45. Ibid., p. 62.
46. Robb, *History of India*, p. 143.

Chapter 9: Resistance to British Rule

1. C. A. Bayly, *Indian Society*, p. 170.
2. Markovits, *History of Modern India*, p. 313.
3. Ibid., p. 314.
4. C. A. Bayly, *Origins of Nationality in South Asia*, pp. 266–67.
5. Spear, *Twilight of the Mughuls*, p. 85.
6. D. Mitra, *Nil Darpan, or The Indigo Planting Mirror: A Drama* (Calcutta: C. H. Mamuel, 1861).
7. C. A. Bayly, *Indian Society*, p. 175; Stokes, *Peasant and the Raj*, p. 272.
8. Markovits, *History of Modern India*, p. 280.
9. C. A. Bayly, *Indian Society*, p. 178. Benares witnessed a formidable protest against a proposed house tax in the years 1809–11.
10. Quoted in Edwardes, *Raj*, p. 171.
11. Quoted in R. C. Dutt, *Economic History of India*, 1:334.
12. Quoted in Brown, *Modern India*, p. 82.
13. E. Stokes, *The Peasant Armed* (Oxford: Oxford University Press, 1986), p. 25.
14. C. A. Bayly, *Indian Society*, p. 181.
15. Brown, *Modern India*, p. 82.
16. Stokes, *Peasant Armed*, p. 31.

17. Quoted Hardy, *Muslims of British India*, p. 69.

18. Quoted in Spear, *Twilight of the Mughuls*, p. 218.

19. Quoted in Mason, *Matter of Honour*, p. 300.

20. Ibid.

21. Ibid., p. 257.

22. Ibid., p. 273.

23. James, *Raj*, p. 269.

24. Quoted in B. Chandra, *India's Struggle for Independence* (New Delhi: Penguin Books, 1988), p. 33.

25. Stokes, *Peasant Armed*, p. 14.

26. Quoted Ibid., p. 7.

27. Ibid.

28. James, *Raj*, p. 269.

29. Hardy, *Muslims of British India*, p. 65.

30. Spear, *Twilight of the Mughuls*, p. 207.

31. Ibid., p. 67.

32. Quoted in ibid., p. 68.

33. Stokes, *Peasant Armed*, p. 5.

34. James, *Raj*, p. 234.

35. Chandra, *India's Struggle for Independence*, p. 32.

36. R. P. Masani, *Britain in India* (Oxford: Oxford University Press, 1960), p. 45.

37. Stokes, *Peasant and the Raj*, p. 188.

38. Ibid.

39. C. A. Bayly, *Indian Society*, p. 183.

40. Brown, *Modern India*, p. 86.

41. S. B. Chaudhuri, *Civil Rebellion in the Indian Mutinies* (Calcutta: World Press Private, 1957).

42. Quoted in Stokes, *Peasant Armed*, p. 13.

43. C. A. Bayly, *Indian Society*, p. 135.

44. Ibid., p. 188.

45. Ibid., p. 190.

46. C. A. Bayly in Stokes, *Peasant Armed*, p. 235.

47. Ibid.

48. Stokes, *Peasant and the Raj*, p. 202.

49. Spear, *History of India*, 2:144.

Bibliography

Battye, E. *Costumes and Characters of the British Raj*. Exeter: Webb and Bower, 1982.

Bayly, C. A. *Indian Society and the Making of the Indian Empire*. Cambridge: Cambridge University Press, 1988.

Bayly, C. A. *Origins of Nationality in South Asia*. Oxford: Oxford University Press 1998.

Bayly, S. *Caste, Society and Politics in India*. Cambridge: Cambridge University Press, 1999.

Brown, J. *Modern India*. Oxford: Oxford University Press, 1985.

Chamberlain, M. *Britain and India: The Interaction of Two Peoples*. Newton Abbot: David and Charles, 1974.

Chandra, B. *India's Struggle for Independence*. New Delhi: Penguin Books, 1988.

Charlesworth, N. *British Rule and the Indian Economy*. Basingstoke: Macmillan, 1982.

Chaudhuri, N. *The Autobiography of an Unknown Indian*. Basingstoke: Macmillan, 1951.

Chaudhuri, S. B. *Civil Rebellion in the Indian Mutinies*. Calcutta: World Press Private, 1957.

Chesney, G. *Indian Polity*. London: Longmans, Green, 1870.

Coupland, R. *India: A Re-statement*. Oxford: Oxford University Press, 1945.

Cumming, J., ed., *Modern India*. Oxford: Oxford University Press, 1931.

Digby, W. *Prosperous British India*. London: Fisher Unwin, 1901.

Dutt, R. C. *The Economic History of India*. 2 vols. London: Kegan Paul, Trench, Trubner, 1902.

Dutt, R. P. *India To-Day*. London: Gollancz, 1940.

Eden, E. *Up the Country*. London: Virago Press, 1983.

Edwardes, M. *A History of India*. London: Thames and Hudson, 1961.

Edwardes, M. *Raj: The Story of British India*. London: Pan Books, 1967.

Gardner, B. *The East India Company*. London: Rupert Hart-Davis, 1971.

Griffiths, P. J. *The British in India*. London: Robert Hale, 1946.

Griffiths, P. J. *The British Impact on India*. London: Macdonald, 1952.

Gupta, N. *Delhi Between Two Empires 1803–1931*. Delhi: Oxford University Press, 1981.

Hardy, P. *The Muslims of British India*. Cambridge: Cambridge University Press, 1973.

Holderness, T. W. *Peoples and Problems of India*. London: Williams and Norgate, 1912.

Hunter, W. W. *The Indian Empire*. London: Smith, Elder, 1893.

Jack, J. C. *The Economic Life of a Bengal District*. Oxford: Oxford University Press, 1916.

James, L. *Raj: The Making and Unmaking of British India*. London: Little, Brown, 1997.

Keay, J. *The Honourable Company: A History of the English East India Company*. London: Harper Collins, 1991.

Kendall, P. *India and the British: A Quest for Truth*. London: Charles Scribner's Sons, 1931.

Kopf, D. *British Orientalism and the Bengal Renaissance*. Berkeley: University of California Press, 1969.

Kulke, H., and D. Rothermund, *A History of India*. London: Croom Helm, 1986.

Kumar, D., ed., *The Cambridge Economic History of India* vol. 2. *c. 1757–1970*. Cambridge: Cambridge University Press, 1982.

Lyall, A. *The Rise and Expansion of the British Dominion in India*. London: John Murray, 1910.

Macaulay, T. B. *Miscellaneous Writings and Speeches*. London: Longmans, Green, Reader, and Dyer, 1878.

Macaulay, T. B. *Critical and Historical Essays*. London: Methuen, 1903.

Mahajan, V. *Modern Indian History*. New Delhi: S. Chand, 1990.

Maine, H. S. *Village Communities in the East and West*. London: John Murray, 1881.

Mann, H. H. *Land and Labour in a Deccan Village,* vol. 1. Oxford: Oxford University Press, 1917.

Markovits, C., ed., *A History of Modern India 1480–1950*. London: Anthem Press, 2004.

Marshall, P. J. *Bengal: The British Bridgehead in Eastern India 1740–1828*. Cambridge: Cambridge University Press, 1987.

Masani, R. P. *Britain in India*. Oxford: Oxford University Press, 1960.

Mason, P. *A Matter of Honour: An Account of the Indian Army, Its Officers and Men*. Basingstoke: Macmillan, 1974.

Mitra, D. *Nil Darpan, or The Indigo Planting Mirror: A Drama*. Calcutta: C. H. Manuel, 1861.

Monier-Williams, M. *Modern India and the Indians*. London: Kegan Paul, Trench, Trubner, 1891.

Monier-Williams, M. *Hinduism*. London: Society for Promoting Christian Knowledge, 1894.

Moon, P. *Strangers in India*. New York: Reynal and Hitchcock, 1945.

Moxham, R. *The Great Hedge of India*. New York: Carroll and Graf, 2001.

Nehru, J. *The Discovery of India*. Calcutta: Signet Press, 1946.

O'Malley, L.S.S., ed., *Modern India and the West*. Oxford: Oxford University Press, 1941.

Pannikar, K. M. *Asia and Western Dominance*. London: Allen and Unwin, 1953.

Robb, P. *A History of India*. Basingstoke: Palgrave, 2002.

Spear, P. *A History of India*. Vol. 2. Middlesex: Penguin Books, 1970.

Spear, P. *India, Pakistan, and the West*. Oxford: Oxford University Press, 1952.

Spear, P. *The Nabobs*. Oxford: Oxford University Press, 1963.

Spear, P. *Twilight of the Mughuls*. Cambridge: Cambridge University Press, 1951.

Stein, B. *A History of India*. Oxford: Blackwell, 1998.

Stokes, E. *The Peasant and the Raj*. Cambridge: Cambridge University Press, 1978.

Stokes, E. *The Peasant Armed*. Oxford: Oxford University Press, 1986.

Strachey, J. *India*. London: Kegan Paul, Trench, Trubner, 1894.

Taylor, P. M. *Confessions of a Thug*. London: Folio Society, 1974.

Trevelyan, G. O. *Life and Letters of Lord Macaulay*. London: Longmans, Green, 1876.

Urquhart, M. M. *Women of Bengal*. Calcutta: Association Press, 1925.

Wallbank, T. W. *A Short History of India and Pakistan*. New York: Mentor Books, 1958.

Wilson, H. H. *The History of British India from 1805 to 1835*. London: James Madden, 1858.

Yeats-Brown, F. *Martial India*. London: Eyre and Spottiswoode, 1945.

Index

Index 189 content below.

About the Author

IAN ST. JOHN studied for a D.Phil in Modern History at Nuffield College, Oxford, and currently teaches history at Haberdashers' Aske's School. He is the author of *Disraeli and the Art of Victorian Politics* (2005) and *Gladstone and the Logic of Victorian Politics* (2010).

Edwards Brothers Malloy
Thorofare, NJ USA
June 12, 2012